GW01451812

THE IRISH DRAUGHT HORSE

A HISTORY

MARY McGRATH AND JOAN C. GRIFFITH

The Collins Press

First published in 2005 by
The Collins Press
West Link Park
Doughcloyne
Wilton
Cork
Ireland

© Mary McGrath and Joan C. Griffith

All rights reserved.
The material in this publication is protected by copyright law.
Except as may be permitted by law, no part of the material may be reproduced
(including by storage in a retrieval system) or transmitted in any form or by any means,
adapted, rented or lent without the written permission of the copyright owners.
Applications for permissions should be addressed to the publisher.

British Library cataloguing in publication data.

McGrath, Mary
    The Irish draught horse: a history
    1. Irish draft horse – History 2. Ireland – Social life and customs
    I. Title II. Griffith, Joan
    636.1'5'09415

ISBN: 190346482x

Font: 11 point Garamond
Cover and text design by Anú Design, Tara
Typeset by Anú Design, Tara
Printed in Malta

In memory of Joseph J. McGrath
who loved horses

Contents

List of Illustrations

Editors and Contributors

EDITORS

Joan C. Griffith is a librarian, who worked at Dartmouth College, University of New Hampshire and University of New Mexico libraries before moving to Germany where she currently works for a bookseller and subscription agent. She is an Honorary Life Member of the Irish Draught Horse Society, Ireland, a breeder of Irish Draught horses and maintains the websites on behalf of the IDHS and Suma Stud.

Mary McGrath has had an international career as an art conservator and consultant which included working and lecturing at Harvard University, the Getty Museum and the University of Denver. Her lifelong interest in horses led her to research and set up the Irish Horse Museum at the National Stud and to become honorary secretary of the Irish Draught Horse Society for a number of years. She currently breeds and shows Irish Draught horses and has, in the past, driven the lord mayor's coach and a team of four Irish Draught mares through the streets of Dublin.

CONTRIBUTORS

John Feehan is a senior lecturer in the Faculty of Agriculture at UCD. He has written extensively on the natural and cultural heritage of the Irish landscape, and on many broader aspects of environmental science. He has won several awards for his work in connection with rural biodiversity and the sustaining of rural community.

John Flynn was involved in human blood-typing during the 1970s in Dublin, where he was attached to a number of hospitals, before moving to the Irish Equine Centre to set up Weatherby's blood-typing laboratory for foal registration. He expanded this service to the non-Thoroughbred sector, which provided the basis for comparative studies in horse-population genetics (including the Irish Draught). John and his staff of thirteen have now established a multi-species DNA-testing laboratory that is recognised as one of the leading institutions throughout the world.

Fergus Kelly is a senior professor in the School of Celtic

Studies at the Dublin Institute for Advanced Studies. His interests centre on the study of early Irish (Brehon) law, and his publications include a *Guide to Early Irish Law* (1988) and *Early Irish Farming: a study based on the law texts of the 7th and 8th centuries AD* (1997).

Stuart N. Lane lives in an eighteenth-century farmhouse on the Meath–Kildare border with his wife, two dogs, an unknown number of cats and seven horses. He has been involved in horses all his life, having bred hunters and Sport Horses, hunted with most of the Irish packs and some of the English, point-to-pointed, show jumped and ridden stock horses in Canada and Australia. He took his master's degree some years ago in Trinity College, Dublin, and is currently working for his PhD in NUI Maynooth, his subject covering the economic history of the Irish horse in the nineteenth century.

Colin A. Lewis lectured at University College, Dublin for over twenty years before moving to South Africa, where he is professor of geography at Rhodes University. For over a decade he was hunting correspondent for *The Irish Field* and a well-known judge of horses and hounds. Professor Lewis' books include *Hunting in Ireland* (1975) and *Horse Breeding in Ireland and the Role of the Royal Dublin Society* (1980), both published by J.A. Allen and Company.

Finbar McCormick is a senior lecturer in the School of Archaeology and Palaeocology at Queen's University, Belfast. His interests centre on early medieval archaeology and the study of faunal remains from Irish archaeological sites. He has published extensively on early livestock farming and diet from a zoo-archaeological perspective.

Dáithí Ó hÓgáin holds a BA in modern languages (UCD), MA in Irish language and literature (UCD), and a PhD in folklore (National University of Ireland). Author of 30 research books dealing with a wide range of culture, as well as five collections of poetry in Irish, three collections of short stories in Irish and four radio plays in English, he has also published many research papers on folklore, literature and related topics. An associate professor of Irish Folklore at University College, Dublin, his collected poems in English, entitled *Footsteps from Another World,* was published in 2002 by Philomel.

Marjorie Quarton has farmed, dealt in horses, cattle and sheep, bred Border collies and written thirteen published books; her best-known horse book is *Breakfast the Night Before.* Marjorie can honestly say that she made her living almost entirely out of horse dealing for 35 years. She had a sketchy education and cared for her elderly parents until they died. The first of her books appeared in 1984, and she had a column in the *Irish Field* for many years. Having retired from farming at the age of 68, she is currently supervisor of the National Council for the Blind of Ireland's second-hand bookshop, Bookends, in Abbey Lane, Nenagh.

Norman Storey B.Agr.Sc. is equine specialist adviser at Teagasc, Kildalton College, Piltown, County Kilkenny. He is responsible for the development and management of the equine breeding unit at the college. An active member of the Irish Draught Horse Society for a number of years, he served as chairman of the breeding committee. He is secretary of the Kilkenny branch of the society, and speaks and publishes regularly on Irish Sport Horse breeding.

Foreword

Five years ago a self-described young middle-aged woman made contact with us through our newly-produced website. She was seeking a really nice riding horse with manners that was easy to keep and fun to be with. At the time we were schooling a five-year-old Irish Draught mare, Crosstown Sky by Glenagyle Rebel out of the Pride of Shaunlara daughter Tara Sky, and the two of them fell in love. Little did we know at the time that the passion we had unknowingly stirred in Joan Griffith's life would ultimately lead to this collaboration with Mary McGrath.

Joe McGrath, Mary's father, was a staunch supporter of the Irish Draught from way back so we cannot claim to have introduced Mary to them, but she did have her first real showing success with Suma's Folklore, who she had bought from us as a foundation mare. Joan and Mary met when, after the success of Sky in Joan's household, her husband Friedemann was smitten with the Irish Draught bug and wanted a gelding to join in the fun and games. The gentle giant Harry, whom Mary had bought as a possible part of a driving team until he grew too big, was the answer and this pairing produced two more instant friendships, Friedemann with Harry and Joan with Mary. Sharing far more in common than horses, such as their love of books and their quest for the history and traditions of the Irish Draught horse, they have both already contributed vastly to the breed. We ourselves are humbled by the enormous efforts they have made and it puts our own contribution into perspective.

Our self-instructed brief in 1977 was to find and help restore the Irish foundation stock which was being overtaken by modernisation, both on the farm and as breeding stock to produce top-performance horses. Like so many others down the road we made the acquaintance of Billy Cotter in Cork and John Joyce in Mayo, and these two were responsible for our first mares, and more especially, our first stallion, Pride of Shaunlara. We broke all the mares, and Pride, when they came up to us because, to us, to be part of the end of the twentieth century, riding is what it is all about. I have to say, very few of them failed to please us.

Folklore herself was a typical Suma mare. By Pride of Shaunlara she was the last foal of Miss Gethins, a Ballylaughton product from Sligo whom we had bought along with her first foal, by Solohead, at Ballinasloe fair. In true horse-fair tradition, a great tale of woe as to why she was being sold was spun, which included the death of the young man's father, whom, not much to our surprise, we subsequently met in the best of health! Miss Gethins, like so many Irish Draughts, had been ridden and worked and was currently not in foal, so on her return to Suma she was sold to a hard-hunting airline pilot. After their first day out together, when they were one of the few pairs to see the end of the hunt, he telephoned to find out where she had hunted before. In fact, she had never crossed the country at all, but was intelligent, willing and loved the whole game. She represented to us everything that is good in an Irish Draught. She had a lovely head, good length of rein, moved like a dream and had super style over a fence. To show how roomy she was, the following year she conceived twins, and not only delivered them alive and well but went ten days overtime. The colt made 16.1 and the filly 16.3! She even went in foal again that year.

The Solohead mare, Carlisheen Molly, went on to produce fifteen foals including two full Irish Draught international showjumpers, a stallion in Canada and a string of lovely pure-bred daughters. She was also Reserve Champion at the Royal Dublin Society!

When we talk of Irish Draughts we are talking an international language. There is probably no other breed that can produce such an instant rapport and then long-lasting friendships. Is it because of the characteristics of the breed itself? – open, friendly, intelligent, loves the outdoor life, works hard, enjoys (is even passionate about) its food, has a bit of a middle-age spread but loves a good tussle and fights to the last.

Irish Draughts are an intrinsic part of the Irish horse, loved all over the world. We are glad that it is in our lifetime that the breed has been recognised for itself, and with so many enthusiasts such as Joan and Mary it can be said – as with Mark Twain – that the report of its death has been greatly exaggerated.

Marily Power and Susan Lanigan-O'Keeffe
Suma Stud, Navan,
County Meath

Acknowledgements

The authors would like to thank the following people and organisations for their assistance in preparing this work: Marily Power and Susan Lanigan-O'Keeffe of Suma Stud; Helen O'Toole at the Department of Agriculture and Dermot Ryan at the Irish Horse Board; the Irish Draught Horse Society, especially Helen Kelly; Sharyn Alexander, Eiline Brennan, and Billy and Kitty Cotter; Phillip Sheppy at the Royal Agricultural Society of England library; the National Museum of Ireland; the National Library of Ireland; the Irish Photographic Archives; Mary Kelliher at the Royal Dublin Society library, Derek Cullen at the Tourist Board of Ireland; the Folklore Commission; the National Ploughing Association of Ireland; Seamus Mac Philib and Albert Siggins at the Country Life Museum, County Mayo; Dublin City Archives; 'Tucks' Bergin, Basil Blackshaw, Mario Corrigan in Newbridge Library, Leo Curran, David and Edwin Davison, Mary Davidson, Mairead Dunlevy, Michael Finlay, Desmond Fitzgerald, William Garner at the Irish Architectural Archive, Buster Harty, Will Hayes, Fiona Hughes, Andre Kearney in the Department of Foreign Affairs, Breide Kelly, Darine Goodman, Louis le Brocquy, Colm Lennon, Margaret Lynch, Philip McEvansoneya, Clare McGahan at the K Club, Brigid McGing, Peter Pearson, Tony Roche at the Department of Environment, Heritage and Local Government, Ruth Rogers, Katie Simpson at the *Illustrated London News*, Michael Slavin and the Hill of Tara Bookshop, Pat Taylor, Robert Walsh, Guy Williams and anonymous lenders.

Thanks also to Pam Ploeger and William Duffy for text review and comments, and to Patricia McGrath and Gay and Joe Keogh for their help throughout the project, for reviewing the text and for their constant encouragement. Thanks to Friedemann Weigel, and many thanks to our 'chapter experts'. Lastly, thanks to our families for their support and encouragement along the way.

Joan C. Griffith and Mary McGrath

Acronyms

The Ruling Body for Equine competitions is based in France. Therefore all abbreviations are based on competition descriptions are in French.

AID	Appendix Irish Draught
CC	Concours Complet d'Equitation: event where the competitions are exclusively for the discipline of eventing
CCI	Concours Complet d'Equitation International: international competition as above
CD	Concours de Dressage: events where the competitons are exclusively for the discipline of dressage
CI	Concours International: international event
CIC	Concours International Combine: events where the competitions are exclusively for international one-day events. Events are listed 1 to 5 in order of difficulty and the amount of money on offer
CIO	Concours International Officiel: official international event
CS	Concours de Saut d'Obstacles: Events where the competitions are exclusively for the discipline of showjumping
CSI	Concours International de Saut d'Obstacles: international competition, as above
CSI A	An event that does not have as much money as a CSIO event
CSI B	An event that has less money than a CSI A event.
CSIO	Concours de Saut d'obstacles International Officiel: major international event at which a Nations Cup show-jumping competition is held, e.g. RDS Dublin Horse Show
CSI/W	Events where a World Cup Showjumping competition is held
CSO	Central Statistics Office
DNA	Deoxyribose Nucleic Acid: DNA analysis is used for parentage testing in horses
EFI	Equestrian Federation of Ireland
FB	Foreign Breed Stallion
FEI	Federation Equestre Internationale: the body which manages International Equestrian Sport Events
ID	Irish Draught
IHB	Irish Horse Board
IHR	Irish Horse Register
ISA	Irish Shows Association
ISH	Irish Sport Horse
MRCVS	Member of the Royal College of Veterinary Surgeons
NI	Northern Ireland
RID	Registered Irish Draught
SJAI	Showjumping Association of Ireland
TB	Thoroughbred
VDL	Van de Landweg: prefix of horsebreeding family in Holland
WBFSH	World Breeding Federation of Sport Horses
WEG	World Equestrian Games
WNTR	Weatherbys non-thoroughbred

Introduction

JOAN C. GRIFFITH

From the outset, we must admit that we are enthusiasts of the Irish Draught horse. We started out to write a book about the native-Irish working horse as a way of promoting this wonderful breed. We formed a collaboration of two, one of us Irish-born and bred, having grown up with the draughts, the other of us, American-born living in Germany, trying to learn about the breed from beyond the Irish shores. We wanted to offer a broad view of the horse so we decided to invite experts to prepare essays on the Irish Draught in order to highlight the topic from a variety of perspectives, to give a clearer picture of what we believe to be Ireland's horse in the landscape. Together our collective views cover a range of material from archaeology, history, folklore, economics, agriculture, art, geography, equine science and a bibliographic review of the literature.

Often missed or overlooked, an unsung hero in many ways, the Irish Draught horse has played a significant role in Irish life and Irish horse-breeding practices. The writing of this book has been a cultural as well as scholarly journey. There are undoubtedly many people in Ireland who would have a word or two to say about the Irish Draught. We, along with our experts, have chosen to tell a tale that will touch the hearts and minds of anyone who picks it off the shelf, for this is not just another horse book; it is the story of a 'cultural icon' that has survived the test of time. The Irish working horse was once found in abundance in Ireland – some say upwards of 300,000 at the close of the nineteenth century – yet today there are far fewer, listed at approximately 2,000 registered Irish Draught breeding mares and 100 fully registered stallions at stud.

As background, one must consider historic influences and applications of technology in Irish agriculture, transportation, and the military, for it is in these activities that the native-Irish working horse was utilised on a

RIGHT: *Side cart and traps wait outside Noughaval Catholic church, 1959.*
Photo: National Museum of Ireland

BELOW: *Coastal road, County Clare, 1964; the shafts protruding at the back of the cart derive from the earliest horse-drawn vehicles.*
Photo: Bill Doyle

ABOVE: *Harvesting corn in 1905 in what is now Greater Dublin.*

Photo: Irish Picture Library

day-to-day basis by farmers, businessmen and generals. The hardships and successes of each of these endeavours helped to mould the character and traits for which the Irish Draught is known today in the competition arena and leisure riding world. From the breed standard, 'The Irish Draught Horse is an active, short-shinned, powerful horse with substance and quality. It is proud of bearing, deep of girth and strong of back and quarters. Standing over a lot of ground, it has an exceptionally strong and sound constitution. It has an intelligent and gentle nature and is noted for its docility and sense.'

The horse, working in tandem with the steel plough,

had a significant economic impact in the rural areas. During the nineteenth century, in the era of the rise of the horse,

Machination in agriculture causing unemployment in rural areas: The steel plough appeared in Ireland about 1820. This was pulled by two horses and completed as much work in one day as ten men with spades. Towards the middle of the 1840s most landlords and medium tenant farmers possessed a steel plough, leading to massive unemployment for rural spades men.

From *Irish Famine and Castlemagner*[1]

During the twentieth century, in the era of the decline of the horse,

The elimination of the horse and the arrival of mechanisation was the biggest single change in Irish farming … From then on farming changed faster than it had ever done before … There is a lot of interest from visiting farmers in everything to do with the old workhorses … The horse was the symbol of the pace of life in those days. Today, there is still a huge interest in horse ploughing. We get many enthusiasts coming here to read about the different techniques. Pre-modern farming is a growing hobby for many people.

Seamus MacPhilib, *Irish Examiner*.[2]

ABOVE: *Carlow, 1954: three horses stand patiently, still harnessed to the reaper, while farm workers take a break from harvesting.*

Photo: Fr Browne SJ Collection

Above: *Horse-drawn plough, Ring of Kerry.*   Photo: Bord Fáilte

Above: *The working horse was so vital to the economy of Ireland that the Consolidated Banks chose to depict them on early banknotes, known as the 'ploughman notes', from May 1929 to December 1953.*   Photo: Central Bank of Ireland

One might say, 'what goes around, comes around', and in Ireland during the nineteenth century the horse and plough replaced the man and spade; during the twentieth century the tractor replaced the horse but the Irish Draught horse, although listed as a rare breed, has with its adaptability and athleticism found many other niches in which to evolve in the twenty-first century, including showjumping, dressage, carriage driving, foxhunting, eventing, and has become a modern-day competition-and-riding horse. With its temperament and ability, it is truly a horse that every member of the family can enjoy.

This book deals primarily with the history and evolution of today's Irish Draught horse. We have supplemented our own 'hands on' knowledge of the topic with that of nine experts, who explore the topic from a scholarly viewpoint.

The Irish horse-breeding industry includes a wide range of breeds such as the native Connemara Pony, the Irish Thoroughbred, Irish Sport Horses and imported cold-bloods; these will not be discussed in this book as they are covered widely and well in numerous other publications. Our topic is specifically the Irish Draught horse.

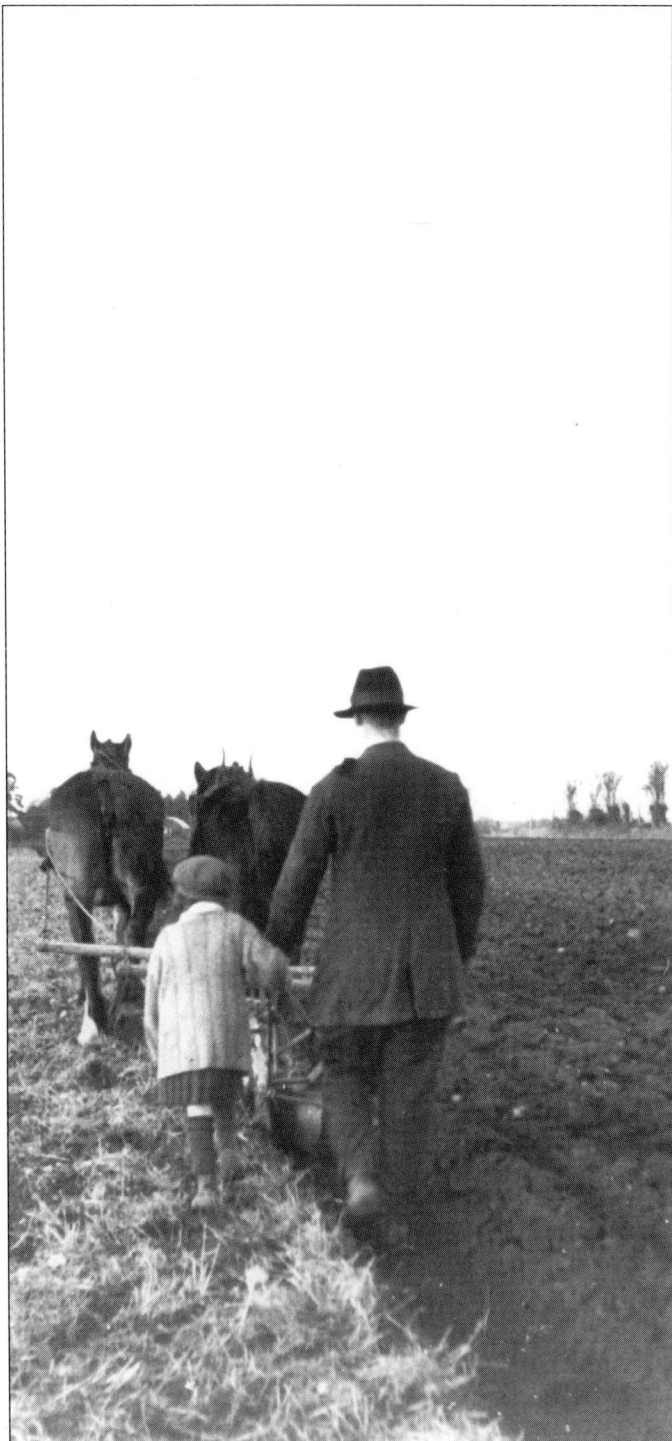

Follower

My father worked with a horse-plough
His shoulders globed like a full sail strung
Between the shafts and the furrow.
The horses strained at his clicking tongue.

An expert. He would set the wing
And fit the bright steel-pointed sock.
The sod rolled over without breaking.
At the headrig, with a single pluck

Of reins, the sweating team turned round
And back into the land. His eye
Narrowed and angled the ground,
Mapping the furrow exactly.

I stumbled in his hob-nailed wake,
Fell sometimes on the polished sod;
Sometimes he rode me on his back
Dipping and rising to his plod.

I wanted to grow up and plough
To close one eye, stiffen my arm.
All I ever did was follow
In his broad shadow round the farm.

I was a nuisance, tripping falling,
Yapping always. But today
It is my father who keeps stumbling
Behind me, and will not go away.

Seamus Heaney, *Death of a Naturalist*
(Faber and Faber Ltd., 1966)

LEFT: *Laois, 1937: ploughman with a pair of horses and a child.*
Photo: Fr Browne SJ Collection

ABOVE: *All Irish horse breeds were depicted on an issue of stamps in 1981, acknowledging their place in the economy of the country, including the horse King of Diamonds, who represented the Irish Draught.*
Photo: An Post

While we could discuss at length the influential older Irish Draught stallion pedigrees, such as Comet, Prince Henry, Young J.P., Woodranger, or the more modern pedigrees of King of Diamonds, Pride of Shaunlara, Clover Hill or Ben Purple, we believe pedigree work has been sufficiently covered by Moore, Begg, O'Hare and Fell. Our goal is to celebrate the Irish Draught horse in broader terms.

The Irish Draught horse is the subject of many opinions and misconceptions. The name conjures up an image of a heavy, farm cart horse, which is one reason why, as a breed, it evaded post-war popular attention and relatively large-scale commercial exploitation until the 1980s. Its popular description, which relates particularly to twentieth-century Ireland up to and during the agricultural mechanisation of the later 1950s and early 1960s, is as a multi-purpose, active farm horse, capable of tilling a small farm, pulling a sidecar to market and milk to the creamery at a steady trot, carrying the farmer out hunting, and breeding a foal each year to sell (usually by a Thoroughbred horse and often to foreign buyers). It had to be quiet to handle, strong and economical to keep. Above all it had to be dependably sound throughout its working life, because the livelihood of the small farm depended on the reliability and efficiency of this horse.

Alex Fell, *The Irish Draught Horse*.[3]

The traits outlined by Fell have served the Irish Draught horse well. However, one could go a step further when comparing the fate of the Irish working horse to that of other Continental European working breeds which, for the most part, faded from the landscape after mechanisation. Being a heavy type of working horse, they could not adapt and evolve, while the Irish Draught, being a light-to-medium-type working horse, survived and continues to be the foundation breed for the world renowned 'Irish hunter', known today as the Irish Sport Horse.

The work of other contributors to this volume represents a wealth of knowledge in Irish cultural scholarship. Each, in their respective field, is outstanding. They too have had a continuing interest in aspects of the Irish horse, as it relates to their broader field of knowledge. Together we shall present, for the first time, an objective view of the role of the working horse in Ireland. We have selected photographs that will conjure up vivid memories of the past that our parents and grandparents will recall, as well as modern-day views which show how the horse in its new role has evolved into a variety of competition and leisure-time activities.

This book is arranged in three parts: 'Setting the Stage,' 'In Search of the Irish Draught Horse' and 'Resources'. Each chapter stands more or less on its own. When viewed as a whole, however, the book creates a historic record that recognises the contribution made by the Irish Draught horse which goes beyond farming and agriculture to the larger themes of Irish culture and heritage.

Part 1: Setting the Stage

Part 1 describes the environment in which the Irish Draught evolved from the perspective of archaeology, Celtic studies, folklore and mythology. Professor Finbar McCormick, senior lecturer of archaeology and palaeocology at Queen's University, Belfast, addresses the evidence of horse remains found in excavations throughout Ireland. His research tells the size, age and uses of horses up to the Anglo-Norman medieval period. Fergus Kelly, senior professor in the School of Celtic Studies at the Dublin Institute for Advanced Studies, translates and discusses his findings about the horse from the early Irish law texts that include types and breeds, colours, qualities, and the legal status of horses under Irish law. Dáithí Ó hÓgáin, associate professor of Irish folklore at University College Dublin, chronicles the superstitions, fears, charms and spells to do with horses in Irish cultural themes.

Part 2: In Search of the Irish Draught Horse

Part 2 reveals the heart of the working horse as cultural icon. Mary McGrath, art conservator and consultant, introduces us to images of the horse as seen through Irish eyes from high crosses to modern art. John Feehan, senior lecturer, University College, Dublin, Faculty of Agriculture, looks at farming methods in regard to the use of the working horse and improving farming technology. Stuart Lane, PhD candidate at the National University of Ireland, Maynooth, shows the important economic, military and transport roles played by the horse in nineteenth-century Ireland. Marjorie Quarton, author and horse dealer, shares with the reader her personal experiences as a horse dealer from 1948 until her retirement. Colin A. Lewis, professor, Geography Department, Rhodes University, South Africa, documents the distribution of Irish Draught horse stallions and mares, as well as the historical development of the recognition of the breed itself. John Flynn, head of the Irish Equine Centre, analyses the DNA of the Irish Sport Horse, the Irish Draught horse, the Irish Thoroughbred and the Connemara Pony. Norman Storey, equine specialist adviser at Teagasc, Kildalton College, reviews recent competitions and reports on the winning Irish Draught and part-bred horses.

Part 3: Resources

Part 3 is a valuable tool for scholars as well as for the enthusiast. Joan Griffith, librarian, has researched the written works dealing with the Irish Draught horse as well as related background documents, and has prepared a selected annotated bibliography. Along with this, the resource guide also has a glossary of terms, chapter reference sources, contributing-author notes and an index.

The Horse in the Landscape

To think of the working horse as icon in Irish culture, one must consider the economic realities and political climate of the past several centuries. One must consider the plight of the poor Irish farmer and the meagre living conditions they and their livestock had to endure. Entire books have been written on topics such as invasions, famine, war and struggle as a continuing way of life. Through good times and bad one constant companion was the working horse, who pulled the farmer's plough, produced the halfbred hunter, took the family to church, and more. Over the years many writers have addressed some of these issues with varying degrees of agreement.

There is an old saying about the Irish Draught: it must be able to 'Plough, sow, reap and mow, go to church and hunt'. But just what is the Irish Draught

ABOVE: *Old Irish Draught mare, 1840.*

Photo: Nineteenth-century book illustration, source not known horse? The Irish Draught has in many ways been an enigma, neither cold blood nor warm blood, perhaps something in between.

To begin, consider the words of others who have been down this road years, decades and even centuries before us.

The Farmer's Horse

The Old Irish Mare. – Much was said of the old Irish mare, but it has been impossible to trace her history, in spite of the interesting treatise on Irish horses furnished to us by Dr Cox, and the map which accompanies it, which shows that from the year 1740 both racehorses and draught horses alike were constantly imported and scattered over the country. The Old Irish mare, within a comparatively recent period, in our opinion, happened to be an accidental product of a hardy dam and a lucky horse, bred without system and molded by the exceptional conditions of her surroundings.'

Earl of Enniskillin, 23 July 1897.[4]

Although the problem of the origin of the Irish horse is of the greatest interest and importance, little research

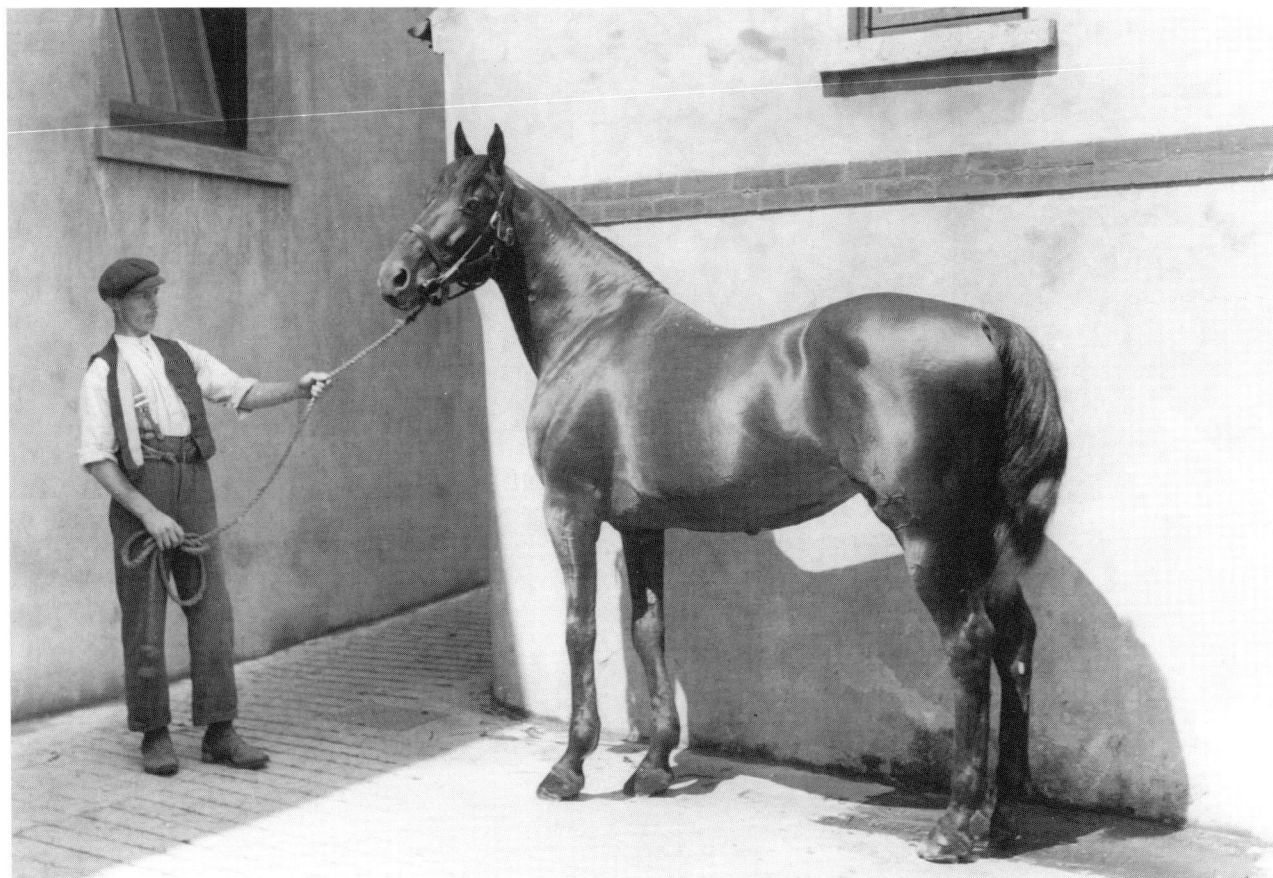

ABOVE: *Mr Widger's Hunter.*

Photo: National Photographic Archive

has hitherto been undertaken to solve it. This is no doubt largely due to the fact that we do not know precisely what the original breed of Irish horse was, or whether several distinct breeds co-existed in Ireland. We are told by some authorities that the Irish Draught horse was the only old breed …

Robert Francis Scharff,
'On the Irish Horse and its Early History'.[5]

In considering the various outside influences which have played a part in horse breeding in Ireland it should be borne in mind that the horse is, perhaps more than any other farm animal, susceptible to climate and environment. Imported breeds become, with the lapse of time, materially altered in their general characteristics, and when crossed with native strains are gradually assimilated by them until there is produced what might be regarded as a single type approximating to that which is indigenous to the country. This is true of all countries, but may be said to apply with double force in the case of Ireland where, it is generally admitted, the soil and climate are singularly well adapted to the development of high class horses of a distinct stamp.

Irish Draught Horse Book.[6]

Irish Hunter Breeding

A description of Irish hunter breeding system is thus, the farmer uses the mare for his ploughing and cart work, and generally crosses her with either a well-bred halfbred or Thoroughbred stallion. She continues to do the farmer's work up to practically the day she foals, is then given about a fortnight's rest, when she is again put to do the necessary ploughing and other farm work. The foal is allowed to run

with the mare while the latter is at work and is, as a rule, weaned during the month of October.

R.G. Carden, 'The Irish Hunter'.[7]

Traditionally, during the nineteenth century, the production of hunters was based on putting Irish Draught mares to Thoroughbred sires. But all the evidence suggests that the Irish Draught was itself the result of the crossbreeding of Thoroughbred and other, Eastern, horses, upon the better and lighter elements of the indigenous Irish horse population, probably upon what had in the earlier days been called the 'Irish hobby'.

Lewis, *Horse Breeding in Ireland*.[8]

The encouragement of horse breeding is a matter of national importance, but it was not until the year 1887 that any attempt was made by Government to foster it.

Irish Draught Horse Book.[9]

Military Service and Slaughter

Replying to the Light Horse Breeders' Society:

It is the light draught horse which is to be the great difficulty in the future, and the solution appears to me to lie in the development for farm work of some breed, with less bulk, greater activity, and altogether tougher fibre than our present heavy breeds – that is, a horse that will eat less, endure more, and is quick enough for field artillery – really a cart horse that will trot.

Lord Derby, Secretary of State for War.[10]

ABOVE LEFT: *Oh Carol RID (Registered Irish Draught) by Pride of Shaunlara, champion mare at Ballina Show, produced Leader Star, reserve champion hunter at the Royal Dublin Society Horse Show, 2003.* ABOVE CENTRE: *Connacht champion filly foal, 1999 by Huntingfield Rebel out of Oh Carol.* ABOVE RIGHT: *Huntingfield Rebel RID by Glenagyle Rebel out of Whippy RID, champion stallion at the Royal Dublin Society Horse Show, 2002.* Photos: Luke Morely and Tony Parkes

1,919 animals were slaughtered, only 417 of these were classified as halfbred females of which 56 were over eight years of age. The vast majority of horses slaughtered were of the heavy workhorse type … we shall continue monitoring the situation to prevent good breeding mares going to slaughter …

from Bord na gCapall (Irish Horse Board).[11]

At that time (1978) there were four approved abattoirs for horse meat within the Republic of Ireland; today there are two. On 4 June 1960, under legislation enacted in October of the previous year to deal with the issue of cruelty to horses en route to abattoirs on the Continent, minimum standards were outlined and the presence of veterinary surgeons was required.

Breeding and Temperament

Breeders must have the patience to persist in the face of any early disappointments; they should cul-tivate the faculty of recognising good breeding animals, and aim at the production of a distinct and well-defined type of horse calculated to meet the requirements of the time.

Irish Draught Horse Book.[12]

Many people buy the draught to use for hunting or simply for pleasure. There is a saying that a farmer doesn't feel he's got a proper farm unless he has a horse on it. There are many farmers who keep a horse, and in particular an Irish Draught, simply for the link with the traditions of the past.

Mark Holdstock,
Great Fair Horse Dealing at Ballinasloe.[13]

The Irish Draught horse has a unique record for pro-ducing top international competition horses which have excelled in all forms of competitive riding, be it the show ring, international showjumping, eventing or dressage. However, the unique qualities of this breed make it equally suited to the keen amateur rider as well as the anxious novice.

Alex Fell, *The Irish Draught Horse*.[14]

There is something special about a draught where hunting is concerned, because of their intelligence and courage and their speed of learning. A good green draught can learn enough the first time it goes hunting if the fences are jumpable to come home almost a made hunter. They look after themselves and they look after the rider.

Pat Gleeson, in *The Irish Draught Horse Book*.[15]

'Above all be proud of your Irish Draught for what it is, a consistently efficient and talented horse that has sustained Man in war and peace, that continues to dominate international competition, and is to those lucky enough to be associated with it a source of great pleasure.

Alex Fell, *The Irish Draught Horse*.[16]

Billy Cotter of Cork (home of the Irish Draught) outlines the typical Irish Draught as a 'clean boned, useful animal of good temperament, whose breeding can be traced back through generations ...' He said the Irish Draught was the foundation of all good hunting and jumping stock in this country and that we should do everything possible to improve our native breed. His concept of the Irish

Draught is a very hardy animal, is between 15.2 hh [hands high] and 16.2 hh and the best type of broodmare has height of about 15.3 hh.

'The Great Debate: A breed or a type'.[17]

The horse [the Irish Draught] in all its aspects had been part of the culture of rural society and even featured large in folklore and storytelling. Indeed, it might be almost true to say that wherever farming folk met within their community, whether at the crossroads for a chat, at the fair or in the pub over a pint, a discussion on rural affairs was not complete without some reference to horses. In this way, knowledge and insight were shared and passed on, as the next generation was educated and imbued with the culture ...

Martin Collins, Irish Draught Horse Society.[18]

The work presented here is a complete and up-to-date account of the history and evolutionary significance of the Irish Draught horse in Ireland, as far as we have been able to determine. By way of facts and figures we believe this book shows many intertwining relationships.

We now invite our readers to take a journey along the cultural road with Ireland's native working horse, the Irish Draught horse. It will be shown as a cultural icon in the Irish landscape supported by way of history, geography, archaeology, folklore, economics, agriculture, art, equine science and a bibliographic review of the literature.

PART 1

Setting the Stage

1

Archaeology:
The Horse in Early Ireland

Finbar McCormick

About 30,000 years ago, wild horses were present across large parts of Eurasia, Africa and even the Americas. Remains from Shandon Cave, County Waterford show that wild horse was present in Ireland about 28,000 years ago. Subsequently, an increase of glacial cover led to their extinction and they did not manage to re-establish themselves when the glaciers retreated. Wild horses are most suited to open steppe areas and it is likely that they were most populous in such areas. It is therefore not surprising that the earliest archaeological evidence for their domestication is in the Ukraine at about 4000 BC.[1] There are, however, problems associated with identifying early domestication. It is extremely difficult to differentiate between the bones of wild and early domesticated horse. There seems to be slight differences in the enamel pattern and skull morphology, but such data can be extremely problematical. Size is not a good indicator as the earliest horses

tend to be similar to their wild ancestors. It is, however, the presence of early horse bits and the tooth wear caused by them that provides the earliest evidence for actual domestication.

The horse was most likely to have been originally domesticated for its meat. Horse remains comprise a significant amount of the food refuse of the early steppe inhabitants of the Ukraine. David Anthony neatly states the case when he states that 'it is doubtful that any prehistoric genius foresaw the potential capabilities of the wild horse as a transport animal, particularly in the absence of any pre-existing tradition of animal riding'.[2] It can therefore be assumed that the horse was domesticated earlier than the first evidence of horses being used for riding.

The earliest evidence for the presence of domesticated horses in Ireland is from early Bronze Age contexts at Newgrange, County Meath, dating to about 2400 BC.

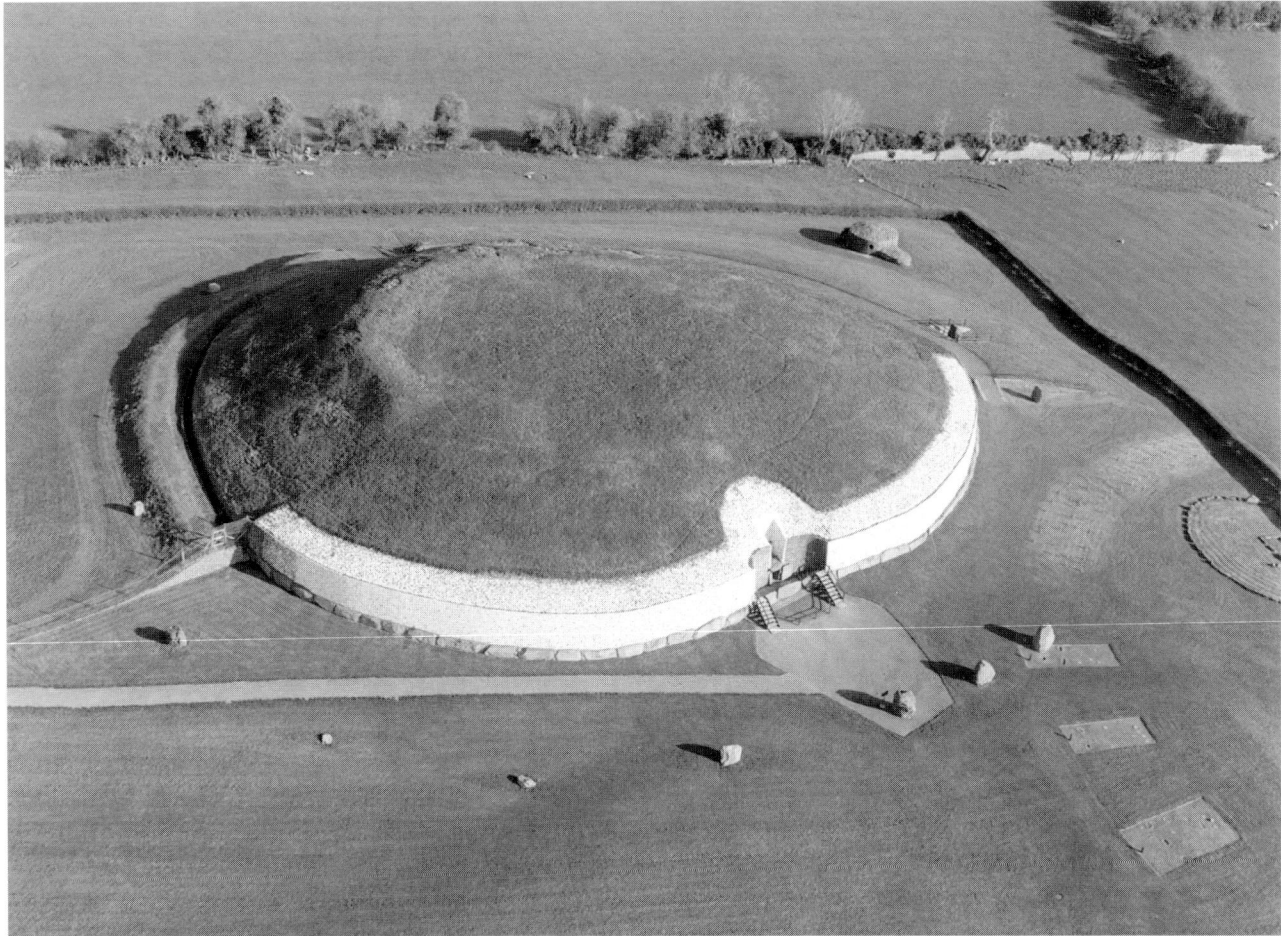

ABOVE: *Newgrange Passage Tomb, County Meath, where horse bones were found in an early Bronze Age context, dating from 2400 BC. The average height of a horse was under 12 hands high.*
Photo: Department of the Environment, Heritage and Local Government

In a few instances, horse remains have been found in Neolithic megalithic tombs but these are likely either to be secondary intrusions or mis-identifications. For instance, a horse skull fragment from the Neolithic Audleystown court tomb on the shores of Strangford Lough, County Down, is likely to be associated with the secondary Bronze Age food vessel burials that were inserted into the tomb.[3] Again, a burnt bone pin from the Neolithic Fourknocks passage tomb, County Meath, was described by the excavator[4] as made of a horse shin bone, but examination of the pin by the present writer has indicated that it was not possible to identify the bone at species level. There is therefore no evidence for the presence of the horse in Ireland before the Bronze Age.

The early Bronze Age settlement at Newgrange was characterised by a type of pottery known as Beaker pottery. The arrival of this pottery coincides with the arrival of metal. Van Wijngaarden-Bakker[5] has noted that in parts of north-western Europe Beaker pottery, metal and the horse appear at the same time. The arrival

ABOVE: *Glenlark, County Tyrone, early twentieth century: on hilly ground, boglands and where there were no roads the slide car was an extremely efficient mode of transport. This type of vehicle has existed from the earliest times. When raised onto block wheels it was known as the low-backed car.*

Photo: National Museum of Ireland

of metal and the horse must have precipitated a social and economic revolution comparable to the arrival of the same commodities to the Amerindians in the sixteenth century. As Anthony remarks, 'trade and exchange systems extended further, became socially more complex, and carried a higher volume of goods than would have been possible with pedestrian transport'.[6] Most importantly, those in possession of horses had a clear military advantage over neighbouring peoples. The horse bones from Newgrange were found intermixed with food refuse from other domesticated livestock. It must be concluded that while the horse may have been kept primarily for transport, they were also eaten. Some of the horses were quite old, up to fifteen years, suggesting they were only killed, cooked and eaten after a useful life of transport or traction had finished. Some of the horses, however, were young, still at their milk-teeth stage, which would suggest some were solely bred for their meat.

One of the horse-foot bones from Newgrange displayed evidence of an arthritic problem that could have been the result of either old age or physical stress due to overwork. The horses were rather small and slender. One complete bone allowed a shoulder height of 121 centimetres, or 11.9 hands, to be estimated.[7] Horse-bone remains are rather scarce throughout the Bronze Age in Ireland, rarely comprising more than 1 per cent of the mammal-bone totals found on early sites. They are in fact totally absent from the Bronze Age levels at Dún Aonghasa, the great stone fort at Inis Mór, County Galway. Horses may simply not have been deemed suitable for the uneven, deeply fissured land surface of the Aran Islands.

The horse bones on Bronze Age sites are generally found mixed with food refuse but one curious example of possible Bronze Age date was found inserted into the top of a Bronze Age burial mound at Farta, near Loughreagh, County Galway.[8] The base of the barrow contained an urn and human cremation of early Bronze Age date, but the mound seems to have been heightened to accept a second burial consisting of an adult human female accompanied by a seven-year-old stallion along with some bones of a red deer. There were no artefacts present that would provide a date for the burial. Human burials accompanied by horses are generally absent in Ireland, although they are known from the Iron Age, Anglo-Saxon and Viking-period Britain. The mystery of the Loughreagh horse can only be solved when the material is radiocarbon dated.

Despite the fact that horses were present in Ireland since the earliest Bronze Age there is no direct evidence as to how they were used. Wear on the front premolars, indicative of abrasion from a bit, has not been found but this is probably a result of the small quantities of horse bones found to date on Irish archaeological sites. No Bronze Age horse bits or harness trappings are known, and the earliest wheeled vehicle, from a bog in Doogarymore, County Roscommon, has been radiocarbon dated to

ABOVE: *Block wheel from Doogarymore, County Roscommon, dating from the second half of the first millennium BC; it provides evidence that wheeled vehicles were in use at this early date.*
Photo: National Museum of Ireland

use of horsehair in textile production. A hoard of late Bronze Age metal object from a bog at Cromaghs, County Antrim, found wrapped in textiles, included a belt with an elaborate tassel made of horsehair.[9]

There is a clear expansion in horse keeping during the Iron Age as horse bones tend to be more numerous on these late archaeological sites. At Dún Ailinne, County Kildare, and Tara, County Meath, horse remains comprise 2.4 per cent and 6.2 per cent of the fragment totals respectively; furthermore horse bits are the most common metal find in early Iron Age Ireland.[10] The use of wheeled transport is implied by the fact that bits are sometimes found in pairs. It can also be assumed that the great wooden plank road at Corlea, County Longford, was built for wheeled transport.[11] Constructed around 148 BC, it runs some 2 miles across a bog. It is estimated that 2-300 large oak trees needed to be felled for its construction. The road was 3-4 metres wide, and at its widest could have easily allowed two oncoming vehicles to pass each other. That said, there was no evidence for ruts caused by wheeled vehicles nor, indeed, was there evidence for wear. It has been argued, on the basis of a jumbled stretch of the road some 7 metres in length, that the construction was never finished, and this probably explains the complete absence of wear and tear on the track.

the middle centuries of the first millennium BC. It is likely that the wheels are Iron Age, that is, dating to after 500 BC. It has been argued that it was only with the advent of the spoked-wheel vehicles that horses rather than oxen could have been used for traction, solid-wheeled vehicles being too heavy for the horse. The Doogarymore wheels are of the latter heavy type. Indeed, as the evidence stands, we have no direct evidence that the horse was used for anything but food during the Bronze Age. The single exception is evidence for the

To get an impression of what wheeled vehicles of the period looked like one must turn to the chariot-burials of the Arras culture of north-east England. Here the remains of numerous chariots have been found as they were frequently put alongside their owners when they were buried. These were light, two-wheeled vehicles with spoked wheels and iron rims, and with a rectangular frame open at the back. A vehicle of this type can be seen at the base of the Ahenny High Cross in County Tipperary, dating to the eighth or ninth century AD. The

❈ THE IRISH DRAUGHT HORSE

ABOVE: *Tara, the legendary capital of Ireland, where a considerable number of horse bones were found. There is evidence that the horses were eaten and they may have been used as a ritual sacrifice. These horses were an average of 13 hands high.*

Photo: Department of the Environment, Heritage and Local Government

circumstantial evidence, the wide wooden track ways and the bridle bits of this period that have been found in pairs would suggest that a similar vehicle was in use in Ireland during the first few centuries BC in Ireland.

The highest incidence of horse bones from an Irish prehistoric site was at Tara, the legendary capital of Ireland.[12] This material dates from roughly the first century BC. No articulated skeletons were present, so once again it is likely that the bones, like the other faunal material, represented discarded food debris. Many of the bones are broken, deliberately shattered for the extraction of marrow. The conclusion that the horse was eaten would seem to be confirmed by the presence of knife cuts and roasting marks on a radius, a bone of the lower front leg.

The ditch at Tara where these particular bones were found was located near the Mound of the Hostages, a site likely to have been a place of royal inauguration.[13] It is tempting to equate the horse bones with the inauguration

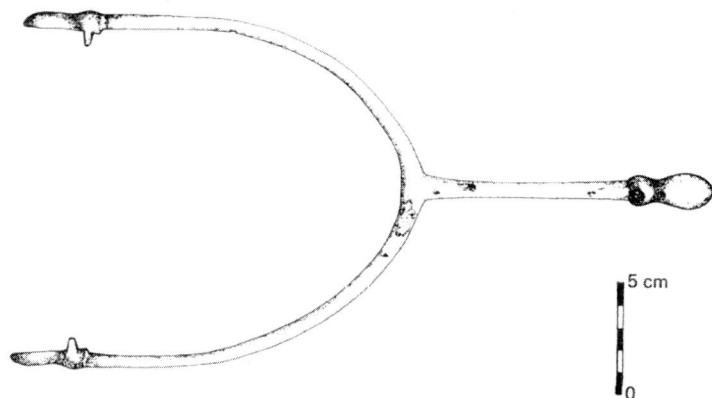

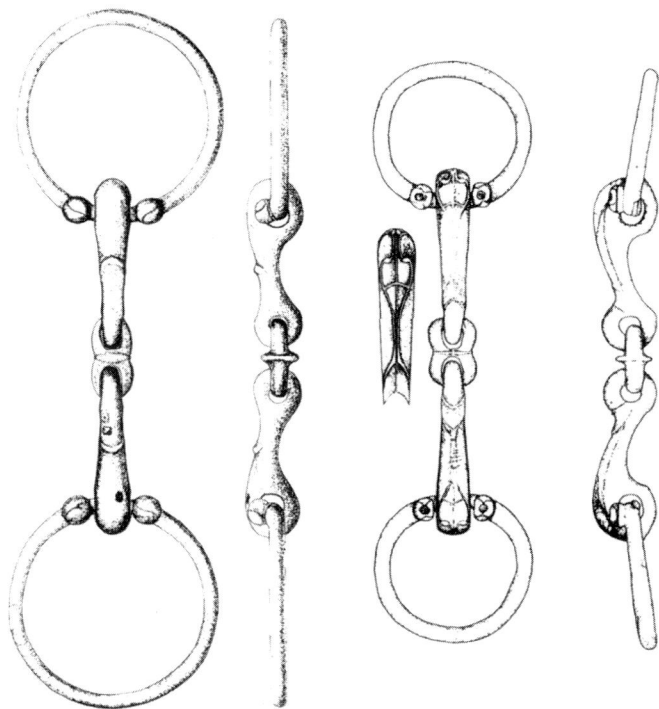

ABOVE: *Horse bits and leading pieces from Attymon, County Galway. These are the most common metal find in early Iron Age Ireland. The use of wheeled transport pulled by two horses is implied by the fact that the bits are usually found in pairs.*

Drawing: B. Raftery Photo: National Museum of Ireland

ABOVE: *Dún Ailinne Hillfort, County Kildare.*
Photo: Department of the Environment, Heritage and Local Government

rite that included the killing, butchery and consumption of horseflesh described by Giraldus Cambrensis. The description is curious, to say the least, and worth quoting in full.

> There is in the northern and farther part of Ulster, namely the Kenelcunill, a certain people which is accustomed to appoint its king with a rite altogether outlandish and abominable. When the people in that land had been gathered together in one place, a white mare is brought forward into the middle of the assembly. He who is to be inaugurated, not as a chief, but as a beast, not as a king, but as an outlaw, has bestial intercourse with her before all, professing himself to be a beast also. The mare is then killed immediately, cut up in pieces, and boiled in water. A bath is prepared for the man afterwards by all his people, and all, he and they, eat of the meat of the mare which is brought to them. He quaffs and drinks of the broth in which he is bathed, not in any cup, or using his hand, but just dipping his mouth into

it around him. When this unrighteous rite has been carried out, his kingship and dominion have been conferred.[14]

Cambrensis' account of Ireland contains much material that is untrue, for one of the aims of the book was to cast a poor light on the morals of the Irish in order to legitimise their reformation by the Anglo-Normans, yet there may still be some truth in this description of the inauguration rite, for the slaughter of the horse is a part of the ritual of kingship in early Indo-European societies.[15] Such a ritual sometimes included a sexual element, although in the Indian *aśvamedha* the encounter is between the queen and a stallion – 'the stallion was smothered to death, whereupon the *mahisí* or chief queen symbolically cohabited with it under covers, while the entourage engaged in obscene banter'.[16] The animal's suffocation would, no doubt, have facilitated this encounter.[17] This element of the rite can be seen as a ritualistic method of ensuring fertility in a kingdom. The sacrificial horse of the *aśvamedha* was subsequently cut up and dispersed, presumably for all to share in its beneficial consumption.

Ceremonial activity described by Cambrensis clearly derives from pagan ritual, and it would be interesting to excavate further inauguration mounds to see if horse remains are present. The Tara material has also provided information about the size of horses at the time. Two complete horse bones indicate shoulder heights of 130 and 133 centimetres (12.8 and 13.1 hands).[18] This is slightly larger than the horse size noted in contemporary Iron Age Britain, where they have a shoulder-height range of 105-48 centimetres (10.3-12.3 hands) with an average of 125 centimetres (12.2 hands).[19]

With the emergence of the early medieval period our knowledge about the early horse, previously derived from archaeology alone, is greatly augmented by the documentary record. The Christian penitentials – those monastic rules that assign penances for individual sins

– made it clear that the Church disapproved of the consumption of horseflesh. The Irish Canons state that 'the penance for eating horseflesh, four years on bread and water'.[20] Despite this, horse bones have been found amongst the food refuse on most sites of the period, including ecclesiastical sites such as Moyne in County Mayo, Church Island in County Kerry and the early Christian Irish foundation at Iona, off the west coast of Scotland.[21] The rule, however, does not seem to have been universal. In a law tract dealing with the maintenance of the sick, the practice of eating horseflesh is not wholly forbidden but noted as being unsuitable for invalids as it tended to 'stir up sickness in the stomach'.[22] Nevertheless, it is probable that the general prohibition of the human consumption of horseflesh adopted by Christianity was derived from Roman and Greek practice, where horses were sometimes used for sacrifice but eating them was regarded with disgust.[23]

If the Irish situation was similar to Continental Europe it is likely that hippophagy (eating of horseflesh) was acceptable until the eighth century, with prohibition introduced later by the Church. It is only *c.* 732 that Pope Gregory wrote to St Boniface, apostle to the Germans, stating that the eating of horseflesh was 'a filthy and abominable practice' and should be prohibited.[24] Perhaps the law on sick maintenance noted above reflects the continuation of a previous toleration of the practice into Christian times.

Horses in early medieval Ireland were used for riding and light traction. The light, two-wheeled chariot was drawn by horses, but heavier traction, especially ploughing, was undertaken by oxen. There is a reference to a horse making up the fourth member of a ploughing team in an early life of St Ciaran, but in that instance it is clearly regarded as a miracle.[25] Horses could only have been used for heavier traction after the introduction of the shoulder harness, which seems to have occurred in Europe during the last few centuries of the first millennium AD. The tale known as the 'Wooing of Etain',

written around 1000 AD, indicates that the shoulder harness was known in Ireland and was appreciated as being superior to the yoke.[26] The story suggests, however, that the harness was used only for oxen, and the earliest evidence for the use of the horse for ploughing is in post-Norman times.

One singular reference in early Irish law suggests that the horse was used for pulling the harrow. This may be the result of a mistaken translation, however, as Fergus Kelly notes that the translation of D.A. Binchy does 'not seem to suit the levelling action of the harrow'.[27] Welsh law also indicates that the horses are used for this purpose,[28] but there is a possibility that the reference may be of post-Norman date.

In England, mixed teams of horses and oxen were used for ploughing for some time before teams made up exclusively of horses came into use. There is evidence for the latter by the middle of the twelfth century.[29] The disadvantage of horse over oxen is that they are much more expensive to feed and when dead their only value was their hide.[30] The earliest evidence for the use of horses for ploughing in Ireland is in the late thirteenth century. However, as in the case of England, mixed teams of oxen and horse seem to have been the norm during the fourteenth century.[31] Oxen generally seem to have been completely superseded by horses for ploughing in Ireland by the fifteenth century.[32]

The early Irish sources make a distinction between horses used for riding and those used for working. Fergus Kelly, in his magisterial study of the documentary evidence for early Irish farming, indicates that the riding of horses was the prerogative of the nobility and well-off free farmer class.[33] Women rarely rode a horse and were transported in chariots. The law tracts make it clear that roads were maintained with chariots in mind. A route way which could boast the title 'highway' was wide enough to allow two chariots to pass each other, while a 'road' could accommodate one chariot and two horsemen passing.[34] Horses were also used for sport, with horse and chariot racing both being referred to in the early texts.[35]

The workhorse in the early sources is often referred to as a *gerrán*, a term that gave rise to *garran* in later sources. Generally, horses carried loads on their back either in the form of bags that hung on both sides or were balanced on some form of pack saddle (*srathar*).[36] References to the actual work undertaken by these workhorses are scarce, but they seem to have been mostly tasks related to agricultural practices. There are references, for instance, to packhorses carrying corn and flour from the mill and also to their carrying loads of wheat, presumably to a mill.[37] A cart (*carr*), as distinguished from a chariot, was also used at this time. References show that the cart was used for the transportation of rods, rushes, manure and corn. These were usually drawn by oxen, but one legal text refers to a carthorse while another reference is to a light *carrus* drawn by a single horse, which was used to transport milk and butter to and from a monastery.[38]

The early sources refer to a variety of colours of horse. Kelly finds references[39] to white, black, grey, dark grey, dun (brown) and orange. Combinations of colours were also known. For information on the size of early horses one must turn to the archaeological evidence. Metrical analysis of material from early medieval rural sites indicates that the horses were mainly between 12.5 and 13.5 hands, but with horses as small as 11.7 and as tall as 13.8 hands also being present. It will be shown below that the Vikings had a profound effect on horse technology in Ireland, introducing the saddle, stirrup, spur and horseshoe. The limited faunal evidence from Viking Dublin shows that there was an increase in the average size of horses to 13.5 to 14 hands and that horses of less than 13 hands are absent.

It is clear that horses were being imported into Ireland during the early medieval period. The laws mention the presence of British horses,[40] the Annals of Ulster in 1029 mention Welsh horses, while the Book of

❊ THE IRISH DRAUGHT HORSE

ABOVE: *Stone cross from Bealin, County Offaly. Ninth-century.*
Photo: Department of Environment, Heritage and Local Government
LEFT: *Drawing of hunting scene on stone cross from Bealin, County Offaly.*
Photo: Department of Environment, Heritage and Local Government

Rights mentions Scottish horses.[41] At the same time, Anglo-Saxon records indicate that horses were being imported from France into England.[42] The Anglo-Saxon Chronicle also indicates that Viking forces were 'horsed' when they arrived in England. The fact that the Vikings made deep incursions into Ireland away from navigable rivers suggests strongly that they brought their horses with them.

The arrival of the Anglo-Normans must have greatly increased the number and range of horses being imported into Ireland. They were obsessive horse breeders, especially of warhorses. The horses brought into Ireland were probably of mixed bloodstock, and it may have been the Normans who introduced Arab strains into Ireland for the first time. The French and English aristocracy imported large quantities of horses from Spain, many of which would have been seized in wars against the Moors.[43] Irish horses were also in great demand. In the year 1171 it is recorded that there was a single shipment of 100 horses from Ireland to England.[44] Some of these horses went further afield. In 1330 Irish horses were being sent to royal studs in France, and during the latter half of the fifteenth century Irish horses were ending up in the studs of the Gonzagas of Mantua in Italy.[45]

The accepted belief is that the Anglo-Normans bred larger horses because of the use of heavily armoured mounted troops. The Irish evidence is equivocal. In twelfth- to thirteenth-century Waterford the horses were generally between 12.5 and 13.5 hands, which is a lower average than in Viking Dublin. Some horses of 14 hands, however, are also present. It is only in fourteenth- to fifteenth-century Ireland that larger horses of up to 15 hands appear, and it is likely that this increased size relates to the adoption of horses for ploughing.

The documentary and iconographic evidence indicates that the early medieval Irish did not use a stirrup or saddle. The texts refer only to a horse cloth that was positioned under the rider.[46] Saddles seem to have been

ABOVE: *Art MacMurrough meeting Richard II, 1399. MacMurrough rides barefoot on a white horse that, without saddle or bridle, was worth 400 cows.*

Photo: By permission of the British Library

a Norse introduction as the Irish for saddle – *sandal* – is derived from Old Norse.[47] The earliest Irish stirrup is from tenth-century levels in Viking Dublin.[48] The prick-spur and the horseshoe also make their first Irish appearance on early eleventh-century levels in Viking Dublin.[49] The horseshoe appears simultaneously in Frankish and Byzantine documentary sources in the late ninth and early tenth centuries.[50] The horseshoe also seems to make its first archaeological appearance in Britain coinciding with Viking settlement in England.[51] It seems, therefore, that the Vikings were making a major

contribution to horse technology both in Ireland and elsewhere. The use of the saddle and stirrup allowed mounted warriors to be used much more effectively in battle, allowing the rider to stand and turn in combat. The Irish, however, do not seem to have immediately adopted all these innovations. Giraldus Cambrensis notes of the Irish in about 1185 that

> When they are riding, they do not use saddles or leggings or spurs. They drive on, and guide their horses by means of a stick with a crook at its upper

end, which they hold in their hand. They use reins to serve the purpose of both of a bridle and a bit.[52]

A mounted horseman holding such an instrument is represented on a ninth-century cross at Bealin, County Offaly.[53]

Cambrensis' assertion that the Irish did not use saddles may not, however, be strictly true. The early-twelfth-century Book of Rights notes that saddles accompanied horses granted as stipends[54] from an over-king to an under-king. It may well be that saddles were only utilised as displays of status, and their military potential, in association with the stirrup, was not realised; perhaps such military 'improvements' were not deemed necessary. Recently it has been shown that the use of heavily armed knight cavalry by the Anglo-Normans in Ireland has been overestimated.[55] Cavalry charges of this type were extremely rare and 'forays, raids, skirmishes and burnings, and the capture of fortified positions were far more common than pitched battles'.[56] Perhaps the particular nature of war in Ireland did not warrant the universal adoption of the stirrup and saddle. Indeed, riding without a saddle must have had its advantages because the Anglo-Norman aristocracy in Ireland began to adopt the practice to such an extent that Edward III introduced legislation to prohibit the activity. The Statutes of Kilkenny, enacted in 1366, noted that 'no Englishman who has to the value of one hundred shillings of land or tenements, or of rent by the year; ride otherwise than on a saddle in the English fashion'.[57] As late as 1399, Irish kings chose not to use the saddle. When Art MacMurrough met the Duke of Gloucester in that year he was described in an account by French historian Jean Creton as follows:

he had a horse without housing or saddle which was so fine and good, that it had cost him, they said, four hundred cows … in coming down he galloped so hard that in my opinion I never saw hare, deer, sheep or any other animal, I declare to you with certainty, with such speed, as it did.[58]

It seems likely that MacMurrough and accompanying soldiers were mounted infantry. Irish mounted infantry on fast, light horses were highly effective in medieval warfare and it may well be that the Irish never utilised cavalry to any great extent. Marie Therese Flanagan has shown that mounted horsemen only seem to have become important in Irish warfare during the later twelfth century.[59] She notes that at a convention at Athboy, County Meath, to confirm the high kingship of Ruadirí Ua Conchobair, some 19,000 horsemen were present from different areas of the country. It seems likely that these were mounted infantry rather than cavalry. The fact that the Irish did not use saddles or stirrups does not imply any military inferiority. Irish infantry mounted on small horses – hobbies – were known to be extremely effective at harassing heavily armoured knights to such an extent that these horses were being hired by Edward I for his campaigns.[60] The first reference to the use of these 'hobblers' was in 1296 when Edward imported 150 of them to help in his war against the Scots, with larger numbers of them being imported into Britain for different campaigns during the succeeding decades.[61]

LEFT: *Kells, County Meath: base of Cross of the Tower, tenth century. Three warriors riding in procession from right to left, and two horses chariots proceeding from left to right. The chariots – on very large, eight-spoke wheels – carry an armed warrior and are driven by charioteers holding the reins and driving the horses on with a whip.*

Photo: Department of Environment, Heritage and Local Government

BELOW: *Mounted infantry carrying circular shields depicted on the base of the ninth or tenth-century Market Cross at Kells, County Meath. The sculptor has created a scene with movement and a rhythm of design that is very modern in feeling.*

Photo: Department of Environment, Heritage and Local Government

ABOVE: *'The Flight into Egypt' on the high cross at Moone, County Kildare. The Virgin is shown riding side-saddle on the off side as was common in Ireland at that time. She is depicted riding on a pony as donkeys were not yet common in Ireland and would probably have been unknown to the sculptor.*

Photo: Department of Environment, Heritage and Local Government

LEFT: *Hunting scene with rider among dragons on tenth-century carved pillar at Clonmacnoise, County Offaly.*

Photo: Department of Environment, Heritage and Local Government

2

Manuscripts:
The Horse in Early Irish Society

FERGUS KELLY

Writings in Irish from the pre-Norman period provide more information about the horse than any other domestic animal, apart from the cow. The Old Irish law texts – ranging in date from the seventh to the ninth centuries AD – are a particularly rich source of information on animal husbandry, and include a short ninth-century text on the qualities which a buyer should look for in a horse.[1] Another law text from approximately the same period deals with the diseases and defects of domestic animals, including seven which are associated with the horse.[2] Horses also feature prominently in sagas, poetry, saints' lives, place-lore and proverbial literature. In addition, many personal names contain the element *ech* – 'horse'.[3] For example, a common name among the early Irish was Eochaid (Echuid), meaning 'horseman'. This is preserved in the modern Irish surname Mac Eochadha, anglicised MacKeough, Keoghoe and Keogh – a Northern

variant gives MacAghy, MacCaghy and MacCaughey. Other early personal names starting with this element include Echmarcach (horse-rider), Echmíled (horse-warrior), Echrí (horse-king) and Echthigern (horse-lord).[4] Many place-names likewise contain words for horse, such as Echdruim (horse-ridge, anglicised Aughrim), Echinis (horse-island, anglicised Aughinish) and Léim ind eich (Léim an eich, horse's leap, anglicised Lemnagh or Leamaneh).[5]

Types and Breeds

Our sources regularly distinguish two principal types of horse. The main law text on status, Críth Gablach, dating from around the eighth century, states that a well-off commoner is expected to own a work pony (*capall fognama*), as well as a horse for riding (*ech imm-rimme*).[6] Higher up the social scale, those who have attained the rank of lord have larger numbers of horses on their farms. A typical lord owns a horse suitable for riding – with a silver bridle – as well as four other horses for more menial tasks.[7]

Various references suggest that imported stock was used to improve the speed and size of the early Irish horse. The law texts assign special value to the horse from overseas (*ech allmuir*). Such horses are often said to be of British origin, and it is likely that they derived from stock brought to Britain from the Continent during the period of Roman occupation. One might expect it to have been more economical to import stallions rather than mares to improve the quality of Irish horses in the early Christian period. However, the importation of foreign mares is indicated by the use of the word *gaillit*, a derivative of *gall* (Gaulish, foreign), to refer to a good-quality mare. Legal glossators clearly regard such mares as being of British origin. A male foal from a foreign mare is termed in one text a *gaillire* – 'the foreign one'.

The small sturdy work pony of the 'Celtic' type is doubtless of more ancient ancestry. Such ponies were generally called *capall*, a term which is cognate with Welsh *ceffyl* of the same meaning. The Latin word for work pony, *caballus* (which gave rise to the Italian *caballo* and the French *chéval*), is almost certainly a borrowing from Celtic. Another early Irish term for work-pony is *gerrán*, which most likely means 'the short one', from the adjective *gerr*, meaning 'short'. In post-Norman sources this type of pony is commonly called a *garran* (*garron*), and in Scotland the same word is applied to the main type of Highland pony, the garron (as distinct from the lighter Western Isles pony).

There is little evidence in early Irish sources of the crossbreeding of the horse (*Equus caballus*) with the ass (*Equus asinus*). The ass was well known to the early Irish in religious contexts because of the frequent mention of it in the Bible. For example, the tenth-century religious poem, *Saltair na Rann*, refers to Christ's entry into Jerusalem mounted on an ass (*assan*).

ABOVE: *Rider, Book of Kells, seventh century (manuscript 58 f89r). The rider has the characteristic Irish riding position. There is no saddle and minimal bridle. Direction seems to be given by means of the hand-held goad.*

Photo: Trinity College Library

In one version of the Old Irish law regulating the observance of Sunday, it is stated that a person should not ride a horse or ass (*imrim for ech nó assan*) on Sundays. However, this portion of text may owe more to Old Testament tradition than to current Irish practice. In another Old Irish version, there is no mention of riding on an ass; possibly the redactor omitted it as being irrelevant in an Irish context. To my knowledge, the earliest explicit reference to an ass on Irish soil is in an anecdote in a legal manuscript, which records that a cardinal came from Rome to instruct certain ecclesiastics. When they stole the cardinal's horses, mules and asses, the Pope sold the tribute and dues of Ireland – which had formerly gone to him – to the English. This incident is alleged to have taken place in the reign of Domnall Mór Ua Briain, king of Munster, who died in 1194.[8] This is also the first Irish reference to a mule, the offspring of a jackass and a mare. It seems to have been an animal which was generally unfamiliar in early

Christian Ireland, so a ninth-century glossator defines the Latin word *mulio* (mule-keeper) in terms of the familiar horse, calling him an *echaire* (horse-keeper).

Colours

There is no evidence of types or breeds of horse in early Ireland being associated with particular colours. However, there is little doubt that the most prestigious colour for a horse was white, and the poetic term *gabor* is used especially of a horse which is white or partly white. There are also references in the literature to horses which were coloured black (*dub*), grey (*líath*), dark grey (*dubglas*), dun (*odor*), brown (*donn*), or yellow (*buide*). Colour combinations include roan (*crón*) with a white head, and grey (*glas*) with speckled mane.

Horse Qualities and Values

As one would expect, early Irish texts devote a great deal of attention to the qualities most admired in a horse. In the case of racehorses, it is obvious that speed is the most important requisite, and the names given to outstanding horses often reflect this quality, such as *Grip* (Swift), *Gáeth* (Wind), *Athach* (Gust) and *Síde* (Whirlwind). The ninth-century law text on the qualities which a buyer should look for in a horse gives us a more detailed insight into the criteria used to judge horseflesh in the early period. It lays down a number of guidelines for a horse intended to be ridden. Firstly, the ideal horse should be 'large, healthy, young and docile'. It should be neither too tall nor too small, and should be broad-chested but narrow-legged. It should not have an excessively large mouth. In temperament, it should be mettlesome, fiery and lively hearted (*béochraide*), but at the same time gentle, calm and 'easy in the hand'. It should not be clumsy, lazy, shivering or in the habit of leaping around. It should not be lame nor should it walk stiffly. It should not be 'yoke-backed' (*mámdruimnech*) –

this may mean that the horse should not bear the marks of excessive subjection to a yoke (*mám*). Any wound caused by castration should have healed, and there should be no lump on its back. It should not be given to kicking or tail-swishing. It should be a good jumper and of good stock. The purchaser of a horse may return the animal for any reason with a full refund within 24 hours of the sale. If the horse develops a disease or other serious ailment within a year of purchase, the buyer is entitled to return the horse and obtain a refund.

In general, horses were regarded as being of considerably more value than cows. One law text states that for a poem in a certain type of metre, a poet is entitled to receive a horse worth two milch cows (*ech dá bó*). Other law texts refer to horses worth five milch cows and even fifteen milch cows. Legal commentary from about the twelfth century provides a detailed – and rather legalistic – account of the value of young and adult horses. At birth a foal of either sex is said to be worth one-twelfth of its mother's value if it resembles her. If it resembles its father it is worth one-twelfth of his value. If it resembles neither of them, it has one twenty-fourth of the value of each parent. Before birth, a foal is said to be worth more than after its birth, having one-ninth of its mother's value. The commentator explains this anomaly as being due to the fact that the death of the foal in its mother's womb is more likely to harm her than its death afterwards. As with other livestock, legal commentary takes one-third of an adult horse's value to be for its body, one-third for its potential and one-third for its work. If a horse has no potential and is incapable of work it is said to have no value because its carcass (*mart*) is worthless – it is implicit here that the meat of the horse is not held to be of any value. Indeed, there seems to have been a general reluctance among the early Irish to eat horse meat.

The main categories of livestock used in the early Irish currency system were cattle and sheep – the most common unit of value being the milch cow (*bó mlicht*). In a few instances, however, a fine or value is given in terms of horses. Thus, one law text states that the fine for a particular injury should consist of one-third cattle, one-third horses and one-third silver. It is further specified that one-third of the horses should be mares. It is clear from a short Middle Irish satire that professional poets looked down on patrons who rewarded them with cattle rather than with horses. An unknown patron is lampooned in the following terms: 'I have heard that he gives no steeds for poems; he gives what is native to him, a cow.'[9]

The Care and Training of Horses

Early Irish written sources provide a small amount of information on the care and training of horses. The Old Irish tale, 'Fled Bricrenn' ('The Feast of Bricriu'), refers to the feeding of horses, and makes it clear that a type of grass called *airthenn* was regarded as a special treat. This grass is to be identified with fiorin-grass (*Agrostis stolonifera*), a species particularly prized by agricultural improvers in Ireland in the eighteenth and nineteenth centuries.[10] The same tale also refers to the feeding of barley to horses.

The training of horses normally starts in their third year. In one law text, untrained horses (*anindle ech*) are described as 'stallions and colts still with their mothers'. Training was initiated by getting the young horse accustomed to having a bit (*glomar*) in its mouth. Attached to the rings of the bit is the bridle, which fits around the horse's head. The texts distinguish a smaller bridle (*srían*) designed for a work pony or riding horse, and a larger bridle (*all*) for a chariot horse. It is well known that the training of horses takes time and patience. Any rush to use an untrained horse can only lead to disaster. For this reason, the proverbial expression, 'a pack-saddle on a colt' (*srathar for serrach*), is used to define an impossible undertaking.

The Work of Horses

One of the most important functions of the early Irish horse was the carrying of loads. *A Life of St Patrick* refers to a load being carried by a work pony (*gerrán*). This load consisted of two bags of wheat, presumably balanced on either side of the horse's back. Loads might be carried in a pack saddle or directly on the horse's back. A legal quotation from about the eighth century warns against a horse carrying a full load on boggy or rocky terrain. As the horseshoe was not introduced to Ireland until about the eleventh century,[11] the hooves of a heavily laden horse would be liable to injury on sharp rocks; on boggy land the horse would sink into the ground.

Early Irish sources contain more references to the use of horses for draught than for riding. It seems that the heavy four-wheeled farm cart (*carr*) was normally drawn by oxen. However, there is also mention of a lighter cart drawn by a horse. For example, a Latin *Life of St Crónán* speaks of a cart drawn by a single horse which was used to transport vessels for milk and butter to and from a monastery. The law text *Críth Gablach* also refers to the use of a pair of draught horses to pull the harrow, though the plough itself was typically drawn by a team of four oxen. It was not until the late thirteenth century that the great plough horse – originally developed on the Continent for military purposes – started to supplant the ox. References in a legal treatise attributed to Giolla na Naomh Mac Aodhagáin (who died in 1309) suggest that both oxen and horses were used for ploughing in his time. By the end of the fifteenth century, however, it seems that oxen had been totally superseded for this purpose.[12]

The two-wheeled chariot (*carpat*) was the regular means by which persons of rank travelled the countryside. It would appear from *Críth Gablach* that even the most prosperous grade of commoner is not expected to own a chariot. Chariot ownership is repeatedly associated with kings, lords, clerics and others of high rank. Such chariots were drawn by two horses and driven by a charioteer (*arae*). He wielded a rod (*echlasc*) which

ABOVE: *Topographica Hiberniae by Giraldus Cambrensis, 1180s (manuscript 700 f.40r). The rider is shown using reins but no saddle or bridle, and is carrying a staff to direct the horse.*

Photo: Produced with the permission of the National Library of Ireland

may have had a metal hook at the top. The chariot was constructed by a professional chariot-builder (*carpat-sháer*). It was largely made of wood, and one law text states that the shafts were commonly of holly. Each wheel had a metal rim, and the inside of the chariot was covered with hides to provide some comfort for the passenger.[13] A short legal passage from about the eighth century deals with road maintenance and other aspects of the highway code.[14] A highway (*slige*) should be constructed so that two chariots can pass one another. Responsibility for the maintenance of such highways fell on the local client farmers. They were obliged to dig out the ditches on either side of the road, fill in potholes and cut away bushes. The text specifies that there are three particular occasions when roads have to be cleared. The first of these is defined as 'the time of the horse-rush' (*aimser echrúathair*), which apparently applies when an assembly is to be held. They must also be cleared so that lords can use them to make their winter visitations to their clients. Finally, they must be cleared in time of battle. This text also tells of the existence of privately owned roads which were used for bringing herds of animals to the mountains or woods – a toll of one animal from each herd was payable every second year by the herd owners.

Horse riding does not seem to have had the same aristocratic associations as travel by chariot, and an ordinary well-off commoner was expected to own a horse for riding (*ech immrimme*). The law texts stressed the importance of the horse as a means of relaying warnings of impending danger and other urgent messages. The law provides special protection for the 'horse of warning' and the 'horse of a man who strives for the honour of the territory'; that is, one on important public business. For such purposes a king was expected to have in his service a professional messenger (*techtaire*) with a swift horse at his disposal. There are few references to women riding horses in early Irish literature, and it is clear that it was more usual for women – especially those of high rank – to travel by chariot. The mounted warrior features only rarely in early Irish sources. In the method of warfare described in the sagas, the combatants came to battle in horse-drawn chariots, but then dismounted and fought on foot. Fighting from horseback is difficult without saddle and stirrups, and it is clear from the linguistic evidence that neither was used in early Christian Ireland. The Old Irish law texts refer to a horse-cloth (*echdíllat*) under the rider, but the word for saddle (*sadall*) is a Norse borrowing. The words for

THE IRISH DRAUGHT HORSE

stirrup (*stiróip*) and spur (*spor*) are later borrowings from Middle English.

Horse-Racing

Horse-races were a feature of the regular public assembly (*óenach*), and seem to have been held particularly at the feast of Lughnasa in early August. Kings were clearly able to enjoy horse-racing more frequently. The account of a king's weekly schedule in the law text Críth Gablach sets aside Friday for horse-races. The term *ech búada* (horse of victory, prize horse) is used for a swift riding horse, often in the context of horse-racing. For example, a law text states that such a horse cannot be subjected to distrait (distraction) – even for its own offences – at a time when races are being held. So even if such a horse caused injury to a passer-by by kicking or biting, the consequent legal process would be postponed until after the races. There is also evidence that chariot races took place: another law text refers to the 'chariot which gains the victory at an assembly'.

A vivid description of early Irish horse-racing is found in the Old Irish tale 'The Voyage of the Boat of Máel Dúin' (*Immram Curaig Maíle Dúin*). Part of it reads:

> when they [the voyagers] had gone a short distance from land they saw many people by the island shore, who held a horse-race (*grafand*) after reaching the green of the island. Each horse was swifter than the wind, and great was their noise and tumult. Máel Dúin then heard the blow of the horse-sticks at the meeting. He also heard what each of them was saying: 'Bring the grey horse.' 'Drive the dun horse over there.' 'Bring the white horse.' 'My horse is faster.' 'The jumping of my horse is better.'[15]

Diseases and Ailments of Horses

The annals contain a number of references to mortalities of domestic animals, usually as a result of exceptional weather conditions and a consequent shortage of grazing. For example, the Annals of Inisfallen record that in 1172 bad weather resulted in the death of 'most of the livestock of the men of Ireland'.[16] Such losses were especially likely to occur during the hungry months of spring: the Annals of Ulster refer to a great starvation of livestock in the spring of 879.[17] It is frequently clear from entries in the annals that the full brunt of such mortalities fell on cattle, the mainstay of the early Irish economy. For example, the Annals of Ulster record an outbreak of cattle mortality (*bó-ár*) in England in 699 which spread to Ireland in the following spring, and triggered off three years of such severe famine that men were reduced to cannibalism.[18] Occasionally, epidemics specifically affecting horses are mentioned in the annals. Thus, the Annals of Inisfallen refer to a contagious cough called *galar na placodi*, which was widespread among horses and people in 1259.[19] This was perhaps an epidemic of 'strangles' caused by *Streptococcus equii* and which is characterised by coughing and swollen lymph glands in the neck. It is known to be transmittable to humans.

Legal commentary refers to diseases and other ailments which may appear after purchase in cattle, horses, goats, sheep, dogs and poultry (and also in slaves). This commentary deals with the legal implications of whether an animal has contracted an infectious disease or whether it suffers from an inherent ailment. This distinction may be difficult to establish, so the category of a 'disease of uncertain origin' is also recognised in law. Seven diseases or ailments affecting horses are listed. Their identity is not always apparent, but the following suggestions – which I have discussed with Tadhg Ó Scannaill MRCVS and Mícheál Ó Dochartaigh MRCVS – may be of interest to readers.

The first disease listed is called *seirthech*, which is likely to be a derivative of the word *seir* (heel, hock), and to refer to some affliction of the hock, such as bone spavin. Next is *deilgnech*, which is explained by a glossator as 'stomach worms' and clearly contains the element *delg* (thorn). Presumably it refers to the thorn-like appearance of some parasitic worms. A later treatise on horses refers to another type of internal parasite called *maílchinnáin* (bald-headed ones), which is described as the worst type of worm.[20] The legal commentary then lists the disease of *echmaig*, which can safely be identified with *farcy*, an ailment of horses characterised by pustules, nodules and ulcers.[21] On recovery, these form star-shaped scars. The next disease is *fothach*, which refers to the nasal and pulmonary disease of glanders. It has now been eradicated from Ireland, Britain, western Europe and North America, but was formerly a widespread and often fatal affliction of horses. It is transmittable to humans. The Annals of Connacht record cases of fatal glanders in the year 1464.[22] Muircheartach Mac Airt Uí Mhaoilsheachlainn and his wife, along with three others, are said to have contracted the disease through going to see a horse which died of glanders. All five died within twenty-four hours of each other. Next on the list of horse diseases is *ech-idu*, which is best translated as 'colic'. Colic in horses may be caused by internal parasites, anthrax, incorrect diet, etc. *Fothach* is followed on the list by an ailment called *lec ós crú*, which literally means 'stone above the hoof'. It may refer to ringbone, a calcium deposit encircling the posterior bones of the front legs.[23] It may also occur on the hind legs. The last disease or ailment on the list is *aife seralach*, which has not been identified.

Finally, there is a reference in another legal commentary to the disease of *tetnais* (tetanus, lockjaw), which is generally fatal to horses and is transmittable to humans. A glossator explains it as *merechduin* which is apparently a compound of *mer* (mad, violent) and *ech* (horse). This term presumably refers to the violent symptoms of the disease, caused by overreaction of the reflex and motor stimuli. Death is ultimately by asphyxiation.

As well as diseases, horses – like other domestic animals – may suffer death or injury in accidents. The law texts make particular mention of the hazards of drowning and of the breaking of limbs. Where liability can be fixed on an individual, the value of the animal must be restored to the owner. For example, if an animal is impaled on a fence which has been constructed in a dangerous manner by a neighbour, he must pay the owner for injury or death caused by this negligence. Similarly, if a woodcutter fails to drive away any livestock which are near a tree he is cutting and death or injury results, the value of the animal must be paid to the owner. A herdsman may likewise be liable where livestock under his care suffer death or injury due to his negligence. In cases of attack by wolves he is free from liability for 'the first seizure of a wolf', but is expected to prevent any further predation on the animals under his care. Naturally, there is no liability if animals are killed by an act of God, such as lightning. Disasters in this category are occasionally recorded in the annals. In the year 1490, the Annals of the Four Masters record a *maidhm talmhan* – presumably an earthquake or landslide – at Sliabh Gamh (the Ox Mountains, County Sligo) which killed 100 people, as well as many horses and cattle.[24]

Horses in Law

The horse – for all its useful and attractive qualities – can be dangerous. Consequently, the Old Irish law texts devote a good deal of attention to the legal implications of injury or death to humans or other animals caused by horses. If the owner of a horse knows his horse is a biter (*daintech*) and it bites someone, he is obliged to pay a heavy fine, which takes into account not only the severity of the injury, but also the fact that he has not taken adequate steps to prevent the attack.

The annals contain many records of death or injury resulting from a fall (*escar*) from a horse. For example, the Annals of Ulster tell us that in the year 1004, a king of Tara named Máel Sechnaill fell from his horse and was so badly injured his life was in danger.[25] However, he recovered from his injury and lived for a further eighteen years, dying in 1022 at the age of 73. Others were not so lucky: the same annals record the death in 1297 of Uilliam Ó Dubhthaigh, bishop of Clonmacnoise, after falling from his horse,[26] and in 1201 Conchubhar Beag Mac Lachlainn died in battle after a fall from his horse which had been wounded by warriors of the Cenél Conaill.[27] It is clear from an Old Irish law text that the horse owner is generally not held to be liable if a person is killed or injured after being thrown from a borrowed horse. However, the accompanying commentary stresses that the owner must give a warning if the horse is known to be in the habit of bucking or shying. The owner of a stallion is generally free from liability for any offences which it commits while the mares are in heat. Injuries involving horses are particularly liable to occur on roads where people or vehicles are crowded together. The main law text on accidents lays down the general principle that a horse owner is not liable for injuries inflicted by his horse at a fair (*óenach*), nor is he entitled to compensation if his horse is itself injured. Accidents involving chariots are similarly immune from liability when they occur at a fair. To reduce the risk of chariot accidents on the roads, the law text on this topic specifies that a high road (*slige*) should be wide enough for two chariots to pass. A second-class road (*rout*) should be able to accommodate a chariot and two horsemen. The law texts also refer to the case of persons being injured by stones or clods thrown up by horses' hooves. The rider is not held to be responsible, as this is classed as one of the 'seven reboundings' which may cause injury but do not entail liability.

As in the case of other domestic animals, horses are liable to break into neighbouring lands and cause damage to grassland. The main law text on farming matters, Bretha Comaithchesa (Judgements of Neighbourhood), lays down detailed rules regarding grazing-trespass under various circumstances. As one would expect, the fine is heavier in the winter season (November to March) because there is less growth of grass at this time. The quality of the land is also taken into account, with the fine for trespass on preserved pasture being twice as much as that imposed for trespass on after-grass or moor land. If horses are guilty of grazing-trespass by night, the fine is doubled on the grounds that they should either be properly tied up or housed in a stable. One law text contrasts the manner in which cattle crop the grass with the more damaging grazing of horses, which 'graze down to the soil'. Damage to crops by domestic animals is also discussed, with particular mention of the destruction of corn-ricks by horses.

The law texts also cover many of the circumstances in which a horse may be subjected to misuse or injury by a person other than its owner. If a person borrows a horse from another he is expected to treat it properly. He is liable to pay compensation if he causes injury through roughness or stretching it beyond its strength. In general, it is an offence to take somebody else's horse without permission – even with the intention of returning it later. According to one legal passage, a person must pay a fine of one cow for the mere act of mounting a horse belonging to another. If he rides off on the horse he must pay further fines based on the rank of the horse owner, and the distance he travels. However, in the case of a genuine emergency in which a person is in fear or if there is a need to warn of danger, a horse may be taken without liability, provided it be returned to the owner. If a person employs a messenger to carry out some business for him, and entrusts him with a horse, the messenger is not liable if the horse is accidentally killed or injured on the journey.

Early Irish texts express strong disapproval of the stealing of horses, and it seems to have been regarded

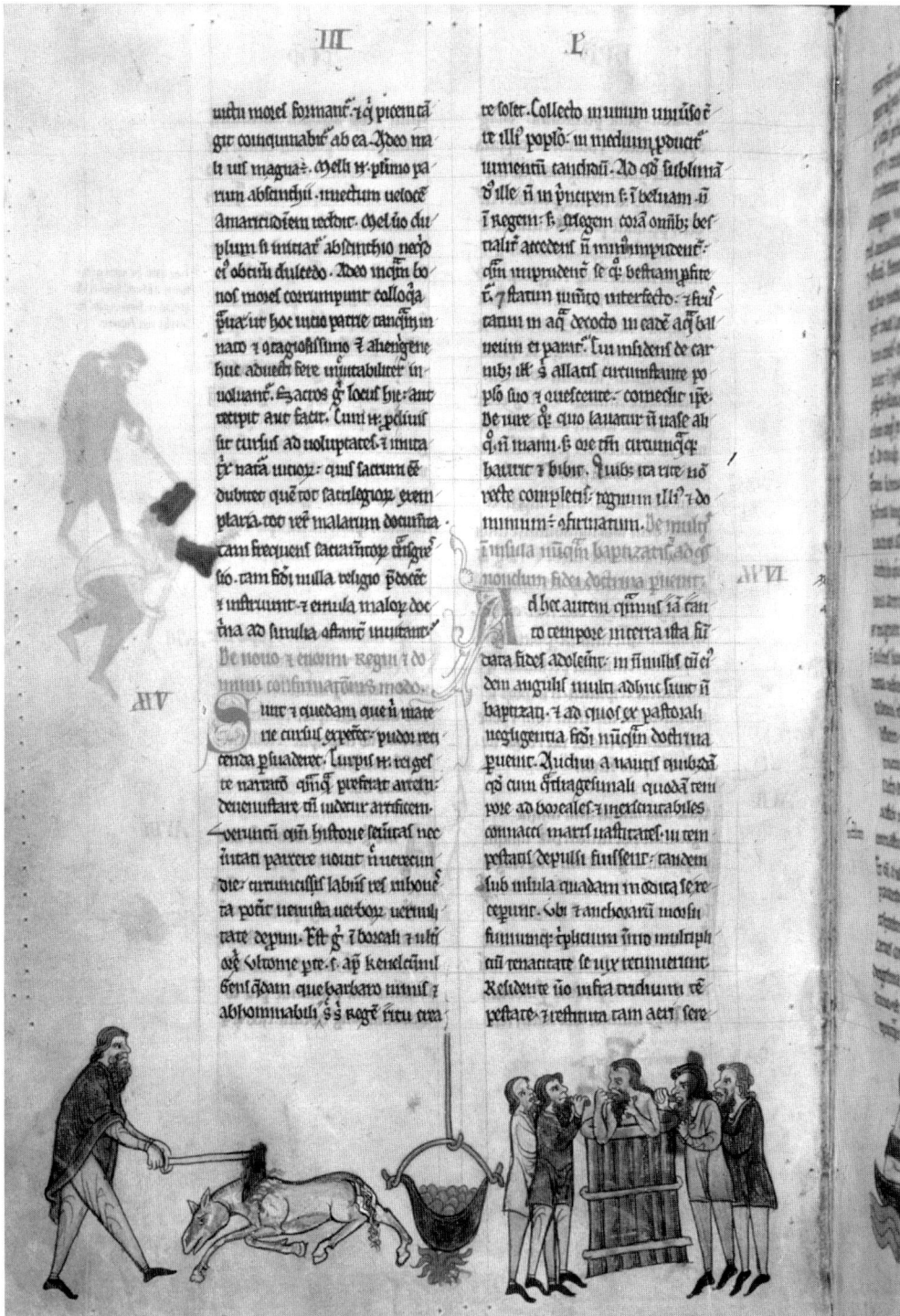

RIGHT: *From* Topographica Hiberniae *by Giraldus Cambrensis, 1180s (manuscript 700 f.39v); it shows a ritual conferring kingship which involved the sacrifice of a white mare, followed by cooking and eating of the flesh.*

Photo: Produced with the permission of the National Library of Ireland

THE IRISH DRAUGHT HORSE

as a particularly base form of theft – the oath of a horse thief is regarded as one of the least reliable of all oaths. One legal passage lists the three public duties (*fubae*) of an ordinary rent-payer as hunting down pirates, horse thieves and wolves. It is clear from sources that horse theft might be carried out on a large scale – another law text refers to the theft of a herd (*graig*) of twelve horses belonging to a number of owners. The culprit(s) must restore the horses (or provide substitutes), and also pay fines based on the rank of the various owners. Finally, the law text on accidents refers to a horse fight (*echtres*) in which one horse kills or injures another. No liability attaches to the owner.

The Horse in Early Irish Myth and Legend

The horse is known to have featured prominently in the early religion of the Celtic-speaking peoples, particularly on the Continent, where the horse-goddess Epona was revered by the ancient Gauls.[28] The supernatural aspects of the horse likewise loom large in early Irish tradition, and continued in the folklore of more recent times (*see* next chapter). Horses play an important part in the Old Irish sagas, particularly in the great epic known as the 'Cattle Raid of Cooley' (*Táin Bó Cuailnge*). The life of the hero of this tale, the warrior Cú Chulainn, was intimately bound up with two horses: the Grey of Machae (Líath Machae) and the Black of Saigliu (Dub Saiglenn). They were twins of about the same age as Cú Chulainn, and grew up along with him. They pulled his chariot, which was driven by his trusty charioteer and confidant Lóeg. There are eloquent accounts of the speed and mettle of these two horses.[29] In the tale of the death of Cú Chulainn we are told how both horses were injured during the fatal attack on their master. After Cú Chulainn's death, the Black of Saigliu rode away with Lóeg, but the Grey of Machae stayed by the body for three days and three nights, allowing no one to approach. Finally, tormented with grief, the horse jumped into a lake and was drowned – this lake henceforth bore the name Linn in Léith (Pool of the Grey).[30]

Horses appear in many different physical forms in early Irish literature. The tale of the death of Cú Chulainn refers to a horse with a dog-like head (*conchenn*) which belonged to the warrior Conall Cernach.[31] A strange legend concerns a 'water-horse' (*ech uisci*) which emerged from a lake in Glenn Dalláin (Glencar, County Sligo) and had sexual intercourse with the daughter of a priest. The result of this union was known as the Beast of Leittir Dalláin, and was counted as one of the seven wonders of Glenn Dalláin. This creature had a human head, but the rest of its body was in the shape of a blacksmith's bellows.[32] Another fanciful tale is recounted in the *Life of St Colmán Mac Luacháin*, and concerns a bull named Grogín, which was in the habit of mating as readily with mares as with cows. The Welsh historian Giraldus Cambrensis, writing in the late twelfth century, includes a number of tales of bestiality in his *Topographica Hiberniae* (Topography of Ireland). This can largely be dismissed as propaganda designed to discredit the Irish. However, there may be a basis of truth in his account of a 'horrible usage' practiced by the people of Tír Conaill, who – as part of a king's inauguration rite – ate the flesh of a white mare with whom the new king had just had intercourse. It is possible that the Church's stern disapproval of the eating of horseflesh – which incurred the heavy penalty of three-and-a-half-years' penance – stemmed from its association with such pagan rites.

Finally, early Irish sources contain many references to the use of magic – and especially the 'evil eye' – to kill or damage domestic animals, including horses. One law text states that a fine equivalent to two-and-a-half ounces of silver is payable if a person injures another's horse through sorcery (*corrguinecht*).

ABOVE: *The forge was a great meeting place where matters of the day and great philosophical questions were discussed at length. The traditional blacksmith's forge, with its darkness, fire and hissing steam, was the source of many stories and fables. The water used for tempering the red-hot steel was used as a cure for warts.*

Photo: National Museum of Ireland

RIGHT: *The wheelwright worked closely with the blacksmith in the manufacturing of cartwheels, which were rimmed with iron bands.*
Photo: Ruth Rogers

BELOW: *Ben Hussey and 'Tucks' Bergin, Kildare, 2004. Nowadays, the farrier comes to the horses instead of the other way round. Cold or hot shoes are fitted on the horse on site.*
Photo: Mary McGrath

RIGHT: *Galway, 1949.*
Horseshoes hammered
into a post were
used for holding
cross pieces at a gap.
Photo: National
Museum of Ireland

✹   THE IRISH DRAUGHT HORSE

3

The Horse in
Irish Myth and Folklore

⊛

DÁITHÍ Ó HÓGÁIN

The horse has a long and distinguished history in Ireland. There is some evidence of the presence of wild animals of the species before the final Ice Age, but these must have died out. Bone remains at the celebrated archaeological site of Newgrange in County Meath suggest that, by the end of the third millennium BC, there were domesticated horses in use, these probably having been imported. They were small – only about 122 centimetres (12 hands) in height at the withers – and it is unlikely the size increased very much for a long time. The horse, however, is at all times a beautiful and dramatic animal and, apart from its utilitarian value for work, it must have served a symbolic function, representing wealth and, due to its use in fighting, military power.

By the Iron Age, elaborate harnessing was in use, some of it for ceremonial purposes, and it is reasonable to surmise that the animal played a leading role in myth and ritual. Such indeed is the picture presented to us by the earliest Irish literature which – although dating no further back than the sixth century AD – undoubtedly preserves many elements of much older tradition.[1]

Mythical Horsemen

In the mythical portions of that literature, horses play a very dramatic role, showing the respect in which these animals were held. One can underline this by reference to some well-known deity names. The father-god of the ancient Celts, Dago-Devos, meaning 'good sky' (later called in Ireland the Daghdha), was envisaged as having the sun as his eye, and one epithet for him was 'Atepomarus' – the *epomarus* here meaning 'great in horses'; that is, having many horses. Continental *epos* (stallion) was, in the Celtic of Ireland, pronounced *ekvos*, meaning that *epomaros* in Irish Celtic would have been

43

ekvomaros, which became in the Irish language of the historic period *eachmhór* (great in horses). So it comes as no surprise that in Irish tradition the father-deity had a further designation: Eochaidh Ollathair (which signified 'horseman, father of all'). Several mythical kings of early Ireland were indeed given the name Eochaidh, which shows how much their traditional portrayal owes to the debris of ancient pre-Christian lore.

A good example of such debris is furnished by a medieval story which, although humorous, has a primordial ring to it. It concerns a fictional character called Eochaidh Mac Maireadha, claimed to have been the son of a prehistoric king of Munster. We read that Eochaidh fell in love with his father's wife, a young woman called Eibhliu, who had been fostered by the divine Aonghus of Newgrange. Eochaidh carried Eibhliu away, accompanied by many of his retainers. On their way, a stranger killed their horses, but Aonghus appeared and gave them a marvellous steed which carried all their baggage. Aonghus warned them not to allow the steed to rest and urinate else it would cause their death. On reaching Ulster, however, the horse did urinate, causing a spring to rise. Eochaidh built a house by the spring and settled there, but one day a woman forgot to replace the cover on the well and it flooded the area, drowning Eochaidh and most of his family. Thus was formed Loch nEachach (Lake of Eochaidh; that is, Lough Neagh).

There are other variants of this story, indicating that the narrative itself derives from sources which long predated the medieval literature. The motif of the steed urinating and therefore giving rise to a lake may appear rather flippant, but can be shown to be of an archaic nature, as the idea of a supernatural being bringing the world into being from its own body was basic to many mythologies. In reality, of course, the largest lake in Ireland got its name from the sept Uí Eachach, who inhabited that area in Ulster. Their name, however, meant 'descendants of Eochaidh', and it is quite likely that the sept was so called from the cult of the deity Eochaidh, and that the story is an elaboration of the equine imagery of that deity.[2]

There was, indeed, a tendency to give the particular name Eochaidh to antique characters in the genealogies of several septs. In the pedigrees of the ancient kings of Munster a character called Echdae was mentioned as husband of the goddess Áine. His name would have meant either 'horse-like' or 'horse-god'. Furthermore, a persistent theme in the mythology of Celtic goddesses was the race in which these ladies showed their speed, sometimes in contention with horses. The most famous of these ladies was the Ulster goddess Macha. She was originally called the Mór-Ríoghain or 'great queen', which is cognate with the great mythical Welsh horsewoman Rhiannon. Both the Mór-Ríoghain and Rhiannon derive from an ancient Celtic Rigantona, meaning 'revered queen', an alternative designation for the Continental Celtic horse-goddess Epona. The story of Macha in early Irish literature is well known – how she was forced, although on the point of giving birth, to race against the chariot horses of the mythical Ulster king Conchobhar Mac Neasa.

There can be little doubt but that this equine imagery derives from the symbolism of the father-deity in the sky as patron of tribal kings. The man being appointed king was said to be taking over the governing of the people with the consent and support of the tribe's ancestor god. An echo of this, indeed, in the Ulster mythology has one king being called Fearghus Mac Róich, which means literally 'male vigour son of great stallion'. The king was required to have 'male vigour' while his divine patron bore the nickname 'great stallion'.

That this was an Irish development from ancient tradition common to much of Europe and western Asia is clear from the fact that the name of the Irish father-deity, Daghdha (Dago-Devos), is cognate with similar names for the sky-deity in other languages, such as Deus (in Latin), Jovis (in Italic) Dyaus (in Indic), Tiwes (in Germanic) and Zeus (in Greek). Zeus, indeed, was sometimes represented as taking the form of a horse. Such importance attributed to the horse as a symbol of otherworld power was natural, given that the Celts and other Indo-European peoples had depended largely on the horse for their worldly power.[3]

Horses and Kingship

It may be that – as the Norman writer Giraldus Cambrensis later claimed – the early Irish had a horse sacrifice as part of the ritual of installing their kings. Such a horse sacrifice was known in other ancient mythologies which ultimately had the same Indo-European linguistic origins as Celtic. There are, at any rate, some very striking accounts in Irish literature of the use of horses in early kingly rituals.[4]

A clear example is that of the lore surrounding an ancient legendary king called Conaire, who may have been a real personage from the early centuries AD although his fame was first committed to writing in the eighth century. We read that his father was a king of Tara called Eterscéle, but that his mother was a peasant-girl and accordingly he was reared in obscurity. When his father died Conaire went to Tara to claim the kingship, and had to undergo a series of ritual tests there to prove his claim. The tests included mounting a chariot to which was yoked two stallions of one colour which had never before been harnessed. If he were not the true king the horses would rear up against him; but since Conaire was the true king, they stood still when he approached. They then coursed tamely around the citadel, and the upright ritual stone at the head of the course there cried out against the axle of his chariot as it always did for the true king.

Especially striking is the tradition that Conaire was under otherworld taboos not to enter his fortress at Tara after sunset and not to leave it before sunrise.

When he eventually breaks this prohibition he finds himself benighted on Slighe Chualann (the ancient road between Dublin and Bray), with three red horse-men riding ahead of him. It has been prophesied to him that three such riders will lead him to his death, and he is indeed slaughtered in a house spanning the River Dodder in which he rests. The import of all of this is that the sun belongs to the father-deity, and that every earthly king must eventually relinquish his throne, being brought to it by horses and led away from it similarly. It may even be that the horse was seen as a type of psychopomp, bringing the dead king to the otherworld, thus mirroring the ritual role of a horse in his earlier inauguration.[5]

The sun, of course, had similar associations with the supernatural destiny of a king, since that heavenly body continually alternates between the underground world of the dead and the ordinary world above ground. The Irish father-deity in the context of the dead was usually called Donn, and 'the horses of Donn' brought dead heroes to the otherworld.[6] All of which goes to show that horse symbolism in connection with the sun and with kingship must be of very ancient vintage in Celtic culture, and in kindred cultures also of the ancient world. One thinks immediately of themes in Greek mythology such as the white horses drawing Apollo's sun chariot, Bellerophon being supported by and then deserted by the wonderful horse Pegasus, and the horse lore associated with the legendary King Pelops.

The father-deity being the ultimate patron, it was held that a different deity actually presided over the reign of kings at Tara. This was Lugh, master of arts and skills, and it is notable that, in the early literature also, we meet with the fancy that one of the country's favourite pastimes was introduced by this celebrity: 'Lugh son of Eithliu, he was the first to bring assemblies and horse-racing.' This Lugh was the Irish form of the pan-Celtic deity Lugus, whose cult was known from Ireland to Celtiberia (a large part of ancient Spain), and who left the imprint of his name on several places in the Celtic world – including Lyon, Laon, Laudun, Lauzun, Loudun, Leiden and Carlisle.[7]

A comparison of Irish, British and Continental sources indicates that Lugus was a polytechnic deity and a patron of the harvest and of contracts. In Ireland, the special 'cultic' centre dedicated to him was Tailtiu (Teltown in County Meath), a place at which famous ancient games were celebrated. His harvest festival – named Lughnasa after him – continued to be celebrated at many places in Ireland on the first Sunday in August down to the twentieth century, and remnants of it still remain. Horses continued to play a conspicuous part in the celebration of this festival. They were raced, usually in spontaneously organised contests on land but sometimes in swimming races in lakes and rivers.[8]

Otherworld Horses in Folklore

The association of horses with the otherworld continued in the fertile imagination of the folk until recent times. We have already mentioned the god of the dead in early Irish tradition, called Donn, and his horses. It is significant that this Donn lives on in the folklore of several areas, such as at Bull Rock off the coast of south Kerry, at the great sand dunes near Dunbeg on the west coast of County Clare, and at the remarkable hill called Knockfierna which dominates the plain of County Limerick. At this latter place in particular, he is represented as Donn Fírinne, a king of the fairy army, who leads his cavalry to battle against other fairy armies, ensuring that the fertile fields and crops of Munster are protected from spiritual foes. Also, in his role of protector and overseer of his territory, he often rides about alone at night on a fine white horse.

As a ghostly horseman riding with great skill, he appears to benighted travellers, but he is generally courteous and frightens only those who are too self-confident. A favourite story has him visiting a blacksmith one night and asking for his horse to be shod. His request being complied with, Donn wrenches off one of the horse's legs and gives it to the blacksmith to have the shoe put on it. The terrified smith does so, and then Donn replaces the leg on the horse perfectly, saying that he is to lead his cavalry this night in a battle against a rival host far away.[9]

A folk legend told in many parts of Ireland tells of a strange horse which came from a local lake and was captured by a local farmer. This 'water horse' became an invaluable worker or racer, and the man profited much by it. One day, however, he struck the horse, with the result that it raced away again into the water. Some versions say that the man was soon after drowned in the lake, and that stray pieces of his body were seen floating on the water as if he had been eaten by the horse. This legend, found also in parts of Britain and in Scandinavia, was already known in Ireland in medieval times.

Somewhat altered versions of the same story tell of several early Irish saints who, lacking a horse, obtained such an animal. For instance, St Féichín of Fore (in County Westmeath) was once on an urgent mission to secure the release of a hostage when his chariot horse dropped dead. Immediately a water horse from a nearby river pool came and took its place under the chariot. When his mission was accomplished, Féichín returned the animal to its strange dwelling place. Even stranger was an adventure of St Maodhóg of Ferns (in County Wexford) who, visiting St David in Wales, once had reason to return urgently to Ireland. He went to the seashore, found a horse there which he mounted, and the horse swam across the sea to Ireland with the saint on its back.

St Ruán of Lorrha (in County Tipperary) was reputed to have had a bitter quarrel with the high king Diarmaid Mac Ceirbheoil in the sixth century over a hostage. When the two worthies were reconciled, the king released the hostage, and the saint gave the king a gift

"Every foot of vantage ground gained by either was hailed by the cheers of the men on the hill."

ABOVE: *During the festival of Lughnasa horses took part in races on land as well as swimming races in rivers and lakes. Lughnasa, originally a pagan festival, continued to be celebrated on the first Sunday in August down to the twentieth century.*

Photo: Nineteenth-century print, source not known

of 30 beautiful dark grey steeds. These had come to Ruán from a river, and they defeated Diarmaid's other horses when racing. Just as the king was beginning to exult in them, however, they raced away into the sea. Not to be outdone, the celebrated St Brendan the Navigator ransomed a prisoner from the same high king with 50 seals he had transformed into horses. These horses proved unmanageable to Diarmaid's jockeys, however, and they raced into the River Boyne, where they assumed their seal forms and then swam into the sea.

The same legend plot was used in early medieval literature in a particularly dramatic context. We read that two foals were born at the same time as the epical hero Cú Chulainn, and when these two had grown into magnificent horses, they were recovered by him. One of them, called 'the Grey of Machae', came out of a lake, and Cú Chulainn immediately jumped onto its back and rode it around all of Ireland before he brought it back tame at nightfall to the Ulster capital at Eamhain Mhacha (Navan Fort in County Armagh). The other horse, called 'the Black of Saingliu', was acquired by him in similar fashion from a lake. This wonderful pair of horses drew his chariot through all his battles, and they died fighting tooth and nail for him when, vastly outnumbered, his own end drew near.[10]

There were some traditions of horses obtained from lakes or the sea which did not return to the watery realm, but instead became progenitors of a notable line of local racehorses or workhorses. No doubt such lore resulted from poetic conceits, such as statements that the exploits of a certain horse seemed supernatural or were comparable to those of supernatural animals. The statements would be so resounding in tradition that they would in time be taken in a literal sense that the particular horse itself was of supernatural origin.

One such tradition of note in County Galway concerned a particular strain of Connemara Pony, to which a supernatural origin was imputed. It was said that a tailor engaged on his journeywork was passing by a lake one day when he saw a group of horses with their foals lying on a grassy patch. He slipped up on them and, taking off his belt, put it around the neck of one of the foals. The other horses raced into the lake, but he took the foal home with him and it grew into a fine mare, which was ever after known as *Láir na Beilte* (the Mare of the Belt). No other horse could defeat her in a race, or could compare with her in drawing a cart or plough. Her progeny were also noted for their ability, but neither she nor they could ever be allowed within sight of a lake, for if so it was feared they would return to their proper home.[11]

Horses of Extraordinary Prowess

To most people, of course, such ideas were silly, and so noted horses were not usually given an otherworld pedigree. That is not to say they were completely deprived of connections to otherworld forces. The celebrated eighteenth-century mare called Irish Lass belongs to the clear light of history – the little grey mare was

owned by George Archbold of Eadestown near Naas in County Kildare, and later by one Charles O'Neill. There are written accounts of her races, and some music composed in honour of her can still be heard. Yet, as we shall see, she was considered extraordinary to the point of being otherworldly.

Irish Lass was popularly known as the Paidrín Mare, the *paidrín* being a rosary that was hung around her neck before a particular race. These beads – the actual set still survives – were intended to bring her victory in the race, and she did duly win. The race, a match, took place on the Curragh of Kildare in the year 1749. It was between Irish Lass and a noted racehorse of the time called Othello, a jet-black stallion with a ferocious temper. Later lore claimed that the stallion had sinister magical powers, and that it was heard to speak to its jockey during the race. The jockey riding Irish Lass was nicknamed Biorán (Pin) because he was so light, and he was advised by a priest to take the lead from the start and to hold onto it, for Othello's magic would be too strong if the stallion got its head in front. Biorán obeyed these instructions and won the race.

It was said that when the Paidrín Mare died, she was opened and it was found there were a pair of wings attached to her heart, which had helped greatly to increase her speed.[12] This Pegasus-type image was associated with some other great racers also, both horses and men. One account from Kerry folklore of a great local racehorse claims that its owner raised it on goats' milk. Having won many races, the owner could not bear the thought of any horse defeating it as it grew older. 'He had a picture taken of himself mounted on the horse, and then put a bullet through it. The doctors opened the horse when it was dead, and they found wings on its heart. They considered that it was the goats' milk which caused that.' An account from County Mayo refers to an even more incredible trait which, it is claimed, was possessed by less than 'one horse in a million'. This was the ability to draw breath through

THE IRISH DRAUGHT HORSE

ABOVE: *The hippomane, an oval, brown object about 15 centimetres long, is expelled with the afterbirth. Old stud grooms used to hang it outside the stable door for the first few days as the foal's good-luck symbol. It was thought to hold magical powers.*

the anus as well as the mouth – 'any horse so distinctively endowed is supposed to be possessed of well-nigh supernatural staying power'.[13]

In the lore of County Kerry, the celebrated nobleman, patriot, and poet, Piaras Feiritéar (*c.* 1610-53), was said to have been a great horseman. One story tells of how he won a race on the Curragh of Kildare on a fine mare of his. Night befalling him on the last stage of his journey home to west Kerry, he heard hoof beats behind him and, looking around, saw a red horseman riding a little black horse. Piaras spurred his mare into a gallop, but no matter how fast they travelled, the strange horse and rider remained behind them. Reaching a stream, Piaras and his mount flew over it. Ghosts cannot cross running water, and so the ghostly pursuers had to stop, and Piaras heard three sharp neighs from the black horse. Reaching home, he put his mare into her stable, but next morning he found her dead and turned grey from fright.[14]

The point of this little story is that Piaras' mare was so good a racehorse that the otherworld desired her for

themselves, and echoes of the red riders of the dead are found in it. The story also draws attention to the belief that horses are particularly vulnerable to otherworld powers. This is a projection of natural reality into the supernatural realm. Horses were socially very valuable animals for work and travel, and their owners would be particularly worried lest their health should fail, thus causing the likelihood of such failure to be stressed. Also, horses are indeed prone to a variety of health problems, and this tended to be rationalised as envy of good horses by otherworld sources. There was a strong belief that the otherworld community, known as the 'people of the *sí*' or the 'fairies', were always trying to steal good horses away into the otherworld. For this reason, it was thought that when a horse sneezed the owner should spit on it, for the fairies are very fastidious beings and will not go near to human bodily emissions. It is even said that the reason why a horse often sneezes when released into its field is to banish the fairies from its surroundings.[15]

One type of horse which brooked no interference from hostile otherworld beings was the *fíorláir*, or 'true mare'. This was defined variably. Some sources claim that a true mare is the seventh successive filly foal born to its dam without any colt intervening. Others claim she is the first foal of a mare whose dam was a first foal, and so on with first filly foals for seven generations. Perhaps both types qualified for the honour. When she grew up it was claimed that the true mare could be easily distinguished by the savant, as one Kerry account has it: 'The fairies, the devil, or evil spirits can't have any power over her. A person is safe to take her out and travel any hour of the night. If she be a racehorse, no other horse will beat her in a race. A mare gets her bridle tooth at five years, a sire gets the bridle tooth at four years; the *fíorláir* gets the bridle tooth at the age of four years, just the same as the sire.' A Galway account elaborates on the skills of such a mare: 'She will fail at nothing. No spirit or evil thing can catch up with her.

She has a leap and a speed exceeding all other horses.' Several stories told of true mares, when carrying their owners on a journey at night, being approached by spirits. In such stories the true mare races away from the spirit with ease; and even when her way is blocked by a spirit appearing in front of her, the mare fights it with her front hooves and drives it away.

One other interesting motif attaches to the true mare. When such a mare is born of its dam, a four-leafed shamrock grows on the spot where it is dropped on the field. This shamrock is called the *Seamair Mhuire* (Clover of the Virgin Mary), and it brings good luck and protection from all misfortune to its bearer.[16]

Danger to Horses

Because the horse is a very nervous animal and has a keen sense of smell, it notices things of which humans often are unaware. This is the basic reason for the widespread belief that horses can see spirits. Many a story tells of how a horse refused to pass a certain place, despite strong urging by its rider or driver, because some dead body lay hidden there, or even because some terrible crime had once been committed at the spot. People feared, indeed, that not only the mysterious after-effects of events could linger in a particular place, but also that certain places were inhabited or frequented by spirits, some of which could be dangerous.

Many people can tell such stories from personal experience. The usual description is that a horse stops suddenly on the road and begins to snort and to pant, looking sideways. A lather of sweat comes on the horse, and it tries to retreat. No matter how it is coaxed or cajoled, it remains restive and steadfastly refuses to go further. It is said that to discover what is actually causing the horse to stop, the rider should look directly between the animal's two ears. Be it shadow or spirit, the cause of the trouble can then be clearly seen. Sometimes, if the rider makes the Sign of the Cross or recites some prayers, the horse will move on, proof that the spirit has been banished.[17]

Greedy or envious humans could also cause great trouble to one's horse. One often hears of how a certain farmer, who had a good working horse, was surprised to notice that the horse's performance deteriorated over time. Then, one morning, he found the horse in a lather of sweat in the field and, on examining it, discovered a 'witch's stirrup' in its mane. This was a piece of tangled hair in the mane, and was a sure sign that somebody had been using the horse during the night in long rides with the fairies. Some remedy was then required, such as to attach a piece of red ribbon, a twig of rowan or a piece of blessed palm, any of which items could be stitched into the horse's mane and would guarantee protection.[18]

An eighteenth-century Limerick poet listed the dangers to a horse as coming *tré nimh shúl drochduine, tré mhothú drochmhná, tré urchóid chnoic, nó tré ghoin shíobhra bhaininn* (through the poison of an evil person's eye, through the feeling of an evil woman, through assault from the hill, or through a wound from a female sprite). In brief, these were references to the destructive powers of the 'evil eye', of envy, of the fairies in the hills, and to fairy darts which were believed to be shot at valuable animals so as to cause them to pine away and die from this world, thereby becoming the property of the otherworld. We have noted already the fastidiousness of the fairies, and the most usual way to protect a horse from fairy attack was to spit on it so these otherworld beings would be too disgusted to go near it. In a religious sense, a blessed medal could also be attached to the horse as protection.

The notion was widespread and long established that harm could be done to valuable animals or even to humans by people who were envious. Envy is sometimes difficult to detect, however, and the envious person's malice might be disguised by expressions of his infatuation. Hence the belief that 'over-praise' (called

THE IRISH DRAUGHT HORSE

greadmholadh, or scorching praise) was suspect. To avoid such suspicion on the part of the horse's owner it was necessary to add a little pious expression to the praise, such as 'That's a fine horse, God bless it!' Those who omitted the blessing might be suspected of envy or wishing the horse ill. Such envious malice was thought to be most often expressed in the form of an envious or penetratingly hostile look, called the evil eye; and it is not surprising that horses, along with children and cattle, were thought to be especially vulnerable to such danger.

For example, according to a description from County Monaghan, a man was working with his mare, and when he brought her into the stable in the evening she would not eat the hay. She lay down as if she had a bellyache, and the owner feared that she would die. He went to a local healer, who told him to come back very early next morning, as he could only do the curing before sunrise. Next morning, he found the healer on his knees muttering some words. The healer then gave him a bottle of water and told him not to spill any of the water. 'Get good strong men to help you,' he said, 'and get a hold of the mare, and hold up her head, and put the water out of that bottle down into her body. And don't let it go with her breath, and she will be alright!' The owner did as he was instructed, and the mare got up safe and sound and began to eat the hay. Then the owner remembered that a certain individual had passed by on the road on the previous day, when he was working with the mare. That man had the reputation of possessing the evil eye.

Whether or not such explanations of sudden sickness in a horse were *ex eventu* rationalisations, there is no doubting the drama in some of the accounts. For example, a report from County Dublin tells of a man who had a fine-bred young mare pulling his cart at Killenarden, near Tallaght, when he met a tall, thin man on the roadside. The man was staring at the horse, and remarked that she was a 'darling mare'. Feeling uneasy, the owner urged the horse on faster, and when they

had passed the man 'he could feel the stare on his back'. When he turned around to look behind him, 'there was the thin man with his head and neck stretched like an angry goose and his eyes devouring the mare'. For her part, the mare had laid back her ears and was beginning to sweat profusely. By the time the man reached home, the mare was totally fatigued and could do nothing but lie down in the stable. The owner went for advice to a local wise man, George Mathers, who was nicknamed the *Bróg* (Shoe). Mathers told him to quickly organise a search, and they located the offender some miles away at Naas. Following Mathers' directions, the owner and a friend went to talk to the thin man and, while the owner distracted his attention, the friend used a scissors to cut a little piece of cloth from his frieze coat. Hurrying home then, they burned the piece of cloth and mixed the ashes with new milk. They used this as a drench for the mare, and no sooner had she drunk it than she gave a great snort and the look of fear left her eyes. She got up as sound as ever she had been before.

A common term for the use of the evil eye was 'overlooking', and Mathers and his neighbours at Killenarden had a remedy which, if applied immediately, would offset the power of malicious staring before it took effect – one should make the Sign of the Cross with the first two fingers on the right hand, and then point the two fingers at the person who is trying to do the overlooking. In Moybollogue, County Meath, a healer called Phil Gargan was said to have a special cure against the overlooking of a horse. This involved putting nine knots in a thread of wool while reciting a prayer, and then placing the thread around the horse's neck.[19]

Horse Whisperers

The aforementioned George Mathers had another special gift with regard to horses, and he showed this once when a mare belonging to the local priest had been overlooked and lay almost dead in its stable. From a bottle he had in his pocket, Mathers rubbed some water on the mare's tongue, flank, heart and, finally, her ears. Then he leaned down to her and whispered for a while into one of her ears. He finally arose, took her by the tail, and slapped her on the quarters, telling her to get up immediately – which she did, as sound as a bell.

This was an example of the celebrated power, possessed by a few rare individuals, of *cogar i gcluais an chapaill* (whisper in the horse's ear). The belief in such an ability to speak certain words to a horse and thereby enthral is also found in other countries, but the words are kept a secret by the practitioners. In Britain, for instance, the words are sometimes claimed to be 'both in one', thus symbolising the basic desire of any horseman to interact with his mount in perfect unison. In Ireland, the secret words were thought to be an *ortha* or 'charm-prayer' of a kind common in folk religion, but the words are unfortunately not recorded. One account from County Kerry goes as follows: 'A horse will do anything for a person who knows the *ortha*. If a horse is on strike or acting against you, it will make him do your will. If he is out in the field, all you need do is point your finger towards him.'

The father of the present writer, who was a fine horseman of the old school, witnessed this power at Kilkenny market early in the twentieth century. An Irish Draught stallion was on auction, and nobody dared to bid on it, let alone go near its stable. The stallion was 'white with temper' when it heard the noise of the crowd outside. Two young men from Mullinahone bid on the stallion, and got it at a very cheap price. 'So the whole crowd stayed waiting there to know what would go on when they would go in to get the stallion. One lad walked into the stable, and the stallion only came up to him neighing, while the other fellow shut the door after him. Everybody thought there would be a dead man inside, but instead of that he led his stallion out as quiet as a sheep. They walked the stallion away, and took him off to Mullinahone.'

The explanation which my father gave for this trick was that when a foal is born, one should take a jelly-like substance from its mouth and keep it. This is called the *greim searraigh* (foal's bit), and if one approaches a stallion with it in one's pocket, the stallion gets the soothing smell of the foal and becomes calm and settled. To add to its effect, some oils would sometimes be bought from a chemist – oils the smells of which are attractive and soothing to horses. In reality, then, we can see in this skill of the whisperer three levels of activity where, if one failed, the other one or two could be employed. Perhaps in the case of most horse whisperers the real efficacy was in the oils used, and the other two were 'blinds' in order to protect this trade secret. The whisper itself, sometimes called 'the horseman's word', was claimed by the practitioners to be their true trick and, if this were doubted or disproved, the foal's bit could still be used to distract attention from the oils.

Be that as it may, it would be unfair to detract from the real skills of some 'whisperers' in controlling wild horses. An account from County Kerry tells of a horseman whose horse would follow him around from tavern to tavern in the main street of Dingle. This man even claimed that 'My horse would try to go up onto the rafters of a house if I so instructed it'. The leading Irish ethnologist Caoimhín Ó Danachair tells of how he once saw, at the fair of Rathkeale in County Limerick, a colt that was prancing and kicking wildly until a teenage youth approached. This youth, the son of an itinerant horse-dealer, fondled the horse's nose and spoke quietly to it, making it absolutely calm. The same youth was reputed to be able to make any horse stand still without moving, until he decided to release it from his magic power.

The best-known Irish horse whisperer was one James Sullivan, a late-eighteenth-century native of Newmarket in County Cork. It was said that Sullivan got the gift from a soldier who had been accused of a serious offence and had nobody to put up bail for him in court. Sullivan

ABOVE: *Work went more smoothly when people sang or whistled to their horses.*

Photo: Bord Fáilte

had some money by him, and he helped the soldier by using it for the bail. In gratitude for this, the soldier told him the secret of how to control wild or vicious horses, and as a result Sullivan became famous for the valuable and fascinating skill.

A contemporaneous account of this Sullivan goes as follows: 'The wonder of his skill consisted in the celerity [speed of movement] of the operation, which was performed in private and without any apparent means of coercion. Every description of horse, or even mule – whether previously broke or unhandled, whatever their peculiar vices or ill habits might have been – submitted without show of resistance to the magical influence of his art. When sent for to tame a vicious beast, he directed the stable in which he and the object of the experiment were placed to be shut, with orders not to open the door until a signal was given. After a tête-à-tête of about half an hour – during which little or no bustle was heard – the signal was made and, upon opening the door, the horse appeared lying down, and the man by his side playing familiarly with him like a child with a puppy dog.'

Sullivan's most celebrated achievement was the taming of a notoriously savage Thoroughbred stallion called King Pippin on the Curragh of Kildare in 1810, after which the horse was so quiet he could be ridden out onto the course and actually won a race on the occasion. One account states that after Sullivan spent the night in the stable with King Pippin, the hitherto vicious stallion followed him about like a pet, lay down at his command, and allowed its mouth to be opened and any person's hand to be put into it safely. Folklore of his native area claims that Sullivan once tamed a wild horse at the fair of Dromagh, near Banteer in County Cork. At a word from him, that horse lay down on its back with its legs upturned, and glasses filled with drink were placed on each leg without being spilt. The onlookers' wonder was expressed in such fantastic accounts, but there was surely some natural explanation for the power which James Sullivan possessed, and one witness put it down to 'natural intrepidity' and 'an instinctive power of inspiring awe' in the animal.[20]

An old saying in Irish is *capall le ceansacht*, meaning that a horse should be handled with gentleness. It was thought that horses had a special understanding of people, and that 'one should treat a horse like a Christian'. In fact, speaking to horses could have a natural sooth-ing effect quite apart from any quasi-magical one. A County Roscommon source states if a team of plough horses were moving so fast that the plough was in danger of being damaged by large stones the ploughman would start to sing calmly to them. This would cause them to slow down as they listened to the song, as if they were 'timing the verse'. According to an account from County Cork, it was common for an extra man there to walk beside the plough team, whistling a tune to the horses; and people in County Waterford were wont to sing a lullaby to soothe an uneasy or frightened horse.[21]

Reading a Horse's Traits

The means of judging the merit of horses by general appearance were many and varied. For instance, infor-mation from a text written in Irish in 1420 can be translated as follows: 'These are the signs of good horses – a small forelock and large eye, and large nostrils, a large chest and a wide shoulder, and a narrow mane and light quarters. These are all signs of a speedy horse. A large mane is a sign of strength in the horse, and a short narrow back which is high.' Another Irish text, written about 100 years later, agrees with this, and adds the following little triad as an aid to memory: 'These are the three widths which are appropriate to the horse – wide between the two eyes and between the two feet and between the two sides.'

The desired dimensions in a horse would, of course, depend on the purposes for which it was required. When seeking a good all-round working horse, traditional farmers would look for a high-enough tail, feet neither too big nor too small, and reasonable width across the chest. Some farmers claimed that a mare should be stronger in front and a gelding stronger behind. The preferences of old horsemen requiring a good hunter or racer could be somewhat different, but that would depend on whether the horse should be a fast one for short distances or a good stayer. For instance, a sprinter should have most of its power behind, with big quarters, a short thick back, short shins and low hocks, yet strong enough in front and with a thick-enough neck. On the other hand, a good steeplechaser should have a flat shoulder, deep girth, a fairly long back but not too long, and a good sweep with the hind legs.

A not altogether unwise, if somewhat humorous, collection of little triads was very popular in Irish folklore with regard to the selection of a good horse. It occurs also in the sixteenth-century Irish source mentioned above, and also in a source from England in that same century, and we may speculate that it is of medieval origin. To translate one version from the Irish, the question is posed, 'What are the proper traits in a horse?' and the answer is then given as follows: 'Three traits of a bull – bold walk, strong neck, and hard forehead; three traits of a hare – bright eye, lively ear, and swift run; three traits of a woman – broad breast, slender waist, and short back!'

There was a long tradition of attributing certain qualities or faults to particular colours and colour markings. The text from 1420 gives definite views on this issue. Praising dark horses, it expresses a preference for the brighter variants of these colours. Black horses are strong if somewhat restive, but the bay is described as lacking in spirit. Speckled horses are gentle and strong, brown horses are sound and reliable, especially if they have a white blaze on the face, while the chestnut is gentle but not very swift. Not all sources would agree with this, and, indeed, one can say that there is as much variety in traditional ideas concerning horse colours as there is in the colours themselves. The writer of 1420 admits that 'the spirit of the horses themselves makes them good whatever their colour, and their lack of spirit makes them bad.' As many old horsemen would say, it is what lies inside the skin that is important. Thus, variously, we may quote sayings such as 'Black or brown is a good colour, but if you see a roan buy it!' and 'Brown is the choice of all colours, except for the chestnut horse with a blaze'.

The desire for a horse with a white stripe on its face was so general that dishonest dealers would sometimes even fake such a marking on a horse which they had for sale. An all-white horse was generally considered unlucky, because – like white cows – such animals were thought to be attractive to the fairies and would accordingly pine away and die. So the white marking on the face was rationalised by claiming that a horse all of one colour, no matter what the colour, is unlucky. Another refinement of belief concerning colour, however, put limits on this picturesque trait of white markings. As an old verse goes: 'One white foot, buy a horse; two white feet, try a horse; three white feet, look well about him; four white feet, you are better off without him!'[22]

Colour and other aspects of a horse's appearance were often considered to be of significance with regard to good or bad luck. For instance, to meet a white horse when setting out on a journey was an ill omen, as it also was to meet a piebald or speckled horse. And finally, mention can be made of the very common belief that the position of the first horse encountered by a person in the New Year betokens one's future fortunes. If the horse is facing the person, that is a sign that the person will prosper in the coming year; but if the horse's quarters are first seen, all will be by no means well![23] The attempt to read the future by a horse's movements are of very antique derivation, being the practice of several different peoples in antiquity and, as we have seen, part of the kingship rituals in early Ireland. So, from the destiny of ancient kings to the simple guesswork regarding the fate of the modern individual, the Irish people have preserved in their vivid imaginations the marvel and fascination of equine culture.

PART 2

In Search of the Irish Draught Horse

4

Images of
the Horse in Irish Art

MARY MCGRATH

Written history gives us a distilled version of what happened in the past. It is usually seen through the eyes of historians who interpret past actions and happenings with the wisdom of hindsight. By contrast, paintings and sculptures are arrested moments in time. The inspiration for an artwork derives from what an artist sees or feels at that moment.

By studying historic images and especially the details, we can step back into the past and observe the happenings, just as the artist did. Occasionally the artist made things appear bigger or more important in order to please his patron, and sometimes the images and happenings are depicted from a very subjective point of view, but one usually finds that the details are correct and true to life.

Contemporary images have a great number of advantages over the written word. Artists create images for a variety of reasons: a personal vision, documentation,

propaganda and so on. The artist portrayed what he knew and what he saw, in a style of the time, in a form that could easily be appreciated by those he wished to please. Commissioned images had to satisfy the patron, who paid for them, and those he wished to impress; consequently they tell us a lot about current taste and what was thought to be important. Accuracy mattered; nevertheless, how the image is depicted says a lot about how the artist felt about his subject.

Prior to the arrival of Christianity there do not seem to be any surviving depictions of figurative scenes despite many mentions of horses in the sagas handed down in the oral tradition. It is possible, even likely, that these were executed in wood and have not survived. Christianity led to the depiction of religious scenes and symbolic hunting scenes on the carved-stone high crosses erected around the country in association with monastic settlements.

The following images have been chosen, not simply

for their artistic content, but for what they can tell us about the horses they illustrate.

High Cross, Ahenny, County Tipperary

The first images come from that crucial period of Irish history during which Christianity gradually takes over from the mystical, pagan beliefs of the native people.

These illustrations come from the base of a ninth-century, carved-stone high cross in Ahenny, County Tipperary, and date from the ninth century. The base of the cross contains secular images including on one side two mounted horsemen and a chariot drawn by two horses; on the opposite side is a funeral procession.

In the first image from Ahenny two men on horseback proceed at a trot in front of a two-wheeled chariot pulled by two horses trotting with matched strides. All the horses have great presence and carry their heads high with arched necks. Their extravagant movement can be seen by the raised action of their limbs, and they have long flowing tails. The riders sit well back and use no stirrups. The carriage horses are carefully matched for style, size and pace. A well-observed collie-type dog with a curly tail balances precariously on the pole of

BELOW: *Base of North Cross, Ahenny, County Tipperary; 'Funeral Scene' (left), 'Procession' (right), with illustrated renditions.*

Photo: Department of Environment, Heritage and Local Government

THE IRISH DRAUGHT HORSE

the carriage. There are two people sitting in tandem in the vehicle; the charioteer in front and, behind, the warrior who owns the chariot. This is a very fine vehicle with large wheels containing eight spokes. It was not designed to drive on very rough ground for any distance; rather it was intended to make a statement of wealth and power on ceremonial roads and to carry its owner into war with style and attitude.

We know from archaeological evidence that the horses could have worn red-enamelled harness and matching bits. A manuscript description tells us that Cú Chulainn's pair of horses was

> alike in size, beauty, fierceness and speed. Their manes were long and curly and they had curling tails. The right hand horse was a grey horse, proud in the haunches, fierce, swift and wild; the other horse jet black; his head firmly knit, his feet broad-hoofed and slender: long and curly are his mane and tail. Down his broad forehead hang heavy curls of hair. The black was called Dubhfhoilean and the grey Líath Macha.[1]

Lócg the charioteer was Cú Chulainn's trusted friend and adviser.

Chariots were driven at high speed into the heart of the battle with much noise, rattling and shouting. The warrior descended from the chariot for hand-to-hand fighting in single combat. The surviving warrior drove away with his enemy's head displayed in triumph on the chariot. The horse is used in both war and peace as a symbol of power and authority.

In the funeral scene the skill of the artist working in stone has created a completely different, more subdued atmosphere. This is an extraordinary achievement as stone is an extremely hard and unforgiving medium. The attitudes depicted convey the sorrow of the moment. A headless corpse is laid on the back of a horse and carried in procession after a bishop with a crozier and a deacon with a cross. A large bird perches on the back of the body symbolising death. The horse is small, about 12 to 13 hands high and very docile. It completely lacks the presence and attitude of the parading horses on the adjoining panel. It is being meekly led by a bridle at a walking pace. Its tail has been cut short, perhaps as a symbol of mourning. A rather jaunty little dog, identical to that on the previous panel, is the only cheerful note in a sad procession.

These carved-stone images are among the earliest visual examples of working horses in Ireland.

A Battle Scene, 1581

John Derricke's *Image of Irelande* (1581) is a work of propaganda published in support of Sir Henry Sidney's Irish campaigns against the MacSweeneys and the O'Neills in the northern part of the country. It is extremely hostile to all things Irish and the illustrations reinforce this trend. However, the details in the woodcut seem to be correct as is borne out by known examples of armour, clothing, swords and spurs dating from the period.

This picture represents 'A battle between English and Irish'. As is to be expected Derricke shows the Irish in retreat, pursued by the English. Both armies are mounted on horses 14 to 15 hands high with plenty of bone. The warriors on both sides wear coats of chain mail and iron helmets, and carry swords and shields which add considerably to their weight. These are powerful, fast horses specially bred for battle. Unlike the English, the Irish warriors clasp

> their heavy spears about midway up the shaft, they do not hold them under their arms [like the English] but they brandish them above their heads, muscles astrain. They possess extremely docile horses on which they charge into the massed bands of the enemy or if they find themselves in an unequal

ABOVE: *Battle between the English and the Irish.*
RIGHT: *Horseboy and horse (detail).* Artist: J. Derricke, *The Image of Irelande* (published 1581, facsimile edition 1883)

contest they avoid attacks by twisting their mounts aside. All of this is achieved with very little effort on the part of the riders although they use very loose reins. Nothing could be more manageable than an Irish horse. The rider never has to cling to the horse. The ride is so smooth and the fetlocks so high even on bumpy or muddy ground that the boots of the rider are not stained at all with dirt or mud.

When mounting their horses they never use steps nor do they approve of attaching to the animals the kind of trappings which to them are useless props. Instead they catch hold of the front part of the mane, or the left ear, and while the excellently schooled horses bend their heads down quietly, the horsemen take off with marvellous agility, despite being clothed in corselet and armour … and they are mounted in an instant. The mastery of this technique is so taken for granted among them that, rather than it being thought special to be accomplished in it, it is held shameful not to be perfect at it. They rarely ride geldings though they be the most placid Asturians. Mares are fed and nourished only for breeding purposes. Nothing is more shameful in the horsemen's eyes or more apt to evoke raucus laughter than the sight of one of their fellows mounted on a mare.[2]

The Irish harness differs considerably from the English. Instead of a crupper, there is a form of breeching with two large buckles holding the saddle in place from behind. In front there is a breastplate with similar buckles keeping the saddle stable from the front. There are no stirrups. The saddle is built up in a large roll in front of and behind the rider to give some support. The Irish horses are ridden in simple snaffle bits and carry their heads in a very natural position compared with the English horses in their curbed bits. Irish manes are hogged and the forelocks left long. There is a small amount of feather on the horses' heels, and they are shod all round. The horses on both sides are quite similar in size and conformation. Many of the soldiers were mercenaries and mounted themselves on the best horses they could afford as this was their best hope of survival. The horses were probably the strongest and fastest available. They may well be descendants of the great horses brought to Ireland by the Normans back in 1169, now much improved with Eastern blood.

In a detail from another Derricke image, a barefoot horse boy holds a fine stallion similar to those depicted in the battle scene. This horse is ambling or pacing – that is, it moves both legs on one side at a time instead of the diagonal movement that is more common today. For some unknown reason it is not wearing front shoes. Here too the mane is hogged and the forelock and tail left long; this must have been the fashion of the time. Horse boys were

messengers whom the Irish call daltins … or lightly armed footservants. They march weaponless and their duties include acting as grooms to the horsemen, hurling strapped javelins and clearing mud stains from the horses' trappings. In the stalls the daltins scrape the coats assiduously with spiked scrapers to restore them to a brilliant shine. They strain every nerve in their bodies to this task of grooming to the extent that their reputation depends on their industry in this regard. Their speciality is the maintenance of equine elegance and cleanliness.[3]

This stallion is fit, well fed and ready for action, and is obviously its owner's pride and joy. It is tempting to believe that these strong, galloping horses, with plenty of bone and stamina, are the distant ancestors of today's Irish Draught.

The Irish Hobby, 1617[4]

These are very rare images of the famous Irish hobby. The hobby was greatly sought after by royalty and the wealthy classes all over Europe. It was especially valued by those seeking to improve their own breeds of horse.

Gervase Markham described the hobby as possessing 'a fine head and strong neck, a well cast body, strong limbs, sure of foot and nimble in dangerous places, of lively courage and tough in travel'.[5]

These little horses are about 12 hands high. They are compact, well made and strong enough to carry a man with ease. Their heads and head carriage are very attractive, and they have full and rich manes and tails. They have good bone, clean legs, active pasterns and excellent feet. They appear to be shod all round and some

appear to have 'cocks' on the heels of their shoes. They are very lively and are ridden in a curb bit and bridles with no nose bands, 'decorated in the Irish manner'.[6] They appear to be very athletic and to walk, trot and canter easily. Some hobbies were pacers and amblers, and were extremely comfortable to ride. They had many admirers. Their comfortable gaits are one of the reasons the hobbies were so highly sought after. Hobbies were so prized that they were considered a gift fit for a king, and there is a wealth of historical documentation about their abilities and characteristics.[7] The saddles still have the rolls front and aft, but the riders now use stirrups. The rider carries his spear over his shoulder in a jaunty fashion. He wears short riding boots and a tall pointed 'Irish hat'.

The other hobbies are lead by 'stable-boys' wearing caps with turned-up brims and with three feathers upright in front. Their outfits are a little fanciful and it is hard to imagine any establishment, no matter how grand, kitting their employees out like this. The cost of replacing the feathers alone would be prohibitive. They

ABOVE AND BELOW: Aigentliche wahraffte Delineatio Vnnd Abbildung Aller, *1617, by Esaias von Hulsen (folios 50 and 53, reference (shelfmark) Douce Prints d44 (1)).*

Photos: Bodleian Library, University of Oxford

carry whips, perhaps for their masters' use while riding. 'They are not noted for their bashfulness in speaking out in public but for the most part they indulge in scurrility and filthy conversation.'[8]

The hobby clearly has a great deal of Eastern blood which may have come from Spain, or from interbreeding with the stallions ridden into battle by mercenary soldiers from overseas. This elegant little horse had a great influence on the ordinary ponies and horses which were prevalent among the poorer farming people in Ireland at that time. They were also much sought after by the gentry, who used them as riding horses and as stallions to cross with imported mares. The Earls of Ormonde, Kildare and Desmond all had their own private studs 'for the breeding of Hobbies which they raced also in England'.[9] Horse breeding suffered during the rebellions of 1580 and 1598. By 1630 the Earl of Ormonde wrote to Viscount Dorchester that, 'There is nothing in this country worthy of presenting to your Lordship; for the dainty breed of hobbies, which were here, are quite gone.'

The Byerley Turk, 1690

The Byerley Turk was the best known of many warm-blooded Eastern stallions that came to Ireland. The horse was named after Colonel Robert Byerley, who captured him from his Turkish owner at the Battle of Buda, today part of Budapest. He was ridden in Ireland as a charger during the Williamite wars by his owner. The Down Royal Corporation of Horse Breeders state that he raced in Downpatrick on his way to the Battle of the Boyne.[10]

The Battle of the Boyne took place in 1690. By 1695 the Penal Laws were introduced to prevent any Catholic from owning a horse worth more than £5. While these laws did little to further the horse-breeding industry in Ireland, many Catholic farmers conspired with their Protestant neighbours to maintain some old breeding lines. Many horses were exported to England for breeding purposes.

There are two portraits of the Byerley Turk, both attributed to John Wootton (1682-1764). In the first,[11] probably painted early in the horse's career, the horse stands four-square and totally dominates the picture space. The groom in Eastern dress is placed in the painting almost as an afterthought. The background shows a landscape with a horse-race taking place. The horse is simply painted, showing realistic conformation and a well-balanced outline. It is easy to believe that the horse looked much as it does in the painting.

The Byerley Turk was one of the founding stallions of the *Thoroughbred Stud Book*. He acquired a legendary importance, and the later portrait deals with the horse from this point of view. It shows the stallion as a highly impressive, heroic animal. He stands alone; his stance is proud and elegant. His coat gleams with good health. He has long, clean limbs and good feet. The horse is depicted against classical buildings and mature trees; both of these features imply wealth and privilege. The groom is dressed in exotic clothing, emphasising the Eastern origins of the Byerley Turk.

Wootton chose to paint the stallion from ground level thereby increasing its height, importance and stature. This painting stresses the new role of an important individual horse, a powerful influence on the new breed of Thoroughbred horse. In this painting the horse is treated with reverence and respect and is symbolically more important than the man or the hound.

When warm-blooded stallions were imported and crossed with the native horses a gradual change took place. The better horses grew taller and faster, and were greatly sought after. Imported Arab and Eastern stallions were greatly prized by powerful Irish lords, such as the Earls of Ormonde and Cork, who had private studs dedicated to breeding fine horses.

The native Irish horse inherited many good qualities from the Thoroughbred as the inevitable result of cross-breeding. Thoroughbreds have had a huge influence on today's Irish Draught horses. The Thoroughbred blood refined the poorer and coarser working horses, and

ABOVE: *Early portrait of the Byerley Turk, attributed to John Wootton; the pose is uncontrived and the landscape very natural.*

Photo: K Club, Straffan, County Kildare

RIGHT: *Later portrait of the Byerley Turk, attributed to John Wootton; a much more stylised portrait that creates an idealised image of the horse, its groom and the landscape.*

Black-and-white print after the original held in a private collection

✿ THE IRISH DRAUGHT HORSE

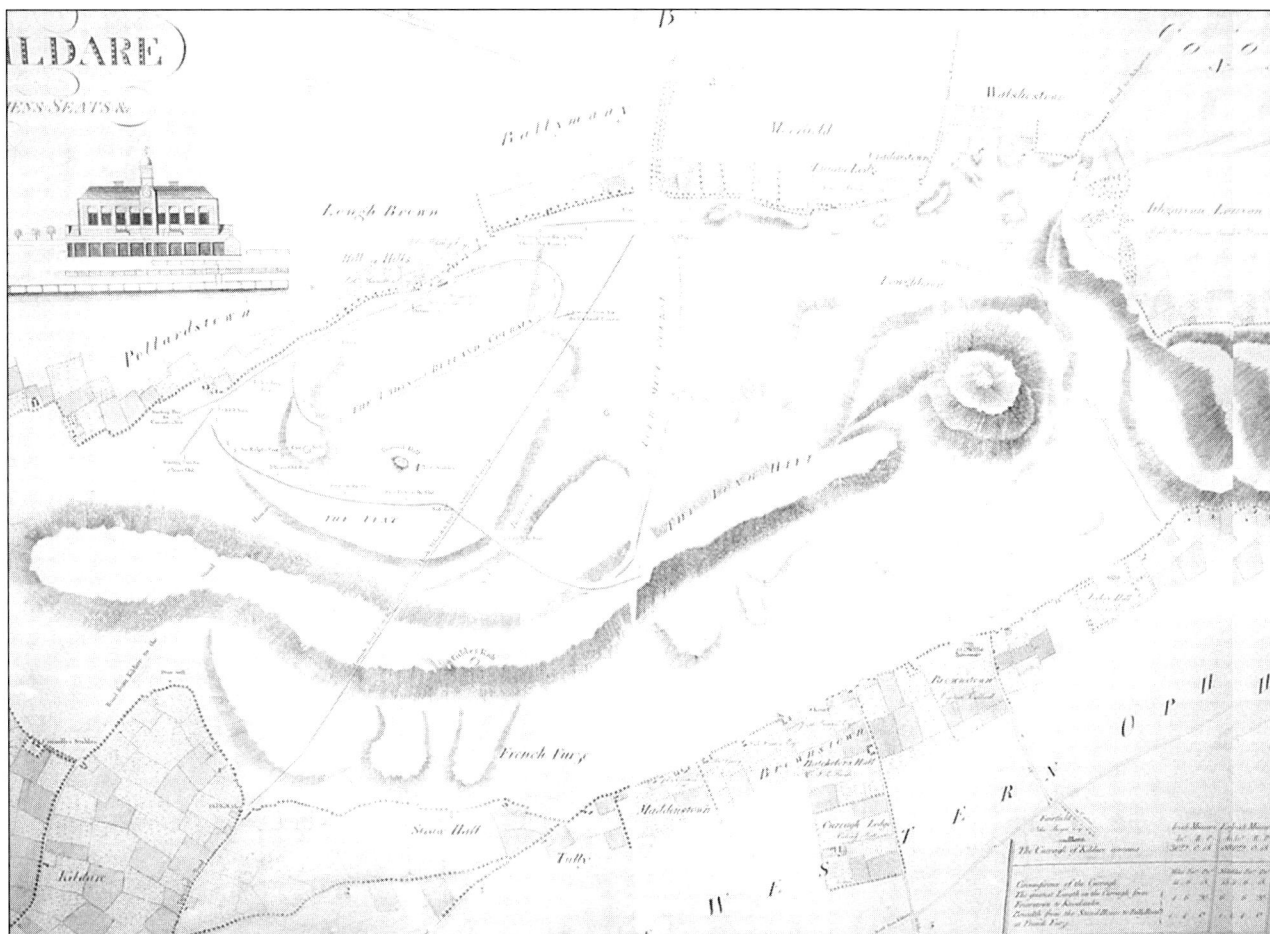

ABOVE: *Map of the Curragh Racecourse, 1807, shows the line of the race depicted in the painting* Race on the Curragh (overleaf). *The starting post is at the upper right. The raised ground of the Round Hill viewing point is clearly marked in a straight line between the start and the tower in Kildare. Parts of this racecourse are still in use today.*   Engraving by H. Walker

contributed to the clean legs, intelligence and good gaits of the draught horses of Ireland.

Race on the Curragh, 1730

The Curragh of Kildare has been associated with horses from the earliest times; the word *cuirreach* meant race-course in Old Irish. A great fair with chariot races was held there every year. It coincided with celebrations at Dún Aillinne and Aileann, two sacred hills in the vicinity. There is an ancient road which runs across the plains, and many forts and mounds from the pre-Christian era that testify to ancient occupation patterns.

Horse-races have always been held on the Curragh. By the eighteenth century, heats were held over a 4-mile course which crossed the main road twice. Sometimes, a horse would run up to three heats in a day before winning the final heat. If there was a close

ABOVE: Race on the Curragh, *1730, anonymous, oil on canvas.*

Photo: Private collection

finish it was called a 'dead heat', and that heat had to be run a second time. The horses were fit and tough. They were walked to the racecourse by a groom, the journey sometimes taking several days as horse boxes had not yet been invented. Contemporary accounts document payment to repair the grooms' boots which had worn out during the long walk.

This picture is a contemporary oil painting. It is set on the Curragh plains, with the round tower in Kildare clearly visible in the background. The artist has captured the excitement and fast movement of the race-horses and the avid interest of the onlookers.

The composition of the painting emphasises the sport enjoyed by the attending crowd. At the start of the race are the officials and a group of dignified observers. In the foreground there is a very elegant lady riding side-saddle on a beautiful horse. In the lower right quadrant there is an altercation taking place between a pedestrian and a man on horseback. They are both using their whips on each other and one wonders what the fight was about. The artist has chosen to use the horse and carriage at mid-left to draw our eyes to the middle ground, away from the race, and back towards the high ground of Round Hill, where many mounted and foot supporters have gathered to watch the race.

The starting post can be seen at the lower right among the officials and dignitaries. The winning post is off to the right of this group and can be clearly seen on Walker's map (on page 67).

Carriages driven by coachmen followed the race from the inside of the circuit. These were owned by people who could afford to enjoy the fun in comfort. The horses pulling these carriages were considerably stronger than the ridden horses and had a good elevated trot. There is now a marked difference between the more powerful carriage horses, the strong galloping hunter types, and finally the Thoroughbred racehorses. The wealthy could now select the type of horse best suited to their needs.

The carriages were accompanied by sportsmen on their finest horses, and together they galloped alongside the racing horses. Other supporters rode directly to the crucial point where the horses turn around and head for home. This would be the likely location for some 'bumping and boring' that no doubt added to the enjoyment of the race. Before the Curragh Racecourse was fenced in, people regularly followed the races in motor cars almost exactly as the carriages are doing in this picture.

The horse pulling the carriage at the lower left moves energetically, with good knee action and active hocks. It has an excellent top-line and carries its head well without the use of bearing reins. The nose band would not come into use for another hundred years. The horse is forward-going with its ears pricked, and is effortlessly pulling a well-sprung two-wheeled vehicle.

Its tail is docked in a workmanlike fashion. (The grey horse in the centre ridden by the jockey in light grey and the darker horse ridden by the gentleman in the foreground have the very latest 1790s-style tails – docked, nicked and cut into a fan shape.[12] In contrast the horses ridden by ladies have flowing, full-length tails.

Carriage horses began to be purpose bred as they were now in great demand. Pairs of matched horses and teams of four or even six were status symbols. Thoroughbred blood was used to improve the quality of the heavier horses, beginning a tradition that still exists today whereby Thoroughbreds are frequently crossed with the Irish Draught to produce a lighter, more active type of horse.

The Brown Linen Market, Banbridge, 1796

The linen industry prospered in the north of Ireland throughout the eighteenth century. A large number of markets for linen and yarn emerged in what had formerly been one of the most backward parts of Ireland. The linen industry was almost entirely domestic, with the bulk of the weaving done in the counties of the northeast. The finishing or bleaching of the cloth required expensive machinery and was in the hands of professional well-to-do bleachers. The weavers sold the linen unbleached. The markets were attended by drapers who bought the cloth and commissioned the bleachers to finish it.

Arthur Young vividly described a similar market: 'When the clock strikes eleven the dreapers jump upon stone standings, and the weavers instantly flock around them with their pieces'.[13] In this picture the weavers enthusiastically hold up rolls of linen to attract the attention of the buyers.

This image focuses on activity outside the market house and in the main street of Banbridge. In the foreground is a draught mare suckling a foal. The mare wears a collar and hames, and a straddle. She may have been unhitched from the wheel car that can be seen inside the market house, with two cloth bundles on its platform. The fact that the mare has no bridle means it is likely she has travelled a long distance, feeding on roadside grass on the way. The foal would have run loose alongside its mother. As the roads were not tarred, the surface would not have been too hard on the foal's feet. Mares worked right up to foaling, and again very soon after. This mare is in very good condition, with a shiny coat and flowing tail. The foal is completely undaunted by the crowd and the bustle as it sucks greedily at its mother's milk. An unharnessed horse stands on the street opposite an inn. There is a pig and two *banabhs* (piglets) wandering down the middle of the street.

The most important single traffic was that in linen from the north to the great Linen Hall in Dublin, the main distributing centre for home and foreign markets. A large number of people derived their income from cartage, each man taking charge of up to eight carts, and on occasion a girl managing up to six. Sometimes, 500 cars were seen in a line en route to Dublin. An indirect effect of the linen trade was the great improvement in the roads and the types of vehicles used.

All land carriage was performed with one-horse carts. The wheel car seen in the market house has solid wooden wheels with rivetted metal rims bolted in place to give better purchase on less-than-perfect roads. It is of an unusual design, with the wheels set outside the line of the shafts. The normal load capacity of early wheel carts was only about 4 hundredweight in 1745.[14] The

Scotch cart was introduced into Ireland around 1800 by the Royal Dublin Society.[15] Its use spread quickly as its large wheels and better springing allowed loads up to 22 hundredweight to be pulled with comparative ease. 'More linen is conveyed from the north to Dublin, than from any other part of Ireland; and these drays are used for that purpose.'

The first Turnpike Road Act was passed in 1729. The idea was to make traffic pay for the damage it caused to the road. As traffic increased and improved vehicles carried increased weights, it became necessary to maintain the roads on an ongoing basis. Stronger and faster horses were required to improve efficiency and delivery times. This led to more organised breeding programmes and, in time, to a better Draught horse.

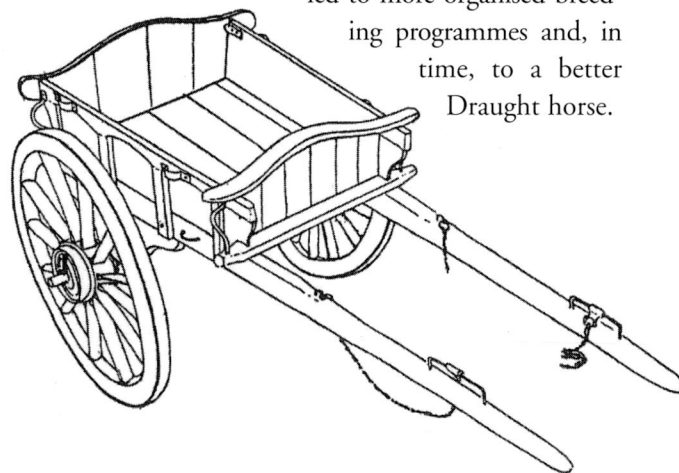

TOP: The Brown Linen Market, Banbridge, 1796, *William Hincks (Linen Industry plate viii).*
Photo: Irish Linen Centre, Lisburn Museum, County Antrim
ABOVE: *Drawing of Scotch cart after G.B. Thompson.*

ABOVE: The Pattern at Glendalough, County Wicklow *(1813) by Joseph Peacock (1783-1837).*   Photo: Copyright Ulster Museum, 2004

A curious fact affecting traffic speed, comfort and safety at this time was the reluctance of drivers to adhere to the left-hand side of the road, or indeed to any side. Eventually, in 1792, a fine of five shillings or three days in jail was brought in for driving on the wrong side of the road.[16]

The Pattern at Glendalough, County Wicklow, 1813

This painting depicts a pattern day in Glendalough in 1813. The term 'pattern day' derives from 'patron day', or the feast of a local saint. On 3 June the faithful came in great numbers to the shrine of St Kevin in Glendalough to pray and to petition the saint for favours. In the late eighteenth and early nineteenth centuries a great many people partook of this pilgrimage and associated festivities. Pattern days eventually became occasions for great drinking, faction fighting and other antisocial behaviour having very little to do with religion. The Glendalough pattern was abolished by the Church hierarchy in 1862.

The painting shows a Glendalough completely denuded of trees, very different to the way it is today. The round tower dominates the scene. Its conical top had been struck by lightning and not yet repaired. The great crowd arrived in carriages, horse carts of all shapes and sizes and on foot from Dublin and elsewhere.

There is a grand open carriage at the lower left of

the picture pulled by a team of quality matched bay horses. One of the passengers – a lady with a pale-coloured dress – holds up a parasol to protect her complexion from the sun. Another lady is helped from the carriage by a groom in formal livery. Behind the grand turnout is a more modest carriage pulled by a pair of grey horses and driven by a coachman. These carriages are parked beside the refreshment tents. In the lower centre of the painting several gentlemen are sitting on riding horses of somewhat mixed quality. They appear to be chatting away and observing the goings-on from their elevated position.

There are a large number of carts heeled up at the lower-right-hand side of the painting. The horses have been removed from the shafts and can be seen tied up and feeding in the distance behind the carts, while their owners partake of the day's entertainment.

Like the fairs the pattern days gave many people the opportunity to sell their wares, including pottery, metalwork, kegs, kettles, candlesticks and miscellaneous animals. There is a toy stall, hats are being sold and, of course, a blind fiddler plays for a singer selling broadsheets. Retail shops were found only in the towns and larger villages, so stalls at fairs provided the opportunity to buy goods that were otherwise unavailable.

In the background a fierce faction fight is taking place. The painting catalogues the extremes of religion and commerce still often seen today in places of religious pilgrimage.

There is an amazing wealth of detail. Apart from its undoubted artistic quality this painting is an extraordinary social document. It teems with activity, showing people and horses from all levels of society mixing and mingling. Only the sounds and smells are missing.

Ejectment of Irish Tenantry, 1848

On 16 December 1858, in the depths of winter, an eviction took place. This eviction was witnessed by a journalist from the *Illustrated London News*. He was obviously outraged and his sympathies lay with the unfortunate dispossessed. The journalist wrote notes and made sketches on site, then sent them to London to be engraved for publication. Engraving onto small woodblocks was very labour intensive, and frequently several artists worked simultaneously on different parts of the picture. A large image such as this would have been composed of perhaps 40 blocks, which would have to be bolted together before use.[17] Despite the laborious technique this image is full of movement and charged with emotion.

The landlord's agent, fat and self-righteous, sits astride a heavyweight riding horse of quality-draught type. The horse has become a symbol of power and wealth as good horses were the property of the middle class and landowners; cottiers made do with donkeys and goats. This horse is completely relaxed, untroubled by the harrowing scene. This is not the first time the horse has attended an eviction. An army of paid wreckers destroy the cottage while armed guards look on. The guards are there to protect the rights of the landlord, not the starving penniless victims. The inevitable curious onlookers gloat as the wretched family beseeches the agent to leave them in peace.

The bailiff is the figure of authority. Amid the frenzied activities the still tableau, formed by the sleek, relaxed horse and rider, towers over the starving family and their pitifully few possessions. The horse contrasts dramatically with the bedraggled donkey and goat that belonged to the tenants. These have now been confiscated and are being driven away.

The bailiff's position on the horse gives him a psychological advantage. If he was not on the horse looking down, he would be seen as equal with the poor. The horse serves as a symbol of power dominating the pitiful tenants.

This moment was captured by the nameless artist and focuses our attention on the cruelty of the eviction

Source: *Illustrated London News*

in the dead of winter. The power of the press was used as an extremely effective tool to highlight the iniquities of the landlord system in Ireland.

Sackville Street, 1850, by Michael Angelo Hayes

While millions of people died of starvation during the Famine, life in Dublin was little affected. This contemporary image of Sackville Street, now O'Connell Street, by Michael Angelo Hayes (1820-77) shows the middle classes going about their lives oblivious to the tragedy

affecting much of the country. The street is dominated by Nelson's Pillar, another symbol of authority but one which manages to reassure citizens of Dublin that all is well with the British Empire.

There are horse-drawn omnibuses full of passengers coming from the newly-built suburbs of Portobello and Rathmines. Indeed, the carriage at lower centre is so full that there are four men and a boy squashed onto the driver's seat, and another man clinging to the back. People are well dressed and the horses sleek and well cared for. There are many fashionable shops to be visited and purchases made. If one did not have a private carriage there were cabs available for hire. Some of these can be seen backed up to the pavement in front of McSwiney Delaney & Co.'s grand shop. This particular type of vehicle was known as a 'whiskey'. The door was at the back and the step extended over the pavement. The advantage of this system was that it allowed ladies and gentleman to step straight from the pavement into the vehicle without getting their shoes dirty. As several hundred tons of horse manure was deposited in the streets daily the gutters were rather unsavoury and the whiskey a most well-designed mode of conveyance.

Alongside the coachman-driven omnibuses, cabs and whiskeys there are also side cars, farm vehicles, broughams and, at the lower right, a very smart 'victoria' with a folding hood, proudly driven by the owner, with his wife beside him. This was a carriage well suited for ladies as there was quite a high dashboard that ensured that the horses' bottoms were hidden from their delicate gaze. The horses depicted here contribute to a sense of purposeful activity. The painting is a celebration of the commercial centre of a capital city. There is an air of Victorian prosperity about this whole scene. It is hard to believe that outside Dublin the Famine raged and three million people were forced to emigrate or

ABOVE: Sackville Street, *Dublin, 1850, by Michael Angelo Hayes.*

Photo: National Gallery of Ireland

ABOVE: The Kilkenny Horse Fair *(1922), Alfred Munnings RA.*

Photo: Royal Academy of Arts, London

died of hunger.

The Kilkenny Horse Fair, 1922, by Sir Alfred Munnings

A.J. Munnings (1878-1959) was a self-taught artist. His father was a miller who apprenticed his second son to a firm of lithographers for six years. He studied art in the evenings after a ten-hour day at work. At the age of twenty he used his savings to buy a carpenter's shop for use as a studio. Very soon afterwards he lost the sight of one eye from a briar while lifting a dog over a hedge. Munnings worked as a poster designer to earn his keep while he began to paint horses. He travelled in the country with a string of horses, ponies and a donkey, lived in a blue-painted caravan and had a flat cart for his canvases and painting materials. His groom was in charge of the whole procession.

Munnings worked out of doors and painted wonderful images of horse fairs and gypsy hop pickers, his work full of light, movement and colour. He painted in a traditional style and despised modern art. 'If you paint a tree, for God's sake try to make it look like a tree,' he said on one occasion.[18]

In 1920 Munnings got married and thereafter he painted commissions for money in order to pay his increased expenses. His talent took him into great houses and elevated society, but his paintings were now executed to please his upper-class clients. *The Kilkenny Horse Fair* falls into this period of his life (though when this painting was completed he presented it to the Royal Academy of Arts in London). He paints an idealised Irish horse fair for an English upper-class audience. The horses are those that would appeal to English sportsmen. All the horses are mature, well turned out and attended by expert grooms. The centrepiece is a fine, grey halfbred being expertly stood up for the dealer and prospective buyer. The horse's stance is for the buyer behind and to the left, and not for us looking at the picture. It has previously been ridden by the gentleman in riding clothes, and has now been stripped of the saddle and rug, which are lying on the ground in the foreground, so that the horse's conformation can be better appreciated.

The heavyweight bay horse on the right shows clear influence of its Irish Draught antecedents. It was bred to carry a heavyweight gentleman across country while at the same time being safe, looking smart and having a calm temperament. This type of horse represented the legendary Irish heavyweight hunter much valued by the English gentry. The horses' tails are cut shorter than would be today as this was the style between the wars.

The composition of the painting was carefully designed to lead our gaze to the centre of the canvas dominated by the grey horse. The subdued range of colours is exceptionally well observed. The light levels are those seen in Ireland when there is a cloudy sky and the shadows are barely visible. There is a stone wall in the foreground and a picturesque ruined church in the middle distance setting the scene firmly in Ireland. The atmosphere is calm and reassuring.

Elsewhere the civil war was raging. Many executions and atrocities took place in adjoining counties. Michael Collins was shot on 28 August that year. Nevertheless, horse fairs continued, the English gentry continued to buy and export Irish horses, and on many levels life went on as usual.

'Energy', 1928

In 1928 electricity was still a novelty. It was a luxury enjoyed by the privileged few primarily in urban areas. The Shannon Hydroelectric Scheme aimed to supply electricity all over Ireland. It was very difficult to explain electricity to a people who had no idea of its power. The Electricity Supply Board chose to use a symbol of power familiar to everyone. Most small farmers and all large farmers were familiar with 1 or even 2 horsepower. Harnessing the River Shannon enabled a hitherto unimaginable 90,000 horsepower to be generated.

The image chosen to get this idea across was a vast herd of horses, all harnessed to a single chariot, galloping as fast as they are able. The driver of the chariot is a heroic figure reminiscent of the Greek god Apollo. His cloak billows out behind him and the lash of his whip is silhouetted against the sky. The horses are pulling hard, their manes and tails flowing out behind them. They wear no bridles and the minimum of harness. This gives the impression of freedom, liberty and dynamism. Their traces are taut, emphasising their strength and power. They move in unison with a single aim, to supply power in the service of man.

It is an extremely effective image, and a new departure for advertising in 1928. It is likely from the style that the artist was German. Many Germans were invited to Ireland to provide expertise in various industrial areas, including the building of the dam on the Shannon to

ABOVE: 'Energy'; *1928 advertisement.*

Image: Electricity Supply Board

harness the energy supplied by the strong flowing river.

Using the draught horse as a symbol of energy demonstrated the importance of the idea of the working horse in Ireland of the Twenties.

Above the Fair, 1946

Jack Yeats was born in London in 1871 but grew up in Sligo with his grandparents. His brother was the poet William Butler Yeats. He began his painting career by doing illustrations for magazines, and watercolours and vivid sketches of life in the west of Ireland. He painted his first landscape in oil when he was 35 years old, and from then on painted constantly in oil.

As Jack Yeats grew older his work became more vivid and more complex. This painting, *Above the Fair*, was painted when he was 75 years old and at the height of his powers. He had always painted with feeling and movement, but here he excels in creating the impression of a bustling fair day, thronged with people and horses. The painting is so full of detail that one must look at it closely in order to see clearly what is going on.

The first thing we see is the beautiful grey horse in the foreground. It carries its head proudly and high and wears no bridle, symbolising strength and freedom. It is white with black dapples, a colour beloved of the ancient Celts. On its back sits a young boy. He is sitting firmly on the horse with his arm raised towards the sky. On the right is the head of a chestnut horse. Yeats has painted it in red, orange and yellow in order to create a vivid image. The horse's head is thrown up. It is likely that the man beside it with his arm raised has been trying to open the horse's mouth to check its age. This natural reaction was well observed by an artist who knew and understood horses. Yeats' horses, while stylized, always display vivid attitudes which imply movement, and a fleeting moment or emotion captured forever in paint. In the centre of the painting is another darker horse being ridden toward the onlooker. Its ears are pricked and its tail is raised with the anxiety and excitement of the occasion. Again the artist's technique involves us in the excitement of the fair and, by directing the horse towards us, captures our attention and draws our gaze back into the crowded street. There are at least eight horses mingling with the crowds in this painting.

In the foreground there is a crowd of dealers, buyers, middlemen and onlookers such as one finds at any fair. Some wear caps, some are bareheaded and some wear battered slouch hats. Thus, very subtly, by means of their headgear, Yeats has defined the nature of the crowd. Their faces are focused and full of expression. Some are shifty, some greedy, some wondering. All are moving.

The buildings at either side focus our attention on the

ABOVE: Above the Fair, *Jack B. Yeats*

Photo: Courtesy of the National Gallery of Ireland

seething mass of people and horses. In the background are more horses being ridden, and in the distance is a horse-drawn cart heading home from the fair. The backdrop is formed by Ben Bulben and Knocknarea.

The painting becomes a metaphor for human life. The young boy on the white horse represents hope in the future. The bustling greedy crowd is interested only in commerce and money making. The mountains will still be there when all else has passed.

Chariots, by Louis le Brocquy, 1969

Louis le Brocquy is one of Ireland's greatest painters. For many years his work has been chiefly concerned with the Celtic concept of the human head as the essence of man. He couples this with an instinctive appreciation of the human spirit's ability to 'see' and to dream. His painting is largely self-taught.

In 1969, Thomas Kinsella, the poet, published a new translation of the *Táin Bó Cuailgne*. The *Táin* is part of the eighth-century Ulster Cycle of heroic tales. It tells the story of a giant cattle raid. The armies of Connacht under Queen Maebh invade Ulster in pursuit of Donn Cuailgne – the great brown bull of Cooley. The *Táin* describes a series of epic adventures where an entire population of characters – kings and queens, heroes, charioteers, cattle, occupants of the spirit world and ordinary people – interact, love, hate, massacre and fight in single combat. These chariots resemble those depicted on the high crosses.

The book was illustrated with brush drawings by le Brocquy. He has chosen to depict images from the text as 'marks in printer's ink'. His flowing brush conjures up shapes, people, animal and folk memories. This subtle illustration technique works by supplying us with just enough information to stimulate our own imaginations by recreating the atmosphere, movement and excitement of a moment 2,000 years ago.

At first glance the illustration may not mean very much to the casual viewer. This image represents char-iots charging. It shows the exhilarating moment when the warriors and their charioteers, full of hope, urge their horses to a gallop and race towards the enemy.

The vigorous energy is immediately obvious. The chariots are racing each other as they rush into battle. There are two figures in each chariot: the charioteer and the warrior both leaning forward in anticipation. The relative positions of the chariots show that they do not advance in fixed lines like the Romans; rather, they gallop with enthusiasm and abandon towards death or glory.

Louis le Brocquy has used his knowledge and understanding of the Celtic psyche to lead us to appreciate the people and times that produced the *Táin*. Of his images he said: 'It is as shadows thrown by the text that they derive their substance.'[19]

The importance of the horse as an inspiration for the creative artist continues to be as powerful today as it has been throughout history.

> Time present and time past,
> Are both perhaps present in time future
> And time future contained in time past.

BELOW: Chariots, *illustrated by Louis le Brocquy; from* The Táin, *translated by Thomas Kinsella, published by the Dolmen Press, 1969.*
Image: Copyright Louis le Brocquy

5

Horses:
Working on the Land

JOHN FEEHAN

Then, from green, grassy grazing-grounds and pinfolds,
There were brought forth for them their flocks of mares,
And their fine, joyous steeds …

from Táin Bó Cuailgne [1]

Horses were domesticated around 4000 BC in the Ukraine, and were kept at first for their meat. They were present in Ireland by 2000 BC, but do not appear to have been common. In the Ireland documented in the Brehon Laws, a prosperous farmer (*bóaire*) was expected to have two horses, one for riding and the other for work about the farm (but not yet for ploughing). Up to the Norman period the Irish horse was very different from his modern Curragh cousin: a very hardy pony of small stature, small and stocky, used as a beast of burden and sometimes as food, although bloodstock was being imported to improve the breed from as early as Roman times.

The practice of eating horseflesh was at least occasional in pre-Christian Ireland (incidentally, the saints of early Ireland did not approve of it). Here is one famous example of the use of horseflesh as food. On his journey to woo Eimear, Cú Chulainn and his charioteer were feasted on a young foal:

> Now, thereby,
> I meant that little foal which in that house
> Was killed and cooked for us. Thou dost remember
> How for three nomads there we were detailed,
> Having partaken of it. For 'tis gass
> On every chariot that a man should mount it
> For three whole nomads, when he hath partaken
> Of flesh of steeds; because the steed it is
> Which doth bear up the chariot.[2]

The horse was held in very high esteem, especially for

its role in racing and warfare. Races were a standard feature at the public assembly, the *óenach*, which was held especially at the festival of Lughnasa in early August. There was considerable investment in expensive riding equipment, and indeed horse tackle ranks among the most beautiful of Bronze Age artefacts. There are some indications that there may have been herds of feral horses in early Christian times. The stirrup (a Chinese invention probably) reached Europe around the eighth century, and came to Ireland with the Normans. It greatly increased the ability of the rider to control his movement on the horse. Irish horses had a very favourable reputation in the medieval and early modern period. Around 1573 the Duke of Ferrara sought to procure 'eight hobby mares and two hobby stallions to breed from'.[3] William Camden described these 'excellent horses, which we call hobbies, and which have not the same movement as others, but a gentle pacing motion',[4] and in 1600 John Dymmok writes of these 'excellent horses of a fine feature and wonderfull swyftness'.[5]

Although horses were not used in ploughing until the medieval period, they were used to draw a harrow over ground previously ploughed by oxen. The Irish horse of this period was a small, light animal, not very different from a Connemara or Antrim pony. The collar in use was made of soft leather, but it pressed against the trachean artery, interfering with the horse's breathing. Only in the late thirteenth century were plough horses introduced from the Continent. Horses were seldom used for ploughing in Ireland before the sixteenth century, and large farm horses only became common after 1850.

The Horse in Ploughing

Simple scratch ploughs (ards) pulled by a single ox had been in use in the Middle East and the Mediterranean for millennia. From there they spread into northern Europe, where they were in use by 3,000 years ago. Although these simple ploughs were good enough on light soils, they could not work heavy land. That required greater strength – which meant more oxen. The introduction of heavy iron-shod ploughs, with a coulter to cut the earth, a ploughshare to cut the grass at its roots, a mouldboard to turn over the furrow slice and with wheels to regulate the depth, allowed farmers to move onto the heavier soils of the valleys. These soils gave better yields, because they were deeper and richer in nutrients, less prone to erosion, and much more resistant to heavy cropping. Such heavy iron ploughs were initially developed from models in use among the Germanic tribes; Nordic farmers had been using ploughs like this at least since the second century BC. However, it required the strength of two to eight oxen to pull the new ploughs, so more domestic livestock were needed. In the eleventh and twelfth centuries horses began to replace oxen in many areas.

As we saw earlier, horses had been harnessed with a loop around their necks before this. This meant they could only pull half a ton on wheels because they had to keep their heads up in order to stop themselves from being strangled. But in the ninth century a solid padded horse collar was invented and introduced – an adaptation of the Arab camel collar. This rested on the horse's shoulders, enabling it to pull loads as heavy as oxen could pull – but half as fast again, so that ploughing could be 50 per cent more productive. The next step was to breed stronger draught horses which could pull a 3-ton load; these were developed from the heavy horses which up to this time had only been of use for military purposes. Another small improvement of the time was also critically important: the invention of nailed horseshoes, followed by the arrival on the scene of the modern blacksmith.

HAYMAKING

ABOVE: *County Meath, 1860; the mowing bar pulled by two horses cuts the grass and leaves it to dry. It is then turned by hand so that it dries right through.* Photo: Irish Picture Library

LEFT: *The hay is cut and allowed to dry on the ground for a couple of days. Then it is turned to allow the underside to dry. When completely dry the hay was made into cocks.*
Photo: Bord Fáilte

ABOVE: *Ballysokerry, County Mayo, 1948; a tumbling rake at work. It gathers up the hay and can bring it to a cock under construction or be 'tumbled' to leave the hay in a heap as the basis for a new cock.*   Photo: Bord Fáilte

LEFT: *Bringing home the hay. A haycock is winched up onto a 'hay bogey' and carried home to be stored for winter.*
                    Photo: National Museum of Ireland

Howth, County Dublin, 1955; generations of children enjoyed sitting on the back of the bogey as the horse made his leisurely way back to the haggard.

Photo: Bord Fáilte

LEFT: *Ag casadh an tsúgán (twisting the rope). Hay ropes were made to hold the rick in place against the winter storms and equinoctal gales.*

Photo: National Museum of Ireland

LEFT: *As there were no hay sheds at that time, the hay was packed into a large stack or rick which could be sliced as needed for winter feed.*

Photo: National Museum of Ireland

LEFT: *Doolin, County Clare, 1948; on smaller farms neighbours banded together in a* meitheal *to help each other bring home the hay as vital winter fodder.*

Photo: Bord Fáilte

ABOVE: *Clonbrock, County Galway, 30 June 1869: a large force of estate workers load hay onto Scotch carts, each drawn by a draught horse. The foreman, mounted on a good-looking horse, supervises the activity.*

Photo: Irish Picture Library

POTATOES

Ploughing scene, 1952; the horseman is preparing potato drills with a single-board plough. The people in the background have buckets of potatoes to sow. The plough will then split the drill to cover the potatoes.

Photo: Bord Fáilte

CORN

ABOVE: *County Cork, 1967; a spring grubber tills across the ploughed ground to break up the clods before harrowing or sowing a crop.* Photo: Bord Fáilte

LEFT: *County Wicklow, 1940; if the clay was lumpy the ground was rolled twice to create a fine surface layer before sowing seeds for turnips or beet.* Photo: Bord Fáilte

BELOW: *County Kerry, 1953; cutting corn with a reaper and binder. The corn was cut while still a little green and tied into stooks where it would ripen in about three days.*

Photo: Bord Fáilte

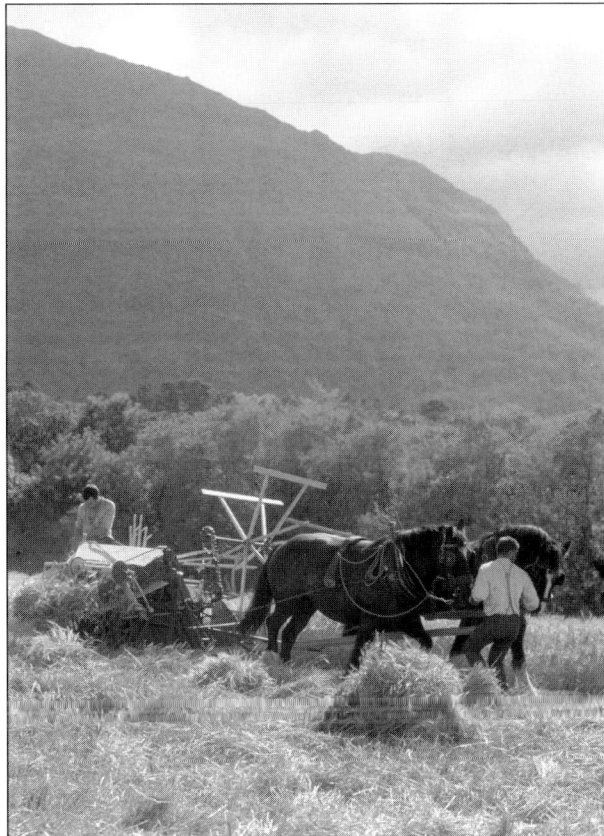

LEFT: *Louth, 1930; the sower broadcasts seed from his* práiscín *(apron). The harrow, pulled by two horses, comes along behind and covers in the seeds.* Photo: Fr Browne SJ Collection

ABOVE: *The stooks are carefully loaded onto a cart and brought to the haggard for threshing.* Photo: National Museum of Ireland

ABOVE: *Ardmore, County Waterford, 1860s; threshing machine powered by four horses. The circling horses turn a shaft which drives a mill. Sheaves are handed into a drum where they are threshed. The corn falls into a sack and the straw is made into a stack for storage. Straw mattresses were made by filling flour sacks with fresh straw. People often spoke of the comfort and scent of a new straw mattress.* Photo: Irish Picture Library

The Mechanisation of Irish Farming

Mechanisation has been part of farming from the beginning; even the simplest hand tools apply the principles of mechanics. Many of the advances that agriculture has made in the course of its long history have been due to improved mechanisation: the rotary quern, the mouldboard plough, the harnessing of water power, the perfection of horse harness, to mention just a few of those that preceded the Industrial Revolution. In those earlier times the farmer fully understood the tools and devices he used, and each community was largely self-sufficient in their manufacture and repair. The forge was the technological heart of the community. But the pace and spread of technology accelerated rapidly after the Industrial Revolution, in due course displacing the blacksmith. For all the benefits it brings to farming, industrial mechanisation impoverishes a community in the fundamental sense that the special skills handed down and elaborated within the community for generations, over centuries and perhaps tens of centuries in some cases, are lost. From our early-twenty-first-century vantage point it is almost incredible that small rural communities, poor by our standards, could produce their own cloth from wool and flax, could fashion their own tools of steel from local iron ore, could attain mastery of the entire sequence of skills and techniques for every stage of so many processes, from raw material to finished product.

Mechanisation was a defining feature of the agricultural revolution, but its effects on Irish farming were very restricted and local until after the Famine. An unlimited supply of cheap labour was one of the main reasons for this. Where agricultural improvement and reform took place, particularly in the pre-Famine years, they mainly involved labour-intensive drainage and reclamation, tenancy reform, co-operative movements and the improvement of varieties and breeds – but with little mechanisation. On small farms, and more especially on poor land, almost all cultivation continued to be done by spade until the twentieth century. The spade was accompanied by a varied suite of hand-operated implements, many of great antiquity: slanes and flachters, querns and grindstones, straw-rope twisters, furze choppers and lifters, thistle tongs, flails and winnowing trays. This ancient intimacy between hand tools and the management of farm land was loosened by the spread of animal power, but it was the arrival of cheap fossil fuel that finally made most hand tools redundant. Many of the tasks performed with some of these tools were truly back breaking, but in retrospect a note of regret at their passing began to creep in, especially as people began to realise that other valued aspects of rural life had disappeared along with them.

From the earliest days of farming, animal power had been used on all but the poorest holdings for many of the heavier tasks. Whether or not a farmer kept oxen or horses depended to no small degree on whether they could be fed through the year. Oxen continued to be used on Irish farms in preference to horses long after they had become an anachronism elsewhere – in some places into the last century. In general, though, the horse was becoming the great source of power on the farm as the nineteenth century progressed. By 1895 there were 15,000 horse-drawn reapers and 10,000 horse-operated threshing mills in use. There were 564,916 horses on farms in 1901. The donkey also played an important role, particularly in the second half of the nineteenth century, during which their numbers rose from 100,000 in 1850 to 240,000 in 1900.[6]

6

For Everything
there is a Season

MARY McGRATH

An outline of the farming year based largely on conversations with 'Tucks' Bergin, who learned his skills from his father, and who has over 60 years' experience farming the land.

Until the 1960s the majority of the population lived in rural Ireland. Farming and agriculture were their principal activities. The success or failure of the harvest determined how many animals could be over-wintered and how well or badly the family would fare until the following year. Come harvest time or haymaking or threshing, all able-bodied men, women and children lent a hand. The horse was the principal means of power and transport on these occasions. Buried in the folk memory of many town dwellers today are happy scenes of a gathering, or *meitheal*, during their childhood where communal labour and shared aims combined to ensure the crops were saved. The history of those happy scenes began a long time ago.

The Normans introduced new farming methods which had to be adapted to existing field systems but gradually new distribution of lands for different social groups became common:

> three-yearly crop rotation on the manorial farms
> led to further enclosure in the period 1171-1300 …
> the Tudor-Stuart plantations continued the process
> of enclosure and the establishment of rural villages.
> The second half of the eighteenth century was the
> last great period of enclosure and in the early nineteenth century the continuous subdivision of farms
> led to the creation of a patchwork of tiny fields in
> many parts of the country [1]

The ox was the principal draught animal down to the twelfth century, when the horse began to be used. By the sixteenth century the horse was the usual draught animal for ploughing, and many improved iron ploughs were invented to make working the land easier and more efficient.[2]

Much of the tillage was in the areas around villages known as the infield. The soil here would be regularly tilled. The procedure known as 'ploughing by the tail', where the plough was attached directly to the horses' tails, was most likely used in these areas as it would have been impossible 'on the tough sod of the outfield, which was allowed to rest for long periods'.[3] The evolution of the plough has been well covered by Evans[4] and Watson,[5] but it was also necessary for the horse to evolve in order to employ the new improved machinery to its best advantage.

In the mid-nineteenth century it proved impossible to plough lea ground properly, even with three or four horses harnessed abreast, 'so weak and small are the horses'.[6] Faced with the necessity for increased tillage and the nature of the small farms divided into many fields, a new type of working horse was required. It needed to be handy, agile, not too big, versatile, strong and biddable. The large Clydesdale horses used in England and lowland Scotland were simply too big for the small areas to be worked and cost too much to maintain. Many schemes were adopted to improve the breeding of the working horse and these have been well documented elsewhere in this book.

Gradually, a type of horse evolved to fill the needs of the small-to-medium farmer. This was the draught horse, in time to become standardised as the Irish Draught horse. Absolutely essential to life on the farm, it was used in a variety of ways every day and at all times of the year.

Farming conditions changed very slowly in rural Ireland during the twentieth century; in some respects very little before the 1950s.[7] The period up to the 1930s and 1940s was the heyday of the working horse. After the war tillage was compulsory and many of the early registers of the Irish Draught horse in the Department of Agriculture document that mares were not covered as the extra tillage requirement meant they were needed to work extra-long hours in the fields.[8] There was also a fuel shortage after the war, and, as motor vehicles were largely off the road, horse transport was in great demand.[9] You would need two good horses to plough a field as it was very hard and constant work.

Most people would plough in the autumn and let the frost break down the soil over the winter, but some people always ploughed in the early spring – around February and March. The working horses were stabled and 'well minded' during the winter, being fed corn and hay to keep up their strength. The other horses were wintered out and fed hay when the weather was hard.

In the spring – late March or April – the land was tilled. First there was spring grubbing to break down coarse clods of clay. The grubber was pulled by one or two horses; it was a sort of rake that eliminated the worst lumps of earth. The land was then harrowed to break the clay into a fine layer ready to sow.

The seed corn had been saved from the harvest the year before. Often the farmer saved his own seed by storing it in the haggard. The sheaves of corn were stacked on a raised stone base, heads in, tails out and headed off with straw. They were tied well down to keep out rats and mice as far as possible. The seed was well preserved in this way.

In the spring the stored corn was threshed to remove the seed. Before the arrival of steam the thresher was powered by two or four horses. They walked round in a circle stepping over a bar which transferred the power to the threshing machine. The sheaves were fed in, often by the farming women, and the corn came out into a sack while the straw was discarded and the chaff fell onto the ground beside the threshing machine.

The fun would start as the end of the stack was reached. The men with the terriers were there to chase the mice and the odd rat. It caused great excitement. One Mrs Whelan from Tullow found a mouse in her clothes when she had cycled 6 miles home after a day's threshing.[10]

In the early days the seed was hand sown or broadcast and then harrowed in. Later a corn drill pulled by two horses was used to perform the same task. The coulters were staggered to ensure that the seed was evenly spaced. The seed was then harrowed in, again using two horses. After that the field was rolled. Every square foot of land was ploughed, grubbed, harrowed, sown, harrowed again and rolled. The same piece of land was travelled six times in order to set the seed. The work was incredibly labour intensive. Children rushed home from school to walk behind the horses as they worked the land. It was a great thrill to be given the reins and allowed to drive these powerful horses alone.

Often when the corn began to break the surface of the clay a farmer would sow grass seed. It would grow slower than the corn, and when the crop was harvested there would be after-grass for the cattle. Hayseed would be sown by a man with a one-wheeled seed barrow so as not to cause too much damage to the growing corn.

Hay was the most important fodder crop. After land was freshly seeded you could get crops of hay for up to three years. First-crop hay was the sweetest and best. There was no silage then, so saving the hay was one of the most important events in the farming year. Haymaking began much later than today, in June or thereabouts. The ripened grass was cut by a mowing bar pulled by two horses. The mowing machine had a seat on it that meant you did not have to walk every yard behind the horses. After a few days drying, the hay was turned using a sward turner pulled by two horses. When it was completely dry, a horse-drawn wheel rake or tumbling rake was used to pull the hay into rows. Then along came the workers making the haycocks, or loading the hay into carts to be brought home. Everything depended on the weather — if the weather was good every single minute counted. This was one of those occasions when everyone worked together to make sure the crop was saved. In the fields the workers ate sandwiches and drank milk or cold tea. It was thirsty work. The hay that was being brought home immediately was stacked high on carts. Sometimes they would put a rack onto the cart that extended out over the horse's back to increase the size of the load. When the cart was fully loaded the horse was almost invisible.

If the hay was to stay in the fields for a while it was made into haycocks. The procedure was to 'head the cocks and pull the butts'. The cocks were tidied round the lower edges by pulling out excess hay. This was then laid on top of the cock and tied in with *súgán* rope. The rope was made by twisting hay and pulling gently at the same time. It would start at one side and, when long enough, was pulled over the top of the cock and tied in at the other side. Hay was left like this for up to three weeks and was reasonably weatherproof. The haycocks were brought back to the haggard ('hay-garth' – a garth is a piece of enclosed ground) on a bogey pulled by one horse. In the field the bogey was backed up by the horse to the haycock and tipped up. A rope was put around the haycock and it was winched up onto the flat cart. The laden cart was then driven slowly back to the farmyard. Generations of children remember sitting on the back of the hay bogey, feeling part of an important occasion and making sparks on the road with the nails in the soles of their shoes as the light faded.

Back at the haggard the loose hay and the haycocks were stacked into ricks. It would take ten to fifteen cocks to make a rick and there could be several ricks in a yard.

Cattle were traditionally taken off the land around St Patrick's Day (17 March) and moved to the outfield or commonage for summer grazing. Old meadow hay was harvested from the winter grazing land around the end of July. This hay was not such good quality as it grew on poorer ground. The late harvest of this hay allowed birds such as the skylark and the corncrake to nest and raise their brood without being disturbed. Poor hay was often known as 'sheep hay' as it was used for winter fodder for sheep.

If the farmer milked cows, traditionally the farmer's

wife made butter, but following the founding of the co-operative movement by Horace Plunkett in 1898 co-operative creameries were set up around the country. The milk needed to go to the creamery every day as there was no way to keep milk cold on the farm. This was a time-consuming business as the carts formed a long queue on the road outside the co-op as they waited their turn. It was a time to catch up on the news and talk about hurling, football, racing and world affairs.

A farmer might have two vehicles: a flat cart or Scotch cart used for heavy work, and a side car, round trap or back-to-back car for special outings. The heavy cart and the farm implements would be pulled using chain harness, a large stuffed-leather collar with metal hames and a wooden straddle padded with horsehair or rye straw. The harness for the lighter vehicle would be made of leather. Harness makers travelled as journey-men round the country at certain times of the year car-rying out repairs on damaged harnesses.[11]

The draught mare might produce a foal in the spring. She would work right up to foaling and start work again not long after. The foal would be stabled while the mare was working in the fields. When the men came home for their dinner in the middle of the day the mare would be put back with the foal, and afterwards would go back to the fields to work until dusk. The mare would be well fed as feeding the foal and working in the field took a lot out of her.

After about one month the mare would need to be covered or mated for the following year's foal. A foal is carried for eleven months. Local stallion owners and the Department of Agriculture travelled horses around the country covering mares as they went. One man in Kildare, Paddy Behan, had his horses on the road for weeks at a time during the spring and summer, and in the autumn and winter he ploughed the land with his two stallions. The stallions would arrive into town on a fair day and be stabled in a local yard, such as McWey's in Kildare. The farmer would drive his mare

ABOVE: *Block printed stallion advertisements were posted promi-nently in towns and on fair greens. Victor shows considerable Clydesdale influence possibly inherited from his northern ancestors.*

Photo: Private Collection

to town with produce or pigs or calves for sale in the cart. The mare would be unhitched and brought to the stallion and covered. At the end of the day she would pull the cart back home to be reunited with her foal. The next day she would be back at work on the land.

Seamus Murphy in *Stone Mad* has a short passage

which gives the flavour of the times. It deals with two stonemasons, nicknamed the 'Prouncer' and the 'Ghost'.

On Sunday mornings after Mass the pair of them used indulge in a form of banter peculiar to themselves, much of it at the expense of a poor man whose job it was to ring a handbell and chant 'Barto Lynch's Duke won't stall no mares this year' or 'Cronin the Gelder will be here tomorrow and at Rockchapel in the evening'. The Ghost used to shout: 'send him up to the Prouncer, he's doing the devil's own damage to the whole neighbourhood and drastic action is required!'[12]

A foal or young unbroken horse (called a 'long tail') for sale meant some much-needed hard cash for the farmer. The foal sales were held in the late summer or early autumn when the foals were weaned. Some fairs, such as Ballinasloe, are still going strong while others like the 'Fair of the Furze' on the Curragh have long since disappeared. A farmer might buy a working horse at one of these fairs. If it was young it would be broken in before the spring, let off for a while, then gradually introduced to work for a half-day at first alongside an older, experienced horse. Sometimes people made a bit from hazel wood as this was supposed to be gentle on the young horse's mouth.[13]

Surprisingly enough the workhorses were rarely ridden. Occasionally, when the hunt passed by, the horse would be taken out of the plough and ridden in hot pursuit, still wearing the blinkers and harness, but on the whole, workhorses were used for work only and for pulling carts and cars.

On Sundays the family rode to Mass in a side car dressed in their best clothes. There were rings set into the walls of the church so that the horses could be tied up during Mass. Similarly, if there was a wedding, the bride and groom travelled separately to church in side cars and

ABOVE: *'Come day, go day, God send Sunday.' Sunday was a day of rest, when members of the farming community put on their good clothes and drove to Mass.*
Photo: Bord Fáilte

then on together to the bride's family's house for the wedding breakfast and some music and dancing. There was no such thing as a hotel reception in those days.

The priest and the doctor either rode or drove a good-quality horse as befitting their status. The doctor's gig was a fine vehicle easily recognised as he drove about the country on his visits.

The blacksmith was always in great demand. Farm machinery needed mending, gates needed to be made and the horses needed to be shod at regular intervals. The blacksmith also shod wheels with iron bands to protect the oak felloes (exterior rim of a wheel). A visit to the blacksmith's forge was an enjoyable outing and a welcome break from hard physical work on the farm. The fire kept the forge warm and there would always be a gathering of farmers discussing the great philosophical questions of the moment while the horses waited patiently outside. The water in which the red-hot iron was tempered was a known cure for warts.

In August the turf that had been cut earlier in the year was brought home while the bogs were firm enough to take the carts. If the ground was too soft for wheels a slide or slipe car was used to bring the turf from the bog to the road. This was a very ancient vehicle resting on skids that was used throughout Ireland for around 2,000 years. The harness was often made of twisted straw or grass. Days on the bog linger in the memory for great fun, sunburn and insect bites. A shed full of turf was an insurance policy against a freezing winter.

In August or September the corn would be harvested. A reaper and binder pulled by three horses would be used. The cut corn was bound in sheaves by the machine and left on the ground as the harvest progressed. The men and women working behind the reaper and binder would stack the sheaves against one another in even numbers. Two, four or six sheaves made a stook. Six or seven stooks made a stack. Four sheaves would be placed upside down on the stack to protect it from the rain until it could be brought back to the farm.

At the end of September or the beginning of October the harvested corn would be drawn into the haggard in one-horse carts. It was then either threshed or stored in ricks to be threshed the following spring. Ricks were built in the haggard as there were no barns or lofts available for storage.

A certain amount of corn was necessary to feed the workhorses, the milking cows and maybe the cattle over the winter. This corn would need to be dried and brought to the mill to be bruised or crushed to make it more digestible and less likely to germinate. The corn would be taken to and from the mill in sacks stacked in a one-horse cart. This had to be done on a regular basis over the winter as the corn did not last very long once crushed.

The straw from the threshing would be used for thatching, or if it was oaten straw it could be used as fodder for young cattle if there was no hay available. Wheaten straw was used as animal bedding, but barley straw was impossible as it caused all kinds of itches and irritations. The long rye straw that was good for thatching was also valued by harness makers for stuffing collars and straddles. The chaff and the fresh straw was often put into flour sacks and used as a pallet or mattress. It was comfortable and smelt lovely when fresh, but it flattened out quickly and needed to be replaced often. Much better was the horsehair mattress, covered with ticking. When the horses' manes were pulled or their tails trimmed the hair was carefully stored. Once a year or so a man would come to the yard and ask if there was any hair. It was taken, washed and made into cushions, upholstery and mattresses. This continues in some areas up to the present day, but modern synthetic stuffing has made horsehair almost redundant.

After three crops of hay on the land, potatoes or a root crop would be grown. During the winter the land would be prepared. If turnips were to be sown, well-rotted manure was spread over the field from a horse-drawn cart and then ploughed in as fertilizer.

ABOVE: *Preparing to apply manure as fertilizer on the land.*
LEFT: *Forking the manure into the furrows prior to ploughing it
in to enrich the soil.*   Photo: National Museum of Ireland

Potatoes were sown in April. They needed a lot of feeding. The field was ploughed as normal and then rotted manure was spread from a cart pulled by one horse. The horse walked in one furrow and each wheel of the cart would fit in adjoining furrows. The farmer forked the manure into the furrows as the horse walked slowly from one side of the field to the other with little or no guidance. The potatoes were sown by hand directly onto the manure. A special kind of double-boarded plough was then used to split the drills and turn the clay over the furrow. When this was repeated over and over, the drills were turned into furrows and new drills were formed over the potatoes and fertilizer. This was a difficult job and you would need a very good horse to walk along the top of a drill while the other walked in the furrow. You would put your best horse on the drill.

Turnips or swedes, beet and mangles were sown in early April. Seeds were bought from seed merchants in town. Powers of Waterford were well-known seed merchants.

ABOVE: *Harvesting the turnips by hand on a cold, misty morning.*

Photo: National Museum of Ireland

The seed was sown by a seed barrow pulled by one horse. The seeds were very small and too many seeds were sown in each row. When they began to grow they needed to be thinned out. Thinning turnips was an unenviable but necessary task, carried out by hand. Now, with more specialised machinery, seeds are sown one at a time and this back-breaking task is no longer necessary. All of these root crops had a great deal of greenery over the ground that needed to be removed prior to harvest. Every man had a pair of 'snaggers' with which he would 'snag the turnips' or remove the foliage. These were then harvested by hand into a one-horse cart. Turnips were brought home and stored in a pit for winter fodder. Mangles had to be well covered as they were easily damaged by frost. Beet was a cash crop which could be sold to the nearest sugar company. It was brought to the roadside for collection or, if you were lucky

enough to be near a train station, you would be given your own wagon to load in a siding. You would tip the load from a horse cart and then load it into the wagon with a beet fork. It would take several loads to fill a wagon.

The mangles were stored as fodder for the cattle during the winter. There was a machine powered by one horse in the same way as the threshing machine and which pulped the mangles to make them suitable for cattle feed. They were then loaded into the cart, brought to the cattle being wintered out and forked over the side as the horse pulled the cart slowly along. Loose hay was fed to the outdoor animals in the same way.

The stabled animals were fed hay from the rick, and crushed or bruised corn from the mill. During the winter fresh green food was in scarce supply. Furze bushes, or whins or gorse as they are known in the northern part of the country, were rooted out using a specially designed *v*-shaped implement. The roots and dead wood served as kindling and firewood, the green tips were crushed in a purpose-made machine and served as fresh food full of vitamins for the stabled animals. There was an area of the Curragh in Kildare called French Furze where an imported type of improved furze was grown to feed the racehorses stabled around the Curragh edge. Crushed furze was supposed to be a good cure for worms.

The stabled animals and milking cows in at night needed to be mucked out regularly. The soiled straw was loaded onto the cart and removed to a manure heap where it gradually rotted down until it was ready to be spread on the land as fertilizer after a year or so.

It was most important that the horses stayed healthy. Veterinary surgeons were in short supply and so 'cures' were a vital part of horse husbandry. Furze treated worms. There were many cures for warts. Bergin's of Oghill owned a wart stone. This was a large rock which had a hole full of water. The water was full of rusty pins and these were used to cure warts and ringworm. The cure for farcie consisted of herbs and a secret ingredient mixed together and fed to the horse with feed. Strains and sprains were treated with rest. 'Doctor Green' was the name given to field rest, where the horses were turned out and given time to heal. If a horse was lame there were special prayers and invocations:

> Christ was walking on rocky ground when a horse's
> foot was hurt;
> He put blood to blood, flesh to flesh and bone to bone.
> As He healed that
> May He heal this.
> Amen.[14]

Young people found life on the farm very hard. Letters from America urged younger family members to leave the land and travel abroad. The 'American wake' was a party held the night before departure to say goodbye to those taking the boat. The role of the horse was to carry the emigrant and the grieving family to the train station or to the boat. The luggage was unloaded from the well of the car while sad goodbyes were said.

In reality life was hard, people were poor and emigration was common. Patrick Kavanagh, in his book *Tarry Flynn*,[15] took a cold look at the realities of farming. The eponymous Tarry, however, is a dreamer. The slow repetitive tasks with the horses allow him time to imagine and dream, much as Kavanagh himself did as a young man.

> He stooped down under the belly of the animal to catch the girth strap and as he did he caught a glimpse of the morning sun coming down the valley: it glinted on the swamp and the sedge and flowers caught a meaning for him. That was his meaning. Having found it suddenly, the tying of the girth and the putting of the mare in the cart and every little act became a wonderful miraculous work. It made him very proud too and in some ways impossible. Other important things did not seem important at all.

It seemed at the time that this traditional way of life would continue for many years. In the 1950s, however, increased mechanisation suddenly arrived on the farm. The tractor replaced the horse as a source of energy and almost overnight the era of the horse was over. Farming methods were irrevocably altered and the firmly fixed rota of the farm year began to unravel. Frequently, the only horse to remain on the farm was a broodmare kept for sentimental reasons.

Today, those golden days of childhood live on in memory. The sun always shone, there was a certainty about the rhythm of the seasons and life moved at the pace of a working horse.

Plough-Horses

Their glossy flanks and manes outshone
The flying splinters of the sun.

The tranquil rhythm of that team
Was as slow flowing meadow stream.

And I saw Phidias's chisel there –
An ocean stallion, mountain mare –

Seeing with eyes the Spirit unsealed
Plough-horses in a quiet field.

Patrick Kavanagh[16]
Fifty Years of Modern Verse. 1938.

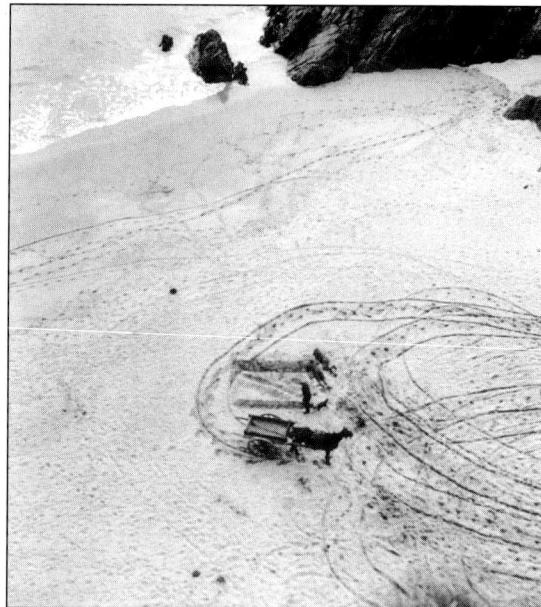

ABOVE: *Kerry, 1920s; collecting sand from the beach. Sand was used for many purposes, including land improvement and building.*
Photo: Irish Picture Library

LEFT: *Wicklow, 1920s; clearing timber. The horse waits calmly while a tree trunk is loaded using a traditional tripod pulley system.*
Photo: Fr Browne SJ Collection

ABOVE: *County Mayo, 26 June 1938; the 'scholars' van', a horse-drawn school bus. This early example of school transport showed the importance placed on education in rural communities.*

Photo: Fr Browne SJ Collection

LEFT: *Slieve Sneacht, County Donegal, 1929; turf sled on skids, supplemented by rollers underneath in case it starts to sink into the bog. The horse is stocky and compact, quite unlike the draught horses of the south.*

Photo: Fr Browne SJ Collection

FAR LEFT: *Bray, County Wicklow, 1870; horse-drawn cabs and carriages waiting outside Bray train station.*
Photo: National Photographic Archive

LEFT: *County Cork, 1950s; before long, motorised transport began to take over. Individual farmers met the creamery lorry along the way and loaded up their churns. It was a sign that the days of horse transport were numbered.* Photo: Fr Browne SJ Collection

BELOW: *There was plenty of time to have a chat and smoke a pipe while queuing up for the creamery.*
Photo: Bill Doyle

THE IRISH DRAUGHT HORSE

ABOVE: *Wicklow, 1950s; traditional travellers' caravan pulled by a good quality draught type. These were a common sight on Irish roads until the 1960s.*

Photo: Bord Fáilte

LEFT: *Kerry, late 1950s; churns of milk had to be brought to the creamery daily as there were no means of preserving milk on the farm.* Photo: Bord Fáilte

ABOVE: *Dr Staunton on horseback, early twentieth century. Doctors were liable to be called out at all hours and in all weathers, so a strong, safe, healthy, reliable horse was essential. As professional men, doctors liked to drive a smart gig or ride a good-looking horse. Horses with some Thoroughbred blood were preferred, though here the draught influence is also much in evidence.*

LEFT: *Blackrock, County Dublin, 1904; upper-class gentlefolk disliked undressing on the beach and walking into the sea. They hired bathing boxes pulled by draught horses, which were slowly backed into the water. The occupants could undress in comfort, don their bathing attire and step down into the sea using the door and steps at the back of the vehicle.*

Photos: National Library of Ireland

7

Economic Role of the Workhorse in Nineteenth-century Ireland

STUART N. LANE

Prior to the advent of the internal-combustion engine, the horse – patient and largely unsung – served a function in the economic life of the country, the importance of which could hardly be exaggerated. The horse acted as man's principal auxiliary in such operations as agriculture, road transport, commerce and industry, military affairs, and much else, and had brought the technology of transport and draught to the stage where the motor car was able to take over in the decade which preceded the First World War. As the economic historian F.M.L. Thompson wrote,

> It is important to recall that the horseless carriage was so named not solely through failure of linguistic imagination, but also because the motor car was first and foremost a horse substitute.[1]

Irish Horse Population Prior to 1900

The national census figures from 1841 to 1900 divide the horse population of two years and older by function: 'Agricultural', 'Traffic and Manufacture' and 'Amusement and Recreation', the latter category presumably representing such activities as hunting, racing and the like. The figures are given by counties, provinces and nationally. Annual figures for horses and mules are given separately from 1847-51. As might be expected, the vast majority of horses were used for agricultural purposes. For example, the number of agricultural horses of 'two years old and upwards' for 1874 were given as follows: Leinster 98,655, Munster 93,529, Connacht 40,207, Ulster 131,480; together, they comprise a national total of 363,871.

The various census figures for the period under review show fairly wide fluctuations in the annual numbers of

ABOVE: *Dublin, 1930s; many horses were old, half-starved, over-worked and ill. At the end of their days they were sold off to the knacker's yard for the price of their hide.*   Photo: private collection

These animals were of very mixed breeding, the mares being usually covered by stallions chosen on no other basis but the cheapness of their fees. A knowledgeable commentator wrote in 1812:

> The condition of the working horse in Ireland is altogether miserable. The mares are always worked even while the foal is sucking, a practice which is highly injurious to both and indeed the whole treatment of this noble and useful animal is exceedingly cruel and barbarous.[2]

However, a better type of workhorse was developed by more progressive breeders. This animal was descended partially from older native breeds and partially from horses that had been imported from England some generations earlier. Over the years these diverse elements had become to some degree homogenised, and by the alchemy of climate, geology and environment had developed characteristics that were distinctively Irish. This mixed race was clean legged and used principally for general agricultural purposes. It tended to be smaller and lighter than its British counterparts, such as Clydesdales and Shires, which tended to specialise in specific functions such as ploughing the extensive areas of tillage found in many parts of that country; the Irish workhorse, by contrast, tended to be a general-purpose animal better suited for the smaller agricultural units characteristic of Ireland. It was used for

> ploughing or harrowing one day, for hauling heavy loads of farm produce the next, and on the third, perhaps for driving to market … Seldom very generously fed, and usually obliged to 'rough it' in all weathers.

The mares of this breed 'have acquired a hardiness, a staying power, and a physical fitness which stands them in good stead in their capacity as breeders.'[3]

horses used in agriculture, with a marked peak from 1859-62. The figures for the other two categories were, however, fairly consistent, each remaining at about 25-30,000 between the years 1854-86. However, there was a gradual rise in the numbers of the second category, 'Traffic and Manufacture', which had reached about 48,000 by 1900, reflecting the increased use of commercial and trade vehicles generated by the increased wealth and prosperity during the latter part of the century. At the same time, figures for the 'Amusement and Recreation' category, which would have consisted largely of Thoroughbred racehorses and halfbred hunters, remained at about 30,000, showing little divergence from the figures for 1854. The section designated 'Traffic and Manufacture' is the one most relevant to the present chapter.

The county surveys commissioned by the Dublin Society in the early years of the nineteenth century reveal that the typical Irish workhorse of the period was generally a poor creature, seldom exceeded 14 or so hands, was usually overworked and was undernourished.

ABOVE: *County Cavan, 1950s; stopping for a chat on the way home. Cattle bought at the fair were driven home along the road in front of the horse and cart.*
Photo: Bord Fáilte

Another factor to influence the development of the breed was the type of farm vehicles used. Ireland, in common with Scotland, Wales and many of the more mountainous parts of Europe, traditionally used light two-wheeled carts drawn by small horses, while four-wheeled wagons drawn by heavy breeds of horses were usual in flatter regions, such as East Anglia and the Netherlands.

The Irish workhorse, known simply as the 'draught horse' during the nineteenth century, was used principally for agricultural purposes. Nevertheless, some strains of the same general breed, sometimes with out-crosses of Thoroughbred and other bloodlines, had been developed to perform certain specialist functions, such as saddle-horses, roadsters, driving horses and the like.

The workhorse population continued to be subjected to out-crossing with various British working breeds, including Suffolk Punches[4] and, as the century progressed, Clydesdales. A general idea of the genetic make-up of the breed during the second part of the century can be gained from national census figures of the numbers and breeds of stallions of the traditional work-horse breeds available to cover mares during the period.[5]

A complicating factor had been the continuing tendency of many of the smaller farmers to sell their best

ABOVE: *Lucan, County Dublin, 1940s; charabanc pulled by a very smart team of draught horses coming home after a day at the races.*
Photo: Dixon Slide Collection, Dublin City Archives

mares, and to breed from the inferior ones using stallions chosen only because they were cheap.[6] The result had been a marked deterioration of the standard of the general horse population during the middle years of the nineteenth century. This was eventually remedied by the holding of classes for working horses by the Royal Dublin Society and various other agricultural-improvement societies, and the establishment of registration schemes for workhorse stallions in the early twentieth century.

While one or two Clydesdale stallions could be found operating in most counties, they were concentrated largely in Ulster and in the neighbourhood of some of the larger towns. However, the coarser Clydesdale blood was regarded by most Irish workhorse breeders as unsuitable for the generally lighter and more finely boned draught horse.[7] Thus, when registration for non-Thoroughbreds was established in the early twentieth century the Department of Agriculture decided that 'no new sires of the Clydesdale or Shire breeds should be registered except for the province of Ulster, the counties of Dublin and Louth, and the district comprised within a radius of the city of Cork'.[8]

Horse Transport in Town and Country

Equines were as ubiquitous in the towns and cities as in the countryside. In the capital itself, before the motor engine had contributed its distinctive effluvia of petrol and exhaust fumes to the cityscape, the homely odours of mingled horse sweat, urine and manure would have been all-pervasive throughout the entire urban area, not only in the many small yards and stables situated in the back alleys and lanes of the working districts, but also in the bustling thoroughfares of the city centre where early photographs show lively street scenes dominated by horse-drawn traffic, and street surfaces littered with horse droppings.

The principal categories of urban horse usage would have been private carriages, hackney cabs, horse omnibuses, horse trams, commercial and delivery vehicles, and general-service vehicles. Private carriages were, of course, a symbol of status, and even today Dublin shopkeepers refer to the top end of the market as 'the carriage trade'. The horses used for this purpose would have been mainly smart 'roadsters' with enough 'blood' to cut a dash.

Hackney Carriages

During the nineteenth century there were various types of street vehicles plying for hire in the major towns and cities. The sidecar, or 'jaunting car', was widely used throughout the century, and there were other types of vehicles used. The intriguingly named 'jingle', which got its name from the noise it made, was common in Dublin during the early part of the century and in Cork until the end of it. The more comfortable London-type 'four-wheeler,' or 'growler' – again called after its characteristic sound – was introduced to Dublin about 1851 and continued to ply the Dublin streets together with the jaunting car until well into the twentieth century.[9] Early photographs, such as those in the Lawrence Collection,

ABOVE LEFT: *Tara Street, Dublin, 1932; horse-drawn commercial delivery vehicles mingle with motorised traffic. Harness makers were once an essential part of the trade infrastructure. Greer and Sons was one of the very few harness makers still trading in the 1980s.*
ABOVE RIGHT: *Ring of Kerry, 1870s; horse pulling a laden sidecar stops by the roadside for a welcome drink.*

Photos: (left) Irish Picture Library; (right) Department of Irish Folklore, University College, Dublin

show that the horses used to pull these vehicles were of the same general type as the light clean-legged draught animals used in agriculture. An interesting reference to Dublin cab horses appears in a volume entitled *Driving*, edited by the Duke of Beaufort in 1889:

> The horses in the hack cars in the streets of Dublin are usually 18 hours 5 or 6 days running in the shafts. They get 28 lbs. of oats a day, and think nothing of running you down to Newbridge, over 20 Irish miles (about 25 miles English measure).[10]

Horse Omnibuses and Horse Trams

Horse omnibuses, which were at first fiercely opposed by hackney-cab proprietors, were permitted to operate in the capital by an Act of Parliament in 1848[11] and provided a limited service to a number of suburbs. The number and type of horses required for the Dublin buses

has not been recorded. However, as London omnibuses of the same period required an average of eleven horses to keep each bus in service,[12] it would seem reasonable to assume that a similar number would be needed in Dublin where the vehicles were of similar type. Horse trams, introduced to the capital in 1872, were technologically more advanced than the omnibuses, as a vehicle running on tracks required less effort to pull than one mounted on wheels in contact with the ground. The Dublin United Tramway Company, which was only one of several tram companies operating in the capital from the early 1880s, was reported to have 136 trams, three omnibuses and 936 horses on 31 December 1882.[13] This would indicate that an average of about six horses was required to keep one tram in operation. Early photographs of Dublin street scenes showing horse buses and trams suggest that the horses used for pulling these vehicles were mostly of the ordinary light-draught type.

Before the coming of the railways, all internal travel

ABOVE LEFT: *Hibernian Hotel, Dublin, 1949; due to the petrol shortage after the war, horse-drawn cabs were still seen on the streets of Dublin up to the 1950s.* ABOVE RIGHT: *The Custom House, Dublin, 1950s; horse-drawn cabs parked outside.*   Photos: Bord Fáilte

in the country, as well as the limited requirements for industrial and commercial freight in a country largely untouched by the Industrial Revolution, was dependant on the horse. Even the limited canal system, which provided facilities for the transport of passengers and freight between Dublin and a limited number of destinations in the provinces, depended on natural horse power. After the advent of the railways, the number of horses used for public and commercial transport actually increased, as the rail networks required additional servicing in the form of the transport of passengers and freight to and from railway stations.

Accounts of visitors to Ireland before the end of the eighteenth century reveal that travel through the interior of the country required a degree of intrepidity. Public

inns and lodgings were very basic, roads were bad and frequented by footpads and highwaymen. The risk of highway robbery was so great that travellers carried weapons to defend themselves, and often travelled in convoy with a military escort.[14] In view of the bad roads, riding on horseback was one of the best and most convenient methods of travel.

Stage coaches had been operating rather intermittently in Ireland since the early eighteenth century, and mail coaches from 1790. The operation of stage and mail coaches was regulated in Ireland by an Act of Parliament of 1810.[15] This limited the number of passengers to be carried on a public coach drawn by four or more horses to six passengers inside the vehicle and ten on top. Mail coaches organised by the Post Office service were

ABOVE: *O'Connell Bridge, Dublin. 1930; exhausted horses frequently died of overwork between the shafts.*   Photo: Fr Browne SJ Collection

of better quality than the commercially run stage coaches. Unlike the latter, they ran on a tight schedule through the night, and with a smaller number of passengers. The number of horses needed to operate a mail coach was approximately the same as the distance of the journey in statute miles. The distances between stages averaged about 10 miles. For this, ten horses were required; of these, four provided a team for the up coach, four for the down coach, and the remaining two rested. Teams were changed with a minimum of delay at the post stages. Two or three minutes were considered

adequate for the operation, and quick changes could be effected in much less time than that. An average mail-coach horse was expected to do one hour's work a day for three consecutive days, and have the fourth off. Their workload was hard and they only lasted an average of four years in first-class service.[16] Generally speaking, the horses used in the mail coaches were of better quality and with more 'blood' than those in the ordinary stage coaches. Mail-coach teams often included grey or coloured horses in front to make them more visible in the dark.[17]

ABOVE: *College Green, Dublin, 1794; the arrival of the mail coach. Coach teams often included a light-coloured horse in front so that they could be seen in the dark. In 1753 a 'flying coach' was advertised doing the journey between Kilkenny and Dublin in one day. Engraving by James Malton.*

RIGHT: *Pro-Cathedral Dublin, 1952; For many self-employed people the draught horse played a vital economic role. It was valued and cared for like one of the family.*

Photos: Irish Picture Library/Bord Fáilte

Bianconi's Cars

An innovative form of horse-drawn transport was introduced into Ireland in July 1815 by Carlo Bianconi, a Clonmel-based Italian immigrant, who realised the potential of a form of cheap public transport at a time when travel by stagecoach was beyond the means of the great majority of the population. The enterprise was launched with a second-hand jaunting car and an army-surplus artillery horse for which he paid £10. Bianconi's first scheduled service was between Clonmel and Cahir, a distance of 10 English miles. The business expanded so rapidly that by the end of the year Bianconi's cars had become an established form of popular transport in the Midlands and south, routes having been set up to link Clonmel with Limerick, Thurles and Cashel. Soon, his cars were covering over 1,000 miles of road each day, linking the principal towns of south Leinster and east Munster. Ten years after setting up the business, the distance covered by Bianconi's cars had reached over 1,170 miles a day.[18] An article on Bianconi in the *Freeman's Journal* reveals that by 1834 Bianconi was the proprietor of 70 cars, most of which were drawn by two horses that

travel on an average, upwards of 2,000 English miles day, including the whole of the province of Munster, a great portion of Leinster, and extensive districts in Connaught … To supply his cars he has between 500 and 600 horses, all excellent animals for the road, and driven daily through 66 towns, besides an immense number of villages.[19]

The horses used in the cars were 15 hands high and of similar type to those sold as army 'troopers'. They were stabled in depots that had been established in the areas serviced by his routes. Their uniformity of height ensured that their harness could, to a large extent, be made to a standard size, making it easier to change teams rapidly at posting stations.[20] The vehicles were a development of the Irish jaunting car, with passengers seated back-to-back, with a 'well' in the centre in which luggage was carried. The cars were open to the elements, the passengers being protected by tarpaulins in rainy weather. As the business developed, Bianconi found it necessary to introduce larger vehicles in order to cater for an increasing number of passengers. The new cars were larger versions of the traditional jaunting-car design, some of which were four-wheelers that could carry fourteen passengers and were drawn by three horses.

Bianconi's reaction to the advent of the railways – which had virtually replaced the stagecoach services by 1850 – was interesting. Instead of fighting them, he co-operated with them and set up 'feeder' services transporting passengers to and from railway stations, and

ABOVE: *Bianconi coach at Hearn's Hotel, Clonmel, 1856; the coach on the right-hand side has been unhitched and is being unloaded. The coach on the left is preparing to leave. Bianconi cars were frequently pulled by two, three or four horses, depending on the road conditions. Here, there will be three horses in an arrangement called a 'unicorn'.*
Photo: Courtesy of the National Gallery of Ireland

extended his own transport network to cover many parts of the country not served by the railway system. Even after his death, in 1875, Bianconi cars continued to provide public transport in the remoter parts of Ireland into the early twentieth century, when they were replaced by motor buses.

Horse-drawn Canal Barges

The two main canals – the Royal Canal and the Grand Canal – that linked Dublin with certain parts of the Midlands and the west of Ireland, were also major users of natural-horse power. They had been created towards the end of the eighteenth century with an over-optimistic vision of including Ireland in the benefits of the Industrial Revolution then burgeoning in Great Britain. Although they never really succeeded in this end, they nevertheless provided a useful form of transport in conveying both passengers and freight by means of horse-drawn 'passage' or 'fly boats' to a limited number of destinations.

The canal companies arranged cross-links by road coaches for the convenience of their passengers. The Grand Canal Company organised link services from its depot at Shannon Harbour to Ballinasloe, Birr, Tuam and Limerick, as well as one between Tullamore and Athlone. At the same time the Grand organised subsidised coach links between Carlow and Athy, and from Mountmellick to Abbeyleix and Mountrath. In 1836 Carlo Bianconi – ever on the look out for business opportunities – offered the Grand Canal Company a deal by which he agreed to take over the existing coach link between Ballinasloe and Galway, and to set up a new route to Tuam. Within a year he had extended the Tuam route to Castlebar, and organised a new service between Shannon Harbour and Roscrea. Passengers on all these routes paid a standard fare of a penny per mile.

As was the case with other forms of horse-drawn transport, the canals lost out to the railways when these were introduced in the 1840s and 1850s.

Urban Commercial and Delivery Vehicles

Early prints of Dublin street scenes depict a limited range of horse-drawn trade vehicles operating in the capital. The majority of these were similar to the ordinary two-wheeled carts used in the countryside. These are often shown carrying barrels which could either have been used as water carriers for street cleaning, or brewers' delivery carts. Unlike in England, where brewers' drays were usually four-wheeled wagons, brewery vehicles in Ireland were principally carts, conforming to a traditional preference for two-wheeled vehicles that were, of course, easier to manoeuvre in narrow streets.[21] Other vehicles common in early-nineteenth-century Dublin were builders' carts. These were sturdy, two-wheeled vehicles with panel sides and straight shafts, drawn by two or more horses. They had typically large wheels and a cranked axle, which enabled the vehicle to be low-slung for easy loading.

After 1850 a greater diversity of delivery vehicles appeared on the streets, reflecting the increased prosperity of the rising middle classes. The great majority of these were two-wheeled carts of various types, and four-wheeled vehicles only appeared in any numbers at the very end of the century. Early photographs of Dublin street scenes show a variety of trade vehicles – mostly two-wheeled general-purpose floats and 'spring carts' used by butchers, grocers, drapers, hardware merchants and the like. The names displayed on the vehicles are sometimes clear enough to be read and can be checked in contemporary trade directories. The best type of horses for slow work, such as pulling the vans used by furniture and piano dealers, were quiet draught animals that could spend eight hours in the shafts without discomfort, as distances were normally quite short and stops frequent. The preferred animals for such quick work as pulling

ABOVE: *Location unknown, c.1900; a well-cared-for draught horse pulling a laden butchers' cart.* Photo: Irish Picture Library

grocery and butchers' delivery floats were hardy cobs, which could average 20 miles a day with constant stoppages. It was usual for such traders to keep enough spare animals so that each horse could get two days rest a week.[22]

Brewery drays were a common feature of the Dublin streets prior to 1900. Photographs in the Guinness archives show that both two-wheeled and four-wheeled drays were used by the firm. Although the majority of the photographs are undated, some information can be gleaned from details such as the draymen's costume, and would suggest that the two-wheeled vehicles tended to be earlier than the four-wheeled ones. Most of the horses shown pulling the four-wheelers appeared to have Clydesdale blood, while ordinary draught horses

ABOVE: *Jameson's Distillery, Dublin, 1960s; a smaller type of Clydesdale-cross is used to pull a two-wheeled cart.*   Photo: Bill Doyle

were used in the two wheelers. Coal carts were also common in Dublin street scenes. These were mostly two wheelers pulled by horses of draught type.

Horses in Industry

Nineteenth-century Ireland was almost entirely an agricultural economy; the Industrial Revolution that had transformed Britain during the eighteenth and nineteenth centuries had almost completely passed it by. However, the country had a few specialised industries, notably the linen industry in Ulster, the butter industry in Cork, a brewing industry which was not specifically localised in any one region but spread over the country, and a small coal-mining industry localised mainly around Castlecomer in County Kilkenny and

THE IRISH DRAUGHT HORSE

Arigna in County Cavan. All of these industries relied largely on horse power for production and delivery, especially before the advent of the railways in the first half of the century, and even after it to deliver to, and collect their respective products from, railway stations. The horses used for this purpose were mainly of small-

TOP: *Guinness Brewery, St James' Gate, Dublin, 1867.*
Lithograph from Midlands Railway Guide. Diageo/Guinness Archive
ABOVE: *Dublin, 1959; horses with Clydesdale blood were used by firms such as Guinness to pull four-wheeled drays. They were often supplied on contract by firms such as Richardson's.*
Photo: Bord Fáilte

draught type suitable for the light two-wheeled carts which were ubiquitous in Ireland.

In the case of the coal-mining industry located around Castlecomer, the transport of coal to the surrounding districts and even further was the responsibility of 'carmen' who delivered the coal in a distinctive type of cart with long 'heels' – extensions of the shafts projecting from the rear of the cart. The standard load was 18 hundredweight (900 kilograms) of coal.[23] As many of the roads in the region during the nineteenth century were hilly and often in poor condition, it was sometimes necessary to use an additional horse or donkey to help the draught horse on the steeper hills. This was known as 'tracing', and entailed the use of two long chains hooked from the collar and hames of the trace animal to the linchpins on the axle of the cart.[24]

In addition to commercial deliveries of coal the Irish collieries produced quantities of coal and anthracite dust known as 'culm' or 'duff' and which was used as fuel in the surrounding areas. This was traditionally collected by horse or donkey carts and formed an important economic resource for the region. Culm was also used extensively in the firing of lime kilns in various parts of the country, and was delivered mainly by horse and cart. After the railways came into being, horses and carts were used to deliver the culm from the railway depots.[25]

Purchase of Horses by the British Army

Ireland had long been a source of supply of army remounts for many of the countries of Europe, and was the largest market in the British Isles for horses for the British Army. By the beginning of the nineteenth century there were two specific breeds of Irish horses of particular interest to the military. The first of these was the Irish Thoroughbred descended from English stock introduced during the eighteenth century. The second was a good type of the ordinary draught horse mentioned

TOP LEFT: *Quarrying stone, Cappoquin, County Waterford, 1948.*
TOP RIGHT: *Arigna Mine, County Cavan, 1933; horses were a vital part of the infrastructure.*   Photo: Bord Fáilte
RIGHT: *Arigna Mine, County Cavan, 1933; the horses used were of a smaller-draught type suitable for pulling the two-wheeled Scotch carts (found mostly in the northern parts of the country) for transporting coal and coal dust.*

Photo: Fr Browne SJ Collection

above. When mares of the latter breed were put to Thoroughbred stallions, the result was the halfbred Irish hunter for which the country became internationally famous. The coarser specimens of this breed fetched a good price as ordinary 'troopers' or cavalry remounts, while better-class animals with a higher admixture of Thoroughbred blood could be sold as hunters or officers' chargers. In fact, the British Army encouraged its officers to hunt, as this developed 'an eye for country' as well as other skills which were considered useful in combat conditions.

Times of war were boom periods for Irish horse breeders. During the Peninsular War of 1808-14, the Duke of Wellington was constantly anxious about the supply of army horses as it was impossible to obtain enough of them from the British Isles to fulfil his needs, even though he was prepared to pay £30 or £40 for ordinary troopers. Good-quality artillery horses were also in demand in this period. The improvement of the road system in Ireland at the end of the eighteenth century had made possible an efficient public coach service which enabled a network of good, rapid communication to be established throughout the country.

This in turn had led to the development of an improved breed of carriage horses that were also used by the army. They made possible a new type of 'flying artillery' that was capable of hauling its field guns at considerable speed and maintaining a fast trot for long periods. They could even gallop on occasion, and were able to keep up with rapidly moving cavalry for a time.[26]

The reduction in military expenditure after Waterloo caused a slump in the demand for horses by the British Army, who were at that time the principal purchasers of remounts in Ireland. During the reigns of George IV (1820-30) and William IV (1830-37), the horsed units of the British Army had been reduced drastically, the Royal Horse Artillery and the field batteries were reduced to virtually nothing, while the cavalry was allowed to deteriorate to such an extent that by 1836 most of its troop horses were reported as being unfit for a campaign.

The purchasing of troop horses for individual regiments of the British Army was the responsibility of the commanding officer of the unit concerned. Up to about 1850, the normal procedure was for the regimental colonel to appoint a suitably knowledgeable officer – often the veterinary surgeon – to buy remounts in the open market, usually at fairs. In Ireland the principal horse fair was at Ballinasloe in County Galway, but there were others as well, notably at Banagher in County Offaly, Hospital in County Limerick, Cahirmee in County Cork, and Mullingar in County Westmeath. However, the regimental officer in charge of buying remounts ran a personal financial risk, as it was possible in theory and sometimes in practice for his commanding officer to reject the purchases, in which case the unfortunate officer would have to pay for them himself.

By the mid-nineteenth century an alarming situation had been noted with regard to the Irish horse population: it had become apparent that the breed of Irish horses was degenerating at an alarming rate. The causes for this deterioration were complex, but, put simply, it appeared that the breeding of the better class of horses on which Ireland's reputation as an international supplier of fine horses was based – once the occupation of the minor gentry – was falling increasingly into the hands of the minor farmers who were ignorant of the finer points of horse management. This class of producer was not prepared to pay for the services of good sires, and would sell off the best mares, keeping the worst ones to breed from. The result was weedy offspring that were largely unsaleable.

In spite of the scarcity of good horses for the army, the outbreak of the Crimean War in 1854 was, not surprisingly, a boom period for the Irish remount trade. The official price paid by the government for remounts for the cavalry and artillery varied from about £30 to £40 each. The same high demand continued into the first half of 1855, but tailed off towards the autumn as the army acquired its quota of replacement horses.[27] Nevertheless, the progressive degeneration of the general horse population that had been observed as early as the 1850s had, by the 1860s, developed into a general groundswell of concern among those who had the well-being of the Irish Horse at heart. On 24 September 1863 the Council of the Royal Agricultural Society of Ireland (RASI) appointed a special committee 'for the purpose of obtaining information upon the cause of the deterioration of the breed of horses in Ireland, and to report to the Council at some future period as to the best mode of providing a remedy for the evil complained of.' After a great deal of discussion, the committee recommended the holding 'of a show of horses in Dublin as a preliminary step'.[28] This was the origin of the Dublin Horse Show which was first held by the RASI on 15 April 1864 on the premises of the Royal Dublin Society (RDS), which at that time were at Leinster House.[29] The RASI continued to hold its annual horse show for several years at various venues in Dublin – including St Stephen's Green in 1867 – until

TOP: *Army manoeuvres at the Curragh, 1943; gun carriages pulled by teams of six horses with outriders.*
Photo: Fr Browne SJ Collection

FAR LEFT: *Grafton Street, Dublin; parade of the Royal Hussars for the queen's jubilee.*
Photo: Fr Browne SJ Collection

LEFT: *Charlie, the last Irish Draught horse in the Irish army, with his handler, Private Barney Stokes, at Kildare Barracks, 1998. Charlie carried out regular fatigue duties in McGee Barracks, Kildare.*
Photo: Mary McGrath

the event was taken over by the RDS in 1868; it has continued under the auspices of the same body until the present day.[30] An interesting innovation of the 1868 show was the introduction of 'leaping competitions' for horses. This developed into the sport of show-jumping, which was to become the main feature of all future horse shows in the world. However, the main feature of the Dublin horse shows were showing-classes with the awarding of prizes and premiums for various types of horses, including Thoroughbreds, hunters, carriage horses and so on. Other regions followed suit in holding shows that had a very positive effect on general horse breeding in the country, and marked the commencement of a genuine renaissance of the Irish horse as an international best-seller.

In 1887 the British Army abolished the old system by which individual units purchased their own remounts in the open market, and adopted a system that had been in operation in France since 1831[31] and in Prussia since before 1800.[32] This consisted of the setting up of a remount depot with the responsibility of central purchasing. The new method of acquiring remounts had immense advantages over the old one. It ensured that from that time on, there would be better standardisation of horses purchased and a pool of remounts available in the case of general mobilisation. Two remount depots were set up in Ireland. One depot was located at Island Bridge Barracks in Dublin under the command of an assistant inspector of remounts who made the purchases of all military horses in Ireland, mainly through a few registered dealers. He was assisted by a staff-captain who was responsible for the registration of the purchases. The second depot was at the Remount Farm, Lusk, County Dublin, where the animals were housed and trained before being issued to individual units.[33]

In the 1880s a new type of mounted unit – mounted infantry – was introduced by the British Army in order to counter the rapid mobility of some of their colonial

ABOVE: *Major Lushington on horseback in full ceremonial dress. His mount appears to be a draught-thoroughbred-cross, ready and able to gallop into battle.*

Photo: National Photographic Archive

enemies, especially the Boers in South Africa. Training camps for the new units were set up at Aldershot and the Curragh, and a large number of remounts were purchased to mount them. Small, hardy cobs such as Connemara Ponies were regarded as ideal for this purpose. The breeding of these animals had been encouraged by the Congested Districts' Board, which had been set up in August 1891 with the object of improving 'the conditions of life of certain of the poorest districts of the western coast of Ireland'.[34] In

ABOVE: *Army farriers, 1890; 'No foot, no horse' is an old saying. Teams of farriers, resident in all large military barracks, were charged with responsibility for keeping the horses sound. These horses are in very good condition. Their manes are hogged and their tails cut short as per army standing orders.*

Photo: Irish Picture Library

the region of 5,000 to 6,000 Irish ponies and cobs, ranging from 14 to 15 hands and at an average price of £30, were purchased for the mounted infantry every year during the course of the South African war, to the great benefit of Irish breeders.[35]

In 1888 a system of voluntary registration of horses was created under the National Defence Act. This gave the government the power to requisition all horses, vehicles and means of transport in the United Kingdom in times of national emergency. In Ireland, the horses registered under this scheme were mainly draught horses belonging to the tramway companies and the breweries. The Belfast Tramways Company registered 400 horses, of which 77 were taken for the Boer War.[36] The Meath and other hunts registered a large number of hunters,[37] but few of these were taken for the war as cavalry horses over 15.1 hands were considered unsuitable for service in South Africa.[38]

French Military Purchases

During the Napoleonic Wars, French cavalry methods, especially their heavy cavalry, were different to the British. Their horses rarely jumped and were generally less skilled at negotiating obstacles across country than the British and Irish cavalry units, whose officers had learned their skills in the hunting field. Consequently, the type of cavalry horses used by the French army at this period were mostly their own agricultural breeds, of which they had a plentiful supply. The Duke of Wellington complained that England and Ireland 'seemed unable to supply one-twentieth of the horses which the French can command', and even considered whether it would be practical to import horses for his own army from America or Brazil.[39]

Following the downfall of Napoleon, the king of France, Charles X, established in 1825 a cavalry school at Saumur under the command of General Oudinot, a distinguished cavalry officer who had earlier fought for Napoleon in Russia.[40] One of his first actions was to acquire 25 Irish horses at an average price of 1,200 francs, as well as 24 saddles of English pattern to enable the cadets to acquire cross-country riding skills.[41] This was the origin of the displays still demonstrated by the elite French equestrian team, the Cadre Noir.

In 1840, under threat of a general European war that did not materialise, the French government felt the necessity of increasing its cavalry numbers to 34,000. Natural resources being unable to provide more than 14,000, it was compelled to seek the remainder abroad.[42] Most of these were imported from Germany, but purchases were made all over Europe, and it is possible that some were bought in Ireland. Following the French colonial adventures in North Africa, many of the cavalry regiments used remounts from that area as well as horses purchased from Prussia.

ABOVE: *Irish horses in India; some army regiments taught horses to lie down under fire so as to provide riders with protection from snipers.*
Photo: Royal Dublin Society

The last major European conflict of the nineteenth century involving France was the Franco-Prussian War of 1870-71. Some years before this, dealers acting on commission for the French government had been actively purchasing military horses in Ireland, the principal agent being a Mr George of Dublin. During the hostilities, about 30,000 horses were exported from the United Kingdom to France, a substantial number probably coming from Ireland.[43] The war proved disastrous for the French and resulted in immense loss of their horses. Large numbers of these had been captured by the Prussians at Metz and Sedan, and upwards of 600,000 reputedly eaten during the siege of Paris.[44] These losses would obviously take a lot of replacing in the post-war period, so it is not surprising to find continuing reports of horse purchases in Ireland on behalf of the newly-established French Republic, which retained Mr George as its principal buyer. According to an article in the *Irish Farmer's Gazette* in 1873, the French government was accustomed to paying higher prices for its military horses than were normally given by the UK government. For example, the French were prepared to pay £48 for heavy cavalry remounts, £44 for light cavalry, £40 for artillery horses, and £32 for draught animals.

> All are purchased at four years old, spend three months at remount depots, nine with their regiments before being worked for the purposes of training, and at five years old they are placed in the ranks.[45]

However, from this time onward, the French army resumed its former practice of buying most of its foreign remounts from Germany, and by the end of the century French purchases in Ireland had dwindled to almost nothing.[46]

Dutch Military Purchases

According to the 1897 Parliamentary Commission into the Horse Breeding Industry in Ireland 'vast numbers' of horses were being bought 'for the Dutch, Italians, French and Danes'.[47] The two principal dealers supplying the Dutch army were John Widger of Waterford and Thomas Meleady of Dublin. Meleady explained that when he first started to buy for the Dutch they gave him £48 for 'strong ones' and £44 for 'light cavalry' and 'riding artillery horses'. He preferred to sell to the Dutch rather than the British, as the former collected their purchases from his yard, while he had to deliver the latter to the army depot at his own expense.[48]

The Dutch army had four methods of acquiring remounts.[49] The first system was by public tender, whereby the war department published its requirements for purchases and invited tenders. The second method was closed tender, by which the government awarded contracts for the supply of horses to one or two principal dealers. From 1879-81 it had obtained its horses from Hungary, and from Ireland from 1881-86, when it probably appointed Widger and Meleady as its official purchasing agents. The third method was private purchase, which was carried out by a 'remount commission' – a panel of military officers that purchased horses on the open market. After 1886, in addition to similar bodies in other countries, the Dutch government set up an Irish Remount Commission that purchased horses at fairs and from various dealers in Ireland. The Dutch had also a registration scheme for horses similar to that of the British by which animals could be requisitioned from companies and private individuals in times of national danger.

Belgium

From 1868 onwards the Belgian army also bought large numbers of Irish horses, mainly through the agency of one major dealer, Ferdinand Delangle of Lille.[50] According to the British Parliamentary Commission into the Supply of Remounts (1902), the Dutch and Belgian

124 THE IRISH DRAUGHT HORSE

armies were still buying large numbers of Irish horses at the very end of the nineteenth century. However, they tended to buy younger horses than the British, preferring three and four-year-olds, while the latter favoured older animals.[51]

Other Countries

Enquiries made to the Royal Danish Military Library in Copenhagen elicited the information that, while the Danish army certainly purchased horses in Ireland during the early years of the twentieth century, it had no records of any such transactions prior to 1900. However, the parliamentary commission of 1897 specifically mentioned military purchases by the Danish government in Ireland during the late nineteenth century, but there is no information as to what sort they were.[52]

Germany, Austria and Russia all purchased horses in Ireland, but these countries, having vast resources of hardy, if rather coarse, native breeds that were suitable for military purposes, bought mainly Thoroughbreds, which were used to improve native breeds by the addition of 'blood'.

Socio-economic Attitudes to Horses

There appears to have been something deep in the Irish character or consciousness that considered the social status conferred by horse ownership as being more important than good economic sense. This applied to all classes and social groups, and probably had its origin in the ancient horse culture of the country. It was especially potent among the gentry, but even among small farmers ownership of a horse was regarded as a desirable status symbol even when their few acres did not justify such a possession in terms of commercial viability.

The Reverend William Hickey, Protestant rector of Bannow, County Wexford, who wrote extensively on agricultural matters during the early years of the nineteenth century under the pseudonym of Martin Doyle, commented on the 'horse madness' prevalent among small farmers in Ireland:

> The small holder who has no money how he is to buy a cow – he has a HORSE. I'll engage that, even if he has but a half dozen acres or even less – he has a horse – let him sell him – the horse must go – car, tackling and all – let him buy a cow and a wheel-barrow, instead.[53]

The same tendency of Irish smallholders to maintain horses to an uneconomic degree is referred to in the preamble to the 1841 Census of Ireland:

> The too great number of horses on small farms has long been the subject of remark. From the table it will be seen, that in farms between five and fifteen acres, there are nearly as many horses as farms especially in Leinster, of which the most remarkable instance is the county of Wexford where they exceed the number of farms.

An exception to this national 'horse mania' was Ulster, where many of the small farmers – with a culture and values inherited from their Scottish Presbyterian forebears – were less horse-minded than their southern and western countrymen, and tended to regard this equine obsession frivolous and uneconomic.

'Hoof Prints on Parchment', The Kerryman, 1983, *by kind permission of Margaret Lynch.*

The Horse Fair

Flotsam and Jetsam

Streets are filled to overflowing.
Horses coming, horses going.
Footpaths lined by countless heads,
Halfbreeds, mongrels, thoroughbreds.
Massive Clydesdales … plumply round.
Aintree-looking sorts … unsound.

Cripples, loose, forlorn, alone,
Droop by footpath's kerbing-stone;
Galled shoulder, trace-worn side;
Sad to see poor shattered pride
Of labourers … whom men discard …
Rewarded by the Knacker's Yard?

Stanislaus Lynch[54]

8

Horse Fairs

A Personal Recollection

MARJORIE QUARTON

My personal experience of horse fairs goes back to the year 1948. Although my whole life revolved around horses from an early age, I had no knowledge of buying or selling them in fairs until I left school. I heard horse fairs mentioned and they sounded wonderful to me. I bought bullocks in the cattle fairs from the age of sixteen and loved it, once I'd got over my fear of spending my father's money badly. Everything that other people complained about – the noise, the smell, the crowds, the dirt – added up for me to an exciting event, where I felt totally at home and confident. Being the granddaughter of a couple of clergymen, I don't know why I developed this intense interest. Perhaps it was my militant suffragette grandmother.

On the farm, we had four, sometimes five working horses and a pony. When one of them was past work, it was put down or pensioned off. Immediately, the bush telegraph got busy and word arrived of dozens of likely horses for sale in the neighbourhood. It only remained to choose the most suitable.

I was seventeen when I bought my first horse for resale, and ten months later I sold her and looked round for a replacement. Although I bought my next two horses off the land, I went to fairs in Limerick and Thurles to check on prices and find out what was available.

The first fair I went to was in Thurles and I had the job of selling a bad carthorse. We would not have owned him in the first place only that one of the workhorses fell with a load of corn, laming himself badly. In the middle of harvest there was no time to be choosy and my father bought Barney, a washy chestnut with a washy temperament to match. I managed to sell Barney and spent the next few hours looking on and trying to learn how to be a horse dealer. I think I had expected to see a lot of private owners trotting up and down on

ABOVE: *Killarney, 1948; fair days brought farmers from a large catchment area into town to sell their produce and also to meet up with neighbours. Horses were their sole means of transport. Once at the fair the horses would have been unyoked and taken to a nearby yard to be fed and watered. Riding horses for sale were often shown under saddle.* Photo: Bord Fáilte

nicely presented horses that they hoped to sell, while other private owners watched hopefully and occasionally made a purchase. The reality was entirely different – as different as a game of croquet from a hurling match.

Thurles horse fair took place on the first Tuesday of the month and was a street fair until the late 1960s, when it was moved to the car park at the cattle mart. It

centred round the cathedral, stretching from the Suir Bridge to the turning for Kilkenny. A funeral on fair day was a misfortune; a wedding was a careless mistake. Horses of every size and shape packed the street – and I mean packed. Motorists nosed their way through the throng and the noise of horns and curses was added to the whinnying and stamping of the horses and the

✿ THE IRISH DRAUGHT HORSE

shouts from the crowd. Carthorses were crowded round the gates of the Protestant church; some foals and yearlings were more or less penned down by the Suir Bridge. The whole street was lined with horses, tails to the road, heads overhanging the pavement. Dealers prowled up and down, occasionally shouting or pointing.

I was used to cattle fairs, so I was not too worried. I had seen this kind of thing with bullocks instead of horses. In fact, horses were better than cattle in the mass. Cow dung can catch you at chest height as you walk behind an alarmed animal; horse droppings

mainly drop, staying on the ground and the soles of your boots. A street fair teaches you less about buying than a fair in a green or field, as there is less room for a looker on, and if you want to watch, you will at best get in the way and, at worst, trampled.

There would be some massive insurance claims if the street fairs existed today. Dealers used to walk along the row of equine backsides facing the street, almost brushing against them. The thinking behind this was that the pavements were impassable and the best place to be, if you must be behind a horse, is as close to his

ABOVE: *Boyle fair, County Roscommon, 30 September 1940; mares frequently worked on the farm before and after foaling. Here, the mare is wearing winkers and was most likely driven to town with her foal at foot to be sold in the market. This foal appears to have some Clydesdale blood on the sire's side, as evidenced by its plain head and its four white legs.* Photo: Fr Browne SJ Collection

heels as possible. You might be knocked over and bruised by a kick, but you would survive without broken limbs. I have twice seen a man's leg broken as he strolled along behind a row of horses; both victims thought they were out of reach, but both were wrong. I never heard of anybody being sued.

Before the auctions started in Goresbridge, a lot of horses from Kilkenny and Wexford found their way to Thurles fair. There was usually a good selection of half-breds and plenty of Irish Draught types as well. A Mr Barton from Cloneen had two Irish Draught stallions at that time, Merville Prince and Irish Chieftain, and they came to the fair, one pulling the trap, the other capering behind, along with a Thoroughbred and a coloured pony stallion. His method was to drive this collection straight ahead, occasionally shouting 'Hoi!' very loudly, and nobody got hurt as far as I know.

Earlier than this, perhaps in the early 1940s, I used to ride my pony in the north Tipperary show in Nenagh. It was a big show then, complete with the army jumping team and an enormous number of broodmares and youngsters. Highlight of the show for me was the parade of Irish Draught stallions – sometimes more than twenty in a smallish ring. Mostly greys, with a sprinkling of bays and browns, they pranced round the ring, screaming and pawing the air. I was fascinated; my mother was terrified. It was a scene never to be forgotten and never repeated. In later years, I remember the snow-white Galty Boy – which made a great mark on the breed – the local sire, Jack Steel, and the plain, heavy Lissarda, which sired my show jumper, Sugar Bush. Sugar Bush was competing with horses like Mr Softee although she was less than 15.1 hands high. She was sold to Switzerland for £4,000 when a 100-acre farm with a nice house on it would have made less.

Limerick fair was held in a big green and there was every opportunity to learn. The fair was held in January, April, July and October on the Tuesday before the last Friday. This strange timing was dependant on the date of the cattle fair, held on the last Friday of the month. The fair green is built over today, but in the late 1940s and 1950s, it teemed with horses, whose owners could – and did – gallop them flat out. The heavy horses were clustered near the gates and, at that time, mostly went for beef. That big and busy fair has vanished completely and no auction or mart has replaced it.

As with other fairs, the railway was the focal point. Horses arrived there in railway boxes, where they travelled three abreast, anchored with massive oily head collars and great rusty chains. They came on the passenger trains and were unloaded with the passengers, but those travelling in cattle wagons were unloaded elsewhere. If sold the smarter horses, having arrived accompanied by grooms, came down in the world, being taken to the siding at Carey's Road and loaded into wagons. Once, a few of us rode our horses down the lines from the main station to avoid going round by the road. We were shouted at, but there was no trouble about it.

This was the first time I remember dealers buying 'gunners' for the Royal Horse Artillery. They were costing about £30 to £40 each and were mainly Irish Draught. I think their price quadrupled by the time they had passed through the hands of three middlemen.

When I started a series of articles on Irish horse fairs for the *Irish Field*, I attempted some research to back up my experience. I discovered that the fair dedicated to horses was a comparatively new arrival. The great traditional fairs were often held to coincide with some pagan festival, and the selling of horses, while fairly common, was of secondary importance. For centuries, Irish farmers ploughed with oxen and good riding horses were in the hands of the wealthy. The Irish Draught, that supreme all-rounder, was chiefly prized as a troop horse. I have heard that an English army buyer coined the name 'Irish Draught' for the type of horse we know so well as a term to describe the troopers he was buying in the Irish fairs. But in almost all fairs, cattle were the chief stock on offer.

ABOVE: *Ballinasloe, 1950s; the green teemed with horses and buyers every October fair.* Photo: National Museum of Ireland

Puck Fair in Killorglin is a good example of the traditional fair. The king goat (Puck is a he-goat), crowned and raised high above the crowd for the duration of the fair, has to have its origins a long way back in history. West Kerry was never horse country, and the horses available at Puck in my time were small, common or both. An old-time fair had the equivalent of the roundabouts and swing-boats of later years. There would be bare-fisted fighting, wrestling, sheaf pitching – a competition that survived longer than most – and sideshows. These would often feature 'freaks', both animal and human. They remained popular until the mid-1900s and I remember a five-legged calf doing the rounds of the fairs. You could peep through a hole in a sack to see it for threepence. In earlier times, the event might also be a 'hiring fair' where

men and women looked for a year's guaranteed employment and young boys looked for apprenticeships. As far as I can discover, the fair for horses alone did not make an appearance until there was a ready market for them.

Ballinasloe could be called a traditional fair because it has been around for a long time. It started its week-long duration for many years on the first Sunday in October, and there may be a significance in the date, but I have heard that it used to fall on the feast of Michaelmas, 29 September, which is not far off. Eating goose on Michaelmas Day is a centuries-old tradition and Ballinasloe used to be one of the fairs where geese were sold. Dealers bought geese in the west of Ireland to be fattened for Christmas in the English Midlands. Even in my lifetime, they were walked huge distances, driven

ABOVE: *Kerry, 22 July 1940; pigs for sale were transported to market and displayed in the farmer's cart.*   Photo: Fr Browne SJ Collection

by young lads. The geese were driven first through soft tar, then through sand, so that their feet would stand the roadwork.

Ballinasloe was a sheep fair first and foremost, centuries back. When I went there first, the horses were all sold on the Sunday or Monday morning, after which the sheep moved in, thousands of them, jamming the roads for miles around. Back in the 1780s, Wolfe Tone stayed

in a Ballinasloe hostelry for a week, and it was the sheep and their owners that kept him awake, not the horses.

This fair is one that has survived, partly because it coincides with a major agricultural show and partly owing to the efforts of an enthusiastic and active committee. In 1974, Bord na gCapall organised several auctions. Cork Racecourse, Gowran Park Racecourse and, of course, Galway Racecourse were the venues. The Galway event was supposed to herald the end of Ballinasloe fair, but it scarcely caused a hiccup. The vast majority of horses presented went away unsold, while Ballinasloe fair was as big and busy as ever. Busier, if anything.

While the traditional fairs grew round a festival of some kind, practical fairs held solely for the purpose of buying and selling took place in every market town and city. My own town, Nenagh, derives its name from the fair of Ormond. Right through the twentieth century, until they disappeared with the opening of cattle-marts, these fairs dealt mainly in cattle, often with sheep being sold on a different day. There would be a pig market and, at Christmas, a fowl market. Horses usually appeared on the same day as the cattle, in a separate area. Sometimes, 40 or 50 yearling ponies arrived from Connemara for auction.

Looking back over the archives of provincial newspapers you can see the same pattern. The cattle dealer was king, the cow was queen and horses fitted in if there was a demand for them. The dealers' Bible was *Old Moore's Almanac*, which is still published each year. The 2004 edition lists monthly sales of horses for Baltinglass, Gort, Castleblayney and Granard, the latter being a fair and mart, the others simply marts. Other regular sales are listed for Listowel, Ballagherdereen, Clifden, Maam Cross, Turloughmore, Bartlemy, Westport and Tullow. Ballinasloe appears, from the 2-10 October, but there is no word of the old Cahirmee fair in Buttevant. Puck Fair in Killorglin is said to feature horses and goats. With the exception of Ballinasloe, I would not like to attend any of these events with an order book and a truck. There is no mention of Goresbridge, the only auction to have had a major effect on the fairs; another auction in Carnew, County Wicklow, seems to have died and the one in Cashel never really got going.

I remember the very first auction of non-thoroughbreds, in Gort, County Galway. A person who would not give his name phoned me, saying that the dealers were boycotting the sale and ordered me not to go. I had not intended to go anyway, but naturally I went after that. There was one other dealer there – cleaning up. Then I knew who had phoned me. As it happened, good horses were in short supply. There, as elsewhere, horses were weighed as they entered the ring like cattle.

The fairs given over to horses were mainly in the southern half of the country. Some of the principal ones were Ballinasloe, Limerick, Kilrush, Buttevant, Spancilhill and Tallow Road. Smaller fairs were held at Miltown Malbay, Kilkee and Ennis in County Clare; Newmarket, Timoleague, Rosscarbery, Dunmanway and several other small towns in County Cork; Thurles, Roscrea, Clonmel and Templemore in County Tipperary; Tallow Road and Dungarvan in County Waterford.

If you look at these places on a map you will see how they are clustered in the south Midlands and the south west. There was a reason for this. Horses were moved to the fairs from the farms on foot, by train or, occasionally, by lorry. From the fairs, they travelled to the nearest port by train, as did the cattle. I do not have reliable figures, but I think that from the 1940s to the 1970s, 80 per cent of animals sold left the country at once. Of the remainder, dealers would have bought another 15 per cent for export as soon as they could find a buyer. These included myself. Very few sales were private.

These figures would be fairly accurate for the big fairs; the smaller ones were nurseries for the bigger ones, so more farmers and fewer dealers attended them. A dealer would not travel from England unless he could be sure of filling at least one railway wagon. The foal fairs in Newmarket, County Cork, and in Kilkee, for example, would not have attracted dealers from outside the country. Farmers bought the foals to rear and probably sell as three-year-olds at Buttevant or Kilrush. Kilrush in County Clare was the only big fair where local farmers and dealers bought a lot of horses to 'grow on'. It was the best area by far to find a two- or three-year-old with plenty of improvement in him.

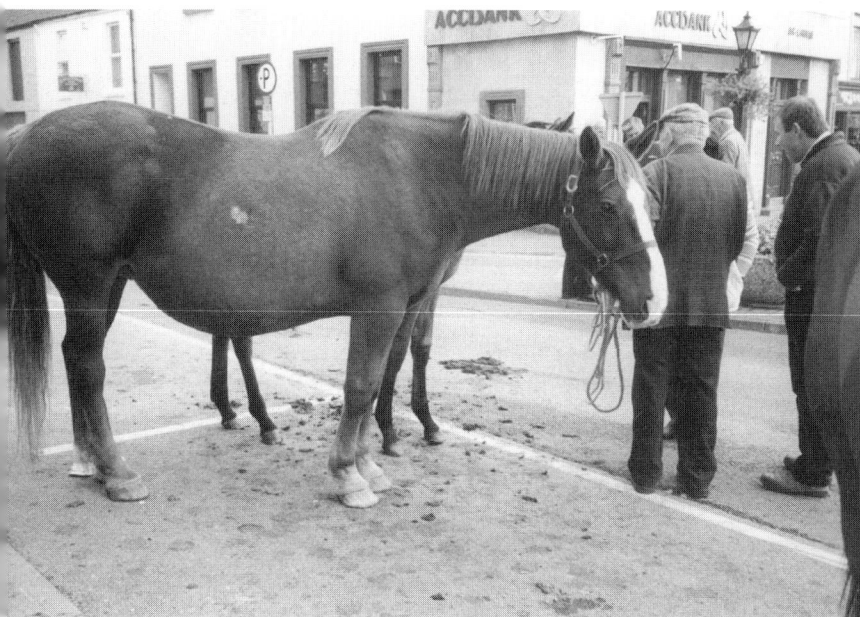

ABOVE: *Kilrush, County Clare, 2003; October foal sale is still going strong despite difficulties with trading laws and safety issues. The quality of foals is very good but their numbers are drastically reduced.*

Photo: Mary McGrath

I once bought a horse by the halfbred Young Protector on the eve of the fair. The owner volunteered to deliver him to my farm 90 miles away for no extra money. Astonished, I agreed. His brother, it turned out, had a garage where he was servicing a Jaguar for Lord Harrington. The horse arrived late at night, in a new trailer towed by the Jaguar. 'What he doesn't know won't trouble him,' is still a useful precept.

The only truly traditional fair to survive as a major buying arena was Spancilhill. This village is too tiny to figure on a road map and used to be impossible to find, even if you knew where to look. The road would fill with hundreds of horses at first light on midsummer's day. In fact, many would be there overnight, and selling would continue while the light lasted. The train left Ennis, 4 miles away, before noon. Nine out of ten horses sold would be travelling by train, so they either had to be led to Ennis by road, or taken there on one of the shaky cattle lorries, which in those days had no ramps.

'Loading banks' were built in fair greens, and some people had them at home, but in the country people had to improvise. Horse trailers were rare. It was lucky for me that Lord Harrington owned one. In order to catch the train, all trade except local transactions was over by 8 am, often much earlier, and boys riding one horse and leading five or six towards Ennis choked the road. The form was to lead a horse either side on a rope, and tie two or three unbroken colts to their tails by their rope halters. A young horse never had his tail cut and they were known collectively as 'longtails'. When a dealer bought one, he tied the end of its tail in a knot. The big dealers used to make a scissor snip on the neck, where the mane would hide it. Each used a different number or pattern of snips. Those buying for the meat trade put snips on the horses' rumps, as they did with cattle, or smeared them with dirt.

Originally, Spancilhill was mainly a cattle fair. Its establishment long ago may have had something to do with its date, the summer solstice having been an occasion for festivities since pagan times. Later, horses almost took over and Spancilhill was one of those fairs scoured by army buyers looking for 'remounts'. Here is a quotation from the *Clare Champion* of 140 years ago:

Buyers from every part of England, Ireland and the Continent attended [the fair] for the purpose of procuring horses for the army as well as for general use … large prices were obtained and very few horses were taken off the green unsold. Mr Manly, who attended to purchase troopers for the British cavalry and artillery, and several French, Belgian and Austrian army agents made extensive purchases in this department …

It is interesting to note that an agent from one country could be bidding against an agent from another country, currently at war with his own. This must have helped to keep prices high. Armies from all over Europe used the strong, active Irish horses and the supply seemed endless. There is a legend that both Napoleon's charger, Marengo, and the Duke of Wellington's Copenhagen were bought in Cahiree fair, to meet again at Waterloo. I doubt it. Marengo might have come from County Cork, but Copenhagen was a clean Thoroughbred, probably one of the duke's hunters trying a new profession.

When the First World War broke out the British government prepared for the type of warfare that required huge numbers of horses. General Haig was one of those who expected cavalry to play a major part. Horses were widely used on the Eastern front, but in Flanders they served mainly to drag guns in the mud and the losses were terrible. Almost 10,000 horses were sent to France at the outbreak of war and over 100,000 were bought compulsorily. Well over a million took part in the fighting and less than half survived. Thousands of these horses were commandeered in Ireland; only those needed to work on the land escaping the buyers.

After the war, the British Army needed few horses, although the Germans used them widely for decades. Then the question arose of the decimation of the breeding stock in Ireland. There had been a scheme to subsidise stallions as far back as 1904. These were Thoroughbred and Irish Draught. The scheme languished through the various conflicts of the twentieth century and was revived in the 1940s. In the meantime, Britain agreed to supply Ireland with a large number of stallions in the 1920s. However, lacking Irish Draught, they sent Shires and Clydesdales.

Ireland is a country of light soil for the most part. Shires and Clydesdales are well suited to the clay of Sussex or Norfolk, but in Ireland they did little besides damaging the Irish Draught breed. The lucky ones went to the cities to pull brewers' drays; the less fortunate went to timber merchants to haul timber.

Even today, the Clydesdale and Shire influence can be noticed, especially in the northern areas where, for some reason, most of them ended up. There were also a few heavy cob stallions. One of them, Bunky Boy, was quite influential in this area. I do not know, but I suspect that when the Department of Agriculture began to refuse licences for common horses, stallion owners north of the border – under a different jurisdiction – were able to continue to breed them. Whatever the cause, the fairs in the border counties had a bigger supply of heavy horses than those further south. Castleblayney in County Monaghan used to be a favourite fair with the 'meat men'.

In the stallion register for 1954, sixteen Shire and Clydesdale stallions were listed in the Republic. In 1956, there were sixteen Clydesdales but no Shires. There were three Clydesdales in Donegal, one in Cavan, one in Cork, one in Dublin, one in Louth, three in Meath, four in Monaghan and two in Wicklow. Significantly, there were none in Tipperary or Clare.

There was a brief bonanza for dealers in working horses at the beginning of the Second World War. Compulsory tillage meant that almost every farmer needed an extra horse – some needed three or four. The problem was to find broken animals in a hurry. I knew a man who made a lot of money then, buying unbroken and selling broken. He said he could sell a horse quiet in shafts and chains, which had been untouched three days before. It worked insofar as the horses were quiet, but their skin had had no chance to toughen and they soon galled under collar and straddle. 'He has no mouth,' said a friend of mine after trying one of them out in Limerick fair. 'Ah, don't worry about that,' was the answer, 'he'll find one after a while.' Of course, the boom could not last; the country was full of horses. By 1943 the trade had 'bottomed out'.

The figures for the drop in population of horses over the 30 years from 1950 are horrific, especially those of native ponies and draught animals. The main reason was that the demand for light draught animals had plummeted after the Second World War. For years there had been hardly any petrol for cars or oil for tractors. Hunting had almost stopped in England, taking away a major market. There was little money to be made except for wheat, which was going to England no matter how awful the quality, as they could no longer import from Canada. With peace came a sudden boom and the cars and tractors returned, while the need for growing big acreages of wheat disappeared.

The horses became redundant in many cases, and the meat trade, feeding hungry countries in Europe, got underway. I will return to this later, but first I will show what markets had been available pre-war. From the end of the First World War, right through the 1920s and 1930s, the horse fairs were enormous. The old Cahirmee fair, held in Buttevant, County Cork, went on for a week. Thousands of horses changed hands, of every shape and size: top-class youngsters, hunters, ponies, draught horses, just about everything, coming in all day and every day, being sold and loaded onto railway wagons. Special trains ran every day to the ports at Dublin (North Wall) and Waterford, where horses were transferred to the boats. Well over 5,000 horses would be sold during the week. Even in my time there was a special train, maybe two, with wagons stretching away out of sight. Eight cobs or smallish horses made a cattle-wagon load – six if they were large – or four big carthorses. Travelling loose, it was routine to dress their manes and tails with Jeyes' Fluid to discourage bored or hungry animals from chewing them off. Hind shoes were pulled off, sometimes in the station, occasionally in the wagon.

Ballinasloe fair in County Galway also went on for a week, and the special trains took horses to Dublin every day. Until trailers became the norm and lorries were equipped to carry horses, a big fair in a town without a railway station simply would not have worked.

In addition, army buyers from many countries shipped Irish horses to Europe and even Canada. In 1939, foreign trade stopped, as did the trade for Thoroughbreds, which could almost be given away. The only animal in demand was the genuine trained working horse, as compulsory tillage continued. There was just one occasion in the five years of warfare when trade looked up and that was before the filming of *Henry V*. The movie, starring Laurence Olivier, was filmed at Powerscourt, County Wicklow, and thousands of horses were required. They had to be broken and ridden, but were of heavy type, such as would have been used to carry a man in armour. Leslie Weaver and Jack White were buying them in my area and they were collected at 'Jerry's Yard' in Nenagh. The film came out in 1943, so I cannot have been more than twelve, but it made a deep impression. I watched the two dealers feeling legs, inspecting teeth and passing or dismissing one horse after another. The Local Defence Force provided extras and good horsemen were in demand for battle scenes. Several young men of my acquaintance went on an unplanned holiday to Powerscourt to take part in the Battle of Agincourt. A very good horseman tried hard

to sell his mare, a confirmed rearer, without success, but ended up riding her himself as a body-double for a herald. When the filming was over, the horses were sold off and trade returned to rock bottom.

The selling of horses for slaughter is an unpleasant subject, but if we are to understand the horse trade from 1945 for at least ten years, it cannot be avoided. I obtained the following figures from a *Yearbook* for 1950:

Number of horses exported for slaughter from the Republic of Ireland, 1950

To England	11,363
To Northern Ireland	3,693
To France	4,839
To Belgium	3,261
To Holland	545
To other countries	394
Total	24,095

These figures were probably down on the previous year and were sustained during the decade. At that time, horse breeding did not pay when compared to almost any other branch of farming. People who had bred horses for a living suddenly found they had no market. Not just a lower price, but no customers at all. If an Irish Draught mare failed to be in foal once, she was unlikely to get a second chance. Only the dedication of those breeders who could not imagine farming without one or two mares kept horse breeding going. Wars upset every aspect of life and halfbred-horse breeders suddenly found themselves unable to make a living, while the Thoroughbred trade made a remarkable recovery.

I am not about to find excuses for the meat trade; I am well aware of the bad conditions and downright cruelty that was involved in the transport of horses for slaughter, but it did put an end to the sight of horses toiling on when they were past work. Factories opened

ABOVE: *Dublin docks, 1950s; horses wait patiently to be exported for slaughter. Being sold by weight, heavier horses were more profitable.*

Photo: Bord Fáilte

in those parts of Ireland where horses were plentiful, and it soon became possible to sell the old horse and replace him for less money with a thinner but younger one. Cold-blooded you think? Maybe, but many a poor farmer in the bad old days literally worked his horses to death, or sold them to questionable buyers. This was especially so in the years of the Economic War, when you could buy a calf for the price of its skin, but the price of strong working horses never took quite such a beating. Hard-hit small farmers simply did not

have the price of a strong horse and had to make the old one last. It was a fact of life.

It seemed in the 1950s as if the value of a horse was always going to be determined by his weight, but this was not the case. Horse riding boomed in England and once again there was a market for the quiet, medium-sized riding animal. Prices rose and the armies and police forces resumed buying from Ireland. In Limerick fair the Doyle brothers bought dozens of cobs in the run up to the fair, to be passed on to the riding-school dealers, mostly from the south of England. I have ridden some of them for buyers in the old hay market. There were lots of low banks there, faced with stone, and these cobs would mostly trot or canter over them without breaking their stride.

That trade was killed off by the rocketing rise of shipping costs in the 1970s, when roll-on-roll-off became the rule and a bad cob cost just as much to ship as a show jumper. It became uneconomic to ship low-priced animals and their price slumped until Irish farmers started to be interested in tourism, often involving pony trekking or fox-hunting.

There was one job entirely suited to a clean-legged active Irish Draught without any admixture of Thoroughbred, and that was the pulling of field guns for the British Army. There are still gun horses and guns, as the Queen's Troop has been preserved for ceremonial purposes and displays. Previously there was also the King's Troop and the Royal Scots greys.

To see Tom O'Donnell of Buttevant buying 'gunners' at Limerick fair was an education. His 'blockers' brought suitable horses to him and he dealt like lightning, handing over banknotes from a vast roll. Some of the horses were heavy, with a mixture of Clydesdale blood. The gun carriages, built for the First World War, had wooden wheels, while the deadweight of the cannons took some pulling. The horses had to be quiet, for during the musical drive and at training sessions the old guns would be fired.

The 'wheelers' nearest to the guns developed huge muscles in their hindquarters, as they learned to trot and gallop with the deadweight of wood and metal behind them. Six horses to a gun, exactly matched in colour, they were ridden by postilions. I say 'were' but of course they still are, and they are still mainly of Irish Draught parentage.

They used to be shipped to Melton Mowbray in Leicestershire for training, and were later kept in St John's Wood Barracks in Knightsbridge, London. They were

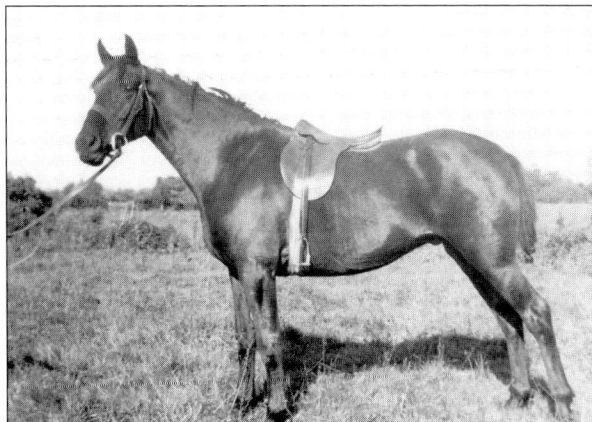

ABOVE: *A four-year-old bought at Limerick fair. On the light side for a trooper, he would have been perfect as an officers' charger, or 'rider', as they were called. Note how his tail is still tied up after coming off the train.* Photo: Marjorie Quarton

not big horses, being compact and powerful with short legs. The officers rode chargers that did not have to be bays and that made a lot more money.

You could buy a 'trimmer' for the guns and maybe double your money. A trimmer is an under-bred horse if you go by the hair on his legs, the mane hanging on both sides of his neck and the rough winter coat. Clip such a horse, pull his mane and tail, and trim his legs, and you give him, as we used to say, 'another two crosses of blood'. Many of these horses had short necks and low withers, but were redeemed by nice heads – once you had clipped off the beard. The army clipped off everything except the tail.

I bought a wonderful trimmer off the land with the army in mind. He was by the Thoroughbred First Melody, but out of a really heavy, hairy mare. My horse had a nice head, low action and flat bone. He was 16.2 hands, but so enveloped in hair that I was able to buy him for £55. I tied him up in the yard and set to work with a steel comb and a pair of sheep shears. Gradually, a nice horse emerged, leaving a pile of horsehair where I had dealt with his tail, a swathe of it under his neck

– all dragged out of his mane – and a large heap of wool behind each leg. I was sweeping up the last of it when Nat Galway-Greer and Willie McCaldin drove into the yard. They did not mess about, but asked the price, and I said, '£80'. I knew even as I spoke that I should have asked double – I simply had not had time to look at First House after his beauty treatment. Just three weeks later he won his class and was reserve champion heavyweight at Dublin Horse Show.

I have mentioned Tom O'Donnell in Limerick, but Buttevant was his town and that of his brothers, Mick and Jamesy. Tom died soon after I started going to the fairs, but his memory lived on. He could neither read nor write, but he sold vast numbers of army horses for many years. I have told how he sold army horses to the British in the parlour of his house on the eve of the Second World War, while his brother was dealing with the German-army buyers in the kitchen. Buying by both armies went on until the boats stopped running.

The fair of Tallow Road started in September 1939. The O'Donnell brothers and a number of other dealers were on their way to Waterford port with several hundred horses when war broke out. They were just outside the town of Tallow in Waterford when they heard. Well, if a war had started, petrol would disappear and workhorses would be needed, the dealers reckoned. So they camped where they were and sent out word that a great fair was taking place of genuine working horses. That is how a tradition starts. Let nobody try to persuade you that the fair of Tallow Road has anything to do with druids, saints or leprechauns. It was the result of an accident and, 40 years later it was still going strong and I was buying there.

I came in on the final act in the annals of the horse fairs. The major events had taken place in or near garrison towns and at or near seaports. The armies of the world decreed the trade for centuries. The Irish Draught can trot or gallop with a big weight behind

him, as I have said. He can carry a soldier on parade with 3 stones of equipment added to his weight, or he can function in action in any kind of going. He's a great 'trooper'.

A trooper, or troop horse, when I was dealing could be a big, sturdy black for the Household Cavalry; he could be a light-grey for the mounted band or he could be a Swiss trooper. In the time I am writing about, the Swiss cavalry provided a living for a lot of Irish dealers. The Swiss also bought big, grey geldings for their mounted police force, but those were horses that would always find a job. The troopers could be any colour except grey or 'coloured', and could be mares or geldings.

The Swiss operated national service for their young men, and they were each allocated a horse to ride on ceremonial duty. First, the government creamed off any potential show jumpers, and a couple I sold went on to jump for Switzerland. When the young men finished their national service and returned to their farms, each was given his horse to keep. This ensured a regular demand for remounts.

I bought and sold Swiss troopers for many years, mainly to Dick Morgan of Waterford, and also to Mick Connors and others. When I started, I asked a buyer in Limerick fair what was needed. He explained that the horse must above all be active, picking up his hind feet well and carrying himself properly. 'I think Switzerland is kind of hilly,' he said. A trooper needed quality, so was seldom pure draught, but he also needed depth through his ribs, width of chest and strong quarters, so he was almost never Thoroughbred. I bought a good typical brown by the halfbred Rosebud, and an even better one by the Irish Draught, Golden Plover, out of a Rosebud mare. You could sell a horse as small as 15.2 hands, but not a narrow or leggy one, or a horse with bad action. Switzerland is indeed hilly.

A huge bonus in buying Swiss troopers was that the Swiss army would accept mares. Most police forces (with the exception of the Metropolitan in London) would not consider a mare. In the fairs, mares made as much as a third less than geldings. Breeding was not paying, the meat trade was disappearing and you bought a mare if you could not afford a gelding. The Swiss, it seemed, were not aware of this and paid a flat rate. A vast number of mares of excellent-breeding type went to Switzerland.

During the 1970s, the Swiss army changed its transport to motorbikes. This came as a huge blow to many. I was warned of what was going to happen and was only caught with a couple of troopers without a job; many dealers had been bringing on a number of them and had to sell at a loss.

The British Household Cavalry rode blacks on parade, and the O'Donnell brothers sold thousands over the years. These horses were often very plain indeed, as size and colour were the most important attributes. I used to go down to Doneraile Park after the army had been buying and pick up a black or two that was too small or too light. It could still be a good hunter and it might 'grow into value'. A clipped-out horse had to be treated with suspicion as they were all shown clipped, and those that 'missed their job' were turned out in Doneraile Park. I have seen several hundred horses running there in the 1950s. Trying to corner and catch one was interesting.

Some dealers bought blacks in County Galway and there was a useful small fair at Dunmore, north of Ballinasloe. There, and in Ballinasloe itself, you could often see bunches of three-year-olds, half-draught and half-Clydesdale, all unbroken. The method of controlling a dozen unbroken horses in a field was to 'ring-tether' them. They all wore rope halters and all the halters were tied together so that each horse could move his head only about a foot from his neighbour's. It worked like a charm. I have seen the method used with ponies too, but ponies are smart and they soon learned to move about all together, some going backwards and some forwards as if they were performing a country dance.

The black horses came from Roscommon, Offaly and the north Midlands as well as from County Galway. Yearlings and two-year-olds blocked the narrow roads while young lads drove them like cattle. They were sold like cattle too, in lots, making about £10 a head. Old horses going for beef were often sold for a 'pound a leg'.

There were two plum jobs that every dealer wanted: one was to find a horse for the queen to ride at the Trooping of the Colour; the other was to find a 'drummer', a horse to carry the kettledrums in the Household Cavalry's mounted band. The kettledrums are made of solid silver and weigh 150 pounds, so the horses have to be extra strong. They have to be extra quiet as well, with the rider beating the drums from their backs. As the rider's hands are occupied with the drumsticks, the reins are attached to the stirrups. There has long been a tradition of using a skewbald or piebald. Irish Draught do not run to odd colours as a rule and the horses were heavier than a pure-bred draught, but they mostly came from Ireland and would be half draught at least. The big dealers had spotters all over the country keeping a look out for these enormous animals, some of them almost 18 hands high.

The queen had two chestnut horses at different times, Imperial and Winston, each being a chestnut with four white 'stockings' to the knee. The search was on to find another, but that particular colour scheme seldom goes with the dead-quiet temperament needed for the job.

Another specialised job was matching up horses for coach teams. Coaching marathons were immensely popular in the 1950s and 1960s, and Irish Draught were ideal. One team consisted of four matched piebalds, but most were bay, chestnut or grey.

I used to sell to six English police forces. They were London Metropolitan, Hull, Salford Borough, Leeds, West Riding and Cleveland. I recently consulted a book about horses, published in 1970, looking for some figures to back up my memory. The short section on police horses started off by stating flatly that they were all bought in Yorkshire. Well, so they were, but only after having been bred and reared in Ireland up to four years old, when dealers transported them to Yorkshire, where the police agents bought them.

Of the forces I have mentioned, only the Metropolitan bought mares. They may have regretted it when, at a race meeting, a two-year-old colt decided to serve the mare that a policeman was riding. The jockey just managed to restrain his mount but nobody was pleased except the people who saw it on television and had a good laugh. After that, the horses on duty at race meetings were never mares. The London police also liked a horse with more quality than many of the provincial forces, but four times Police Horse of the Year, Sandown, was a big, strong gelding by King's Justice out of an enormous heavy draught mare by Mountain Heather. London police horses were trained at Imber Court; if they showed any ability, they found their way into the jumping ring. There were also classes confined to police horses.

I bought Sandown as a four-year-old in Thurles fair, along with his full brother, who was a year younger. The younger colt was named Royal Justice and made a useful jumper. Sandown's active career ended when he was struck by a car and thrown bodily onto the bonnet, giving his rider a nasty fall.

The Hull police liked a big bay gelding with white markings, but did not keep many. Yorkshire West Riding had some very plain animals too. Salford Borough and Cleveland kept better sorts and I sold them some nice chestnut geldings, mostly bought in Kilrush fair. In the old days, fewer dealers went to Kilrush because of the absence of a train service, so there was more choice for other people. When I was on my own, I used to set off for Kilrush in the small hours. After I married, we used to stay in Kilkee overnight. Many horses went to the fair from Kilkee or Carrigaholt, and some were sold the night before the fair. I remember few pleasures like waking by the seaside, with the sound of deals being struck right under the window. Okay, it might not be everybody's idea of a holiday, but it was mine and,

ABOVE: *Crannagh by Rosebud at the Eisteddfod. Bought in Kilrush fair.* Photo: Marjorie Quarton

fortunately, my husband enjoyed these excursions too.

It was when staying in Kilkee for the Kilrush June fair that we went to see a couple of horses that were to be on show next day. The farmer lived close to the sea and, unfortunately, both horses were too small. He offered to show us the sire and took us to a little stable overlooking the Atlantic, where he had a smart bay Irish Draught, probably unregistered as he too was small. The door of his stable was rounded like a horseshoe and decorated with limpet shells. His owner had embossed words in the cement: 'The Irish Draught is the Farmer's Friend'. How right he was.

In west Clare, the Irish Draught was appreciated and valued. At the time when I was first buying, they were going out of fashion. Many a good jumper by a draught sire acquired a new pedigree when he was sold. It was not until sires like King of Diamonds and Clover Hill were so successful that buyers had to take notice that they were recognised. I think the reason Irish Draught were despised was partly that their owners did not look after them. A draught mare would survive and even rear a foal where a blood one would die. As a result, once these grand horses were no longer used for farm work, they were left out all the year round to live on grass, fresh air and spring water. No wonder their foals grew up undersized and with poor constitutions.

In west Clare things were different. The weather in winter was rough, the grass was of poor quality and horses did all kinds of small jobs that would have been done by tractor in richer farming areas. Because he was useful and because wintering outside was outside of the question, the draught horse in that area had a much better time.

Research on the Irish Draught is skimpy. Yes, there are pedigrees of stallions, listed by the Department of Agriculture in the mid-1900s, and the breeding of many mares is also classified. We accept today that most 'Irish Draught' to have influenced the breed of riding horses had at least one cross of Thoroughbred in their veins. King of Diamonds and Clover Hill are well-known examples. We know, but cannot prove, that many fine jumpers and event horses were not by the Thoroughbreds claimed by their breeders, but by Irish Draughts.

One thing is certain: their influence will last as long as horses are used for sport. One of the best show jumpers I owned, Clare Glens, was by an unregistered Thoroughbred called Scratchy, with a frightful record as a sire, but from a draught mare by the great Jack Steel. Another, Hold Hard, was of a popular mix, being by Prefairy from a dam by Milestone. Abervail Dream, which I bred, has similar back-breeding.

The time has gone when, provided you knew your job and were an early riser, you could go to a horse fair with a sporting chance of buying an international show jumper in the making. Sadly, few dealers let the original owners know because it would 'put up the price'. I was fortunate because I used to sell to Billy Bamlet from Yorkshire who always let me know how my horses had gone on. He sold on to Graham Fletcher, Ronnie Richardson and others. Keeping the successes of their horses from breeders was short-sighted in the long run. It is no use raising the price unless somebody will give it. Some breeders just gave up and bought a few extra cows.

Trying to revive a horse fair is comparable to holding a steam-engine rally. Their day has passed and anything we organise in that line will be just an outing for the tourists, since the fairs were comprised of conditions, horses and people that can never be brought back artificially. They served their purpose and brought a living and a lot of fun to me and to others like me.

FAR RIGHT: *Hunting; a brief check while hounds are called in. Full hunt members wore 'pink' coats and top hats. The master and hunt staff wore 'pink' coats, hunting caps and brown-topped boots. Ordinary hunt followers wore black or tweed and bowler hats. In time, younger people began to wear hunting caps. Dress code and etiquette were considered most important.*

Photo: Bord Fáilte

RIGHT: *The Irish Draught was the ideal heavyweight hunter. Here, the father controls the child's pony with a lead rein as they wait with great anticipation for the hunt to move off.*

Photo: Reportage Photographic

BELOW RIGHT: *The Galway Blazers outside Ashford Castle.*

Photo: Ruth Rogers

BELOW LEFT: *Kildare, 1950s; Dodo Beaumont, whose husband was master of the Kildare Foxhounds, always rode side-saddle on a beautifully turned-out horse. Side-saddles show off a horse's conformation. The long ears and good, flat bone indicate close Irish Draught relatives. Pictured is The Seventh Dwarf, at 17.1 hands high.*

Photo: Supplied by the owner

9

Recognition and Development of the Irish Draught Horse

COLIN A. LEWIS

Napoleonic Wars, Horse-drawn Passenger Services and the Rise of the Railways

The eighteenth century ended with the horrors of the French Revolution, which culminated in the seizure of power in France by an adventurous soldier, Napoleon Bonaparte, whose ambition was French control of Europe. Thus began the Napoleonic Wars, in which Britain and Ireland were engaged against the French and their allies. The war ended in 1815 with British victory at the Battle of Waterloo and the crushing of French ambitions.

During the Napoleonic Wars there were good prices for Irish-bred horses suitable for military use, such as troopers and animals suitable for the commissariat. After the war, however, prices fell rapidly. This enabled entrepreneurs such as Charles Bianconi to purchase trooper-type horses and use them to establish horse-drawn passenger services throughout much of Ireland.

In 1834 the first railway was opened in Ireland, from Dublin to Kingstown, Dún Laoghaire.[1] In the years that followed, as the rail network spread its tentacles through the Irish countryside, horses were in demand to move passengers and freight to and from the railway stations. While this should have caused a tremendous upsurge in prices for horses, other events exerted negative pressure on demand.

Repeal of the Corn Laws and the Great Famine

The Corn Laws had been passed in order to stimulate agricultural production and ensure that the population of Ireland and Britain could be fed during the Napoleonic Wars, and their repeal in 1846 led to a decrease in agricultural profitability. On the heels of this downturn came the disaster of the Great Famine in Ireland. Within a few years up to a million people died while, within five years of the onset of the Famine, another one million people emigrated.[2]

Fenian Rebellion and the Land League

By the 1850s conditions were such that new political movements sought to overthrow what many Irish people saw as the colonial government. The Fenian Rebellion of 1867 failed, but was followed less than ten years later by the establishment of the Irish National Land League, an organisation that emphasised the rift between landlords and tenants that had festered in Ireland throughout the nineteenth century, and campaigned against eviction of tenants from their farms and for a reduction of rents. Ultimately, the Land League intended to transform 'Tenant farmers into owners of their own holdings'. From 1879-82 'tenant farmers as a class stood up to landlords', and the Land War took place.

In 1881 the Land Act diminished landlords' income and, in the next three years, rents fell by an average of almost 20 per cent. In 1885 the Ashbourne Act established the principle of state-aided land purchase, which was extended by subsequent Acts.

RDS Premiums for Horse Breeding

An effect of unrest and agrarian agitation was the disruption of horse breeding, a major cause for concern to many landlords since horses were profitable and provided the means by which many tenant farmers had been able to pay their rents. Consequently, it was not surprising that, in 1886, the Royal Dublin Society (RDS), which was then a mirror of landlord society, introduced at its annual Horse Show 'prizes for stallions … designed to encourage the judicious breeding of horses by Tenant farmers in Ireland'.[3]

The stallion prizes offered in 1886 were limited to Thoroughbred stallions, and the owner of any stallion awarded a prize had to guarantee 'that his horse shall serve in Ireland during the ensuing season, and must guarantee to offer ten subscriptions for the use of bona fide tenant farmers' halfbred mares not exceeding four years old'.[4]

In 1887 the society offered sixteen service premiums to Thoroughbred stallions 'suitable for getting Hunters and other Halfbred Horses' on condition that each premium sire served 'if required, not less than fifty Halfbred Mares, the bona fide property of Farmers'. Finance for these premiums came from Her Majesty's government, which had promised to encourage 'improvement in the Breed of Horses and cattle in Ireland'.

For 1887 the society divided Ireland into sixteen premium stallion districts and then appointed a local committee in each district to select mares for service by the premium stallion allocated to the district. In most districts there was intense competition for nominations and, on average, there were 109 mares inspected per district although only 50 nominations were on offer. In the Portadown district, in the north of Ireland, 258 mares competed for nominations, while 168 did so in the Ballymote district in County Sligo and 143 in Dunmanway in west Cork. There was thus no shortage of halfbred mares in Ireland in 1887, although no evidence appears to exist to indicate how many of them were Irish Draught in type. Halfbreds were the progeny of a Thoroughbred sire on a non-thoroughbred but warm-blood mare, which may well have been an Irish Draught, even though that name had yet to be given to Ireland's distinctive light draught horses.

For the next ten years the Royal Dublin Society continued to offer service premiums to Thoroughbred stallions and to award nominations to halfbred mares. The society also introduced veterinary examinations to ensure that stallions were free of hereditary diseases that constituted unsoundness, and insisted on evidence that stallions already standing at stud were fertile. From 1892 the society published an annual *Register of Approved Stallions*, all of which were Thoroughbreds.

Nevertheless, as the years went by, it became increasingly obvious that there was need for a comprehensive enquiry into horse breeding in Ireland.

Royal Commission on Horse Breeding

In 1896 a royal commission was appointed to enquire into the breeding of horses in Ireland. The commission was chaired by the Earl of Dunraven, from Adare in County Limerick. Another influential member was the Earl of Enniskillen. During the meetings of the royal commission evidence was heard from many horse dealers, breeders and others interested in horse production in Ireland. Among them was Colonel de Robeck from County Kildare, who said that in his area

> One man has what they call an Irish cart horse. He has very little hair on his legs, is a very strong horse and looks like a cross of the Clydesdale. [Another man has] what he calls an Irish cart horse … a good useful stamp of horse to get a tram horse or canal horse, but it is not a very hairy-legged horse.

Richard Flynn from Tulsk in County Roscommon introduced the term 'Irish Draught' to the commissioners:

> The Irish Draught was a breed in itself, I think; they were a sort of slow hunter with clean hard legs … they could jump well and gallop fairly fast and were never tired; they were a real genuine Irish breed.

Major C.W. Studdart of Corofin in County Clare was even more informative:

> an old Irish mare is a long, low mare, about 15.2, with good neck, head and shoulders. She might have some hair on her legs, too … she can go eight Irish miles twice a day for … a creel of turf and come back none the worse for it. She trots … five or six miles

an hour. They are produced from old Irish blood, with some crosses of Thoroughbred blood.

When the commissioners finally reported, in 1897, they wrote that 'the number of horses now exported [from Ireland] is nearly 40,000 annually', to the great benefit of the Irish economy. The commissioners divided on their recommendations. Dunraven wrote that the south of Ireland

> was the chief mart in the world for high class horses for both riding and driving purposes. These horses are almost entirely the produce of Thoroughbred sires, or of halfbred sires of the hunter type.

Dunraven and his supporters added that Thoroughbred and certain halfbred sires should be used for breeding, and recommended that if they were registered they should first be vetted for soundness and that state aid should be given for the production of 'hunters, high class carriage horses, and remounts'.

Lord Enniskillen and his supporters thought differently. They stated that the majority of horses in Ireland were used for agricultural purposes: 89 per cent in Connacht, 88 per cent in Ulster, 85 per cent in Munster and 74 per cent in Leinster. The Royal Dublin Society's *Register* included none of the agricultural stallions, of which there were at least 816 in Ireland in 1896; neither did it include any other than Thoroughbred sires, even though there were 651 halfbred stallions in the country (these statistics had been collected by the police). The Enniskillen faction concluded that 'the needs of each class of breeder should be recognised', thinking that it was essential to register Thoroughbred, hunter, carthorse and hackney stallions. The scene was thus set, ready for the dawn of a new century, for the establishment of a new register of stallions and, possibly, a new policy on horse breeding.

Recognition and Registration of the Irish Draught Horse

The twentieth century began with major reorganisation of the ways in which government was involved in the development and administration of agriculture in Ireland. In May 1900 the first meeting of the Council of Agriculture was held, in Dublin. This was the body newly established by the government to take charge of agriculture in Ireland. In his opening address the chairman, the Right Honourable Horace Plunkett MP PC, who had already made a great reputation for himself by his work for the Irish creamery movement, stated that

> We ought to watch very carefully the requirements of the War Office as regards remounts … It is already in contemplation by the Department to constitute a Committee … to deal with this important question of horse-breeding.

The Register of Stallions

In 1901 the Department of Agriculture and Technical Instruction for Ireland issued its own *Register of Stallions* and this included Clydesdales and Shires as well as Thoroughbreds. Thenceforth, there was no need for the Royal Dublin Society's *Register*, nor for the society's premiums for stallions, although some money still existed in the Society's coffers for the award of premiums. The last of this money was disbursed in 1903, when the final ten premiums for Thoroughbred stallions were awarded. In 1901 the society had broken with tradition and among the 28 stallion premiums that were awarded were three for 'agricultural stallions', at least two of which were Clydesdales.[5]

Although the establishment of the Department of Agriculture's stallion register was generally welcomed, fears were expressed that the registration of heavy draught sires throughout the country might damage the quality of Irish horses, which were active, light-draught-type hunters suitable for the carriage and remount trade rather than slow, heavy draught beasts.

Among the opponents of geographically indiscriminate Clydesdale and Shire registration was Patrick J. Hanlon from Grangeforth in County Carlow, an outspoken member of the Council of Agriculture. In 1904, partly as a result of lobbying by Hanlon, the department decided

> that no new sires of the Clydesdale and Shire breeds should be registered except for the province of Ulster, the counties of Dublin and Louth, and the district comprised within a radius of 10 miles of the city of Cork. The object … was to check the great impetus that had been given to the importation of Clydesdales and Shires; for most authorities agree that such sires, if too freely imported, will impair the reputation of Irish horses.[6]

Irish Draught Stallions

In 1905 the department made the momentous decision to offer to 'owners of stallions of the old Irish Draught type and of halfbred stallions of the hunter type, a premium of £50 for selected stallions'.[7] For the first time, in an official document, recognition had been given to the Irish Draught, although it was not until 1911 that the Irish Draught was given formal recognition by the listing of stallions under that designation in the department's register. Thirteen stallions were registered as Irish Draught in 1911 and the same number in the following year. In 1913 and 1914 numbers fell to a dozen, but rose again to thirteen in 1915. No Irish Draught were listed during the height of the First World War, in 1916 or 1917, but there was a steady increase in registrations from 1918 until 1921 (immediately preceding the political partition of Ireland), from 44 in 1918 to 60 in 1921.[8]

Irish Draught Mares

In 1911, in addition to stallion inspections, the owners of mares were invited to submit them for inspection for registration as Irish Draught. Out of 5,040 mares subsequently inspected, only 264 were judged suitable for registration. Thus, through the official government horse-breeding schemes, suitable mares as well as stallions were formally accepted as Irish Draught.

Irish Draught Horse Book

In 1918 the Department of Agriculture published volume one of the *Irish Draught Horse Book*, which listed stallions and mares. Unfortunately, none of the 264 mares passed in 1911 were included in the volume. In 1919, when the second volume of the *Irish Draught Horse Book* was published, it contained the statement that the Department believed that

> A lesson may be learned from the manner in which the various English breeds of live stock have been improved within recent years through the establishment of stud books and the formation of breed societies.

This, presumably, was the rationale that had influenced the department to publish what was, in effect, a stud book for an Irish breed of horse, although no one yet knew whether Irish Draught was prepotent enough to breed true to type, or whether it was just a type that needed occasional infusions of Thoroughbred blood in order to maintain their characteristics.

Study of pedigrees shows that many of the Irish Draught stallions first registered by the Department of Agriculture were descended from the union of Thoroughbred stallions serving under the premium-stallion schemes of the Royal Dublin Society with mares selected by District committees for service by those stallions. Comet (1; numbers in brackets following a horse's name refers to its registration number), for example, the first sire to be registered as an Irish Draught, was by an unregistered stallion of the same name and out of a mare that had been sired by Vanderhum. Kieran Mullins of Flemingstown in Glenmore, County Kilkenny travelled Vanderhum between his own stable and New Ross in 1892. The horse was a 16-hand chestnut Thoroughbred stallion registered by the Royal Dublin Society that year. Comet (1) was a 16.2-hand brown horse, foaled in 1892 and owned by James Doran of Enniscorthy in County Wexford. Another early registered Irish Draught stallion with Thoroughbred ancestry was the 16-hand grey Forester (22), foaled in 1907. This sire traced back to a mare by a Thoroughbred named Liberator.

Carden's Description of Irish Draughts

Although, from 1911, stallions were registered by the Department of Agriculture as Irish Draught (with the exception of some years, as already noted), there was at that time no stated standard for the breed or type. In 1907 R.G. Carden, who was a member of a major land-owning family in County Tipperary, a major authority on hunters and who had been one of the members of the Royal Commission on Horse Breeding, wrote that prior to about the year 1850 there was a breed of horses known as the Irish cart or draught horse:

> It must not be taken that the words 'cart' and 'draught' imply that these animals were purely kept for agricultural purposes, or were in any way of the same type or blood as what are known in England and Scotland at the present day as the Shire and Clydesdale, as there are many instances in which some of these 'Irish Draught horses' proved to be the best hunters of their time.

Carden wrote of Irish Draught as

> a long, low build of animal, rarely exceeding 15.3 or 16 hands high, with strong, short, clean legs, plenty of bone and substance, short backs, strong loins and quarters … slightly upright shoulders, strong necks and a smallish head. They had good, straight, level action, without its being extravagant, could trot, canter and gallop. They were also excellent jumpers … No authentic information in regard to their breeding is now available, though, no doubt, many breeders carefully preserved the strain in their breeding studs for many years, but it may generally be taken that the original breeding of the 'Irish Draught horse' was the result of the cross of the imported Thoroughbred sires on the stronger of the well-bred mares of the country, which latter must have had an infusion of Spanish or Arabian blood in their veins.[9]

Whether horses of the type described by Carden were confined to Ireland is debatable. In 1912 A.W. Anstruther, in presenting a report of the Board of Agriculture and Fisheries in Britain, referred to 'the old breed of Welsh Light Cart Horses', which provided 'light legged mares suitable for Hunter breeding'. The board had initiated a scheme 'to preserve the native hardy breed and ensure its reproduction',[10] but the scheme did not succeed. Another breed, or type, of light draught horse that also disappeared in the early years of the twentieth century was the Devon packhorse; the Irish Draught was lucky to survive, as was the Cleveland Bay.[11]

Inspection Tours and the Selection of Mares

Over 7,000 mares were examined by the official inspectors of the Department of Agriculture in their tours of 1917-19 and, of these, 688 were accepted for registration as Irish Draught. Details of 678 of these mares were subsequently published in volumes one to three of the *Irish Draught Horse Book*, although it is not known why details of the other ten were omitted; perhaps they died before publication. The book usually records the name and official registration number of the mare, the name and address of its owner (and, occasionally, of its breeder), the mare's colour, distinguishing marks, height, year of birth and, in most cases, limited information as to its pedigree. In a very few cases the foals produced by the mare, with the names of their sires, are listed. Two further volumes of the *Irish Draught Horse Book* were published – in 1921 and, after the partition of Ireland, in 1932. Another volume appears to have been almost ready for publication on the outbreak of the Second World War, in 1939, but never appeared.

The three inspectors in 1917 – James Clarke of Navan; Patrick Shelly of Callan in County Kilkenny; and P.J. Howard MRCVS of Ennis in County Clare – reported that:

> In making our selections of mares we adopted a good average standard of merit, and were particularly careful to exclude mares showing coarseness or signs of imported cart-horse blood. No well-made mare that could be regarded as a good, useful farm animal of the clean legged draught type was passed over without careful consideration. With regard to the stallions, in making our selections we set a high standard of merit, and we have not recommended for entry any sires respecting which there was a reasonable doubt in our minds, either on the score of general merit, or in the matter of pedigree. Our main concern was to choose animals having, in the first place, a good general conformation; and secondly, true Irish Draught character and weight. In considering the question of breeding, we have been most careful to exclude such sires as had imported cart-horse strains so far as we could trace. We were not so strict in regard to Thoroughbred

blood, and we have recommended a few sires which have one or two crosses of thoroughbred more or less remote in their pedigree. With these exceptions the selected sires come from old strains of Irish Draught horses.

The question of action also received considerable attention, and whilst we did not look for anything in the nature of extravagant action, we satisfied ourselves that the horses we selected were reasonably straight and true movers.

The Distribution of Mares

The distribution of mares registered in the first three volumes of the *Irish Draught Horse Book* was mapped by Lewis.[12] None were located in the boggy lands of Erris or in Connemara, nor in those of Iveragh and the rocky and boggy peninsulas south of Kenmare, except in the fertile lands at Bantry and along the south coast to Goleen. The uplands of the Wicklow Mountains, the Comeraghs and Knockmealdowns, and other uplands in the south of Ireland, were also devoid of Irish Draught. There were very few in Ulster (including Donegal), Louth and County Dublin, which were all heavy-draught-horse areas. The relatively rich lands extending inland past Ennis from the Fergus Estuary in County Clare were Irish Draught areas, as were the coast lands along the northern shore of the River Shannon west of the Fergus Estuary and the Loop Head peninsula, but the rugged limestone lands of the Burren were not suited to them and they were absent there.

The Size of Mares

The smallest mares registered in the first three volumes of the *Irish Draught Horse Book* were 15 hands high, the tallest were of 16.2 hands. Of those registered, 86 per cent of the mares were between 15.2 and 16 hands and 40 per cent were of 15.3 hands. The typical Irish Draught

mare was therefore of 15.2 or 15.3 hands. Analysis of mare height spatially shows, however, that mares were larger in some areas of Ireland and smaller in others (figure 2). The tallest mares averaged over unit areas of 100 square miles in which there were eight or more mares per area, existed in south and east County Wexford and in County Down. The smallest mares, analysed similarly, existed in the disadvantaged terrain of County Mayo and adjacent areas, where the drumlin landscape of little fields and heavy and generally ill-drained soils probably militated against the development of larger animals. Irish Draught thus seem to have been adjusted to local conditions, at least as far as height was concerned, in the early part of the twentieth century.[13] Whether they were similarly adjusted in earlier times is now a matter for conjecture. Since only nine mares out of the total of 673 for which data exists were just 15 hands high, it is likely that smaller mares were not accepted by the inspectors for registration.

Irish Draught Stallions in 1921

The department's *Register of Stallions* for 1921 records not only the names of Irish Draught stallions, but gives some information about them and about the places where, during 1921, they were to stand at stud. The names of the owners and their addresses are also given. The registered stallions were concentrated south of a line from the Boyne to Galway Bay. There was no registered Irish Draught stallion standing at stud in what was to become Northern Ireland, and only a handful existed north of a line from Dublin to Galway.[14]

One of the horses that travelled furthest for his mares was Rainbow (49), owned by James Dodd, who was a well-known veterinary surgeon in Sligo. Dodd's horse was a 16-hand bay, foaled in 1915, by Starlight (7) out of Lady Dolly. Starlight (7) was a 16.2-hand bay horse foaled in 1904, by Comet (1) by an unregistered sire of the same name. The dam of Comet (1) was by

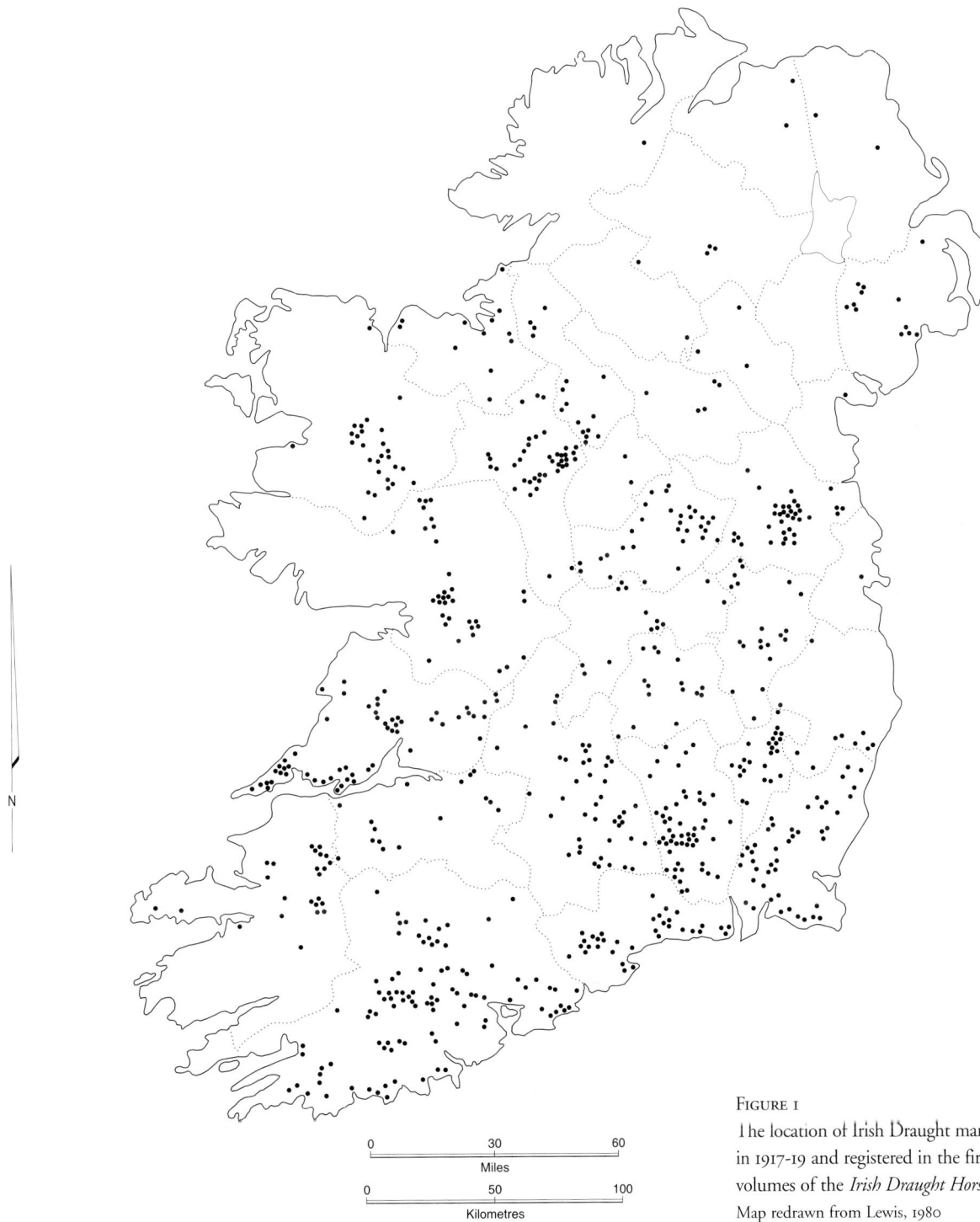

FIGURE 1
The location of Irish Draught mares inspected in 1917-19 and registered in the first three volumes of the *Irish Draught Horse Book*.
Map redrawn from Lewis, 1980

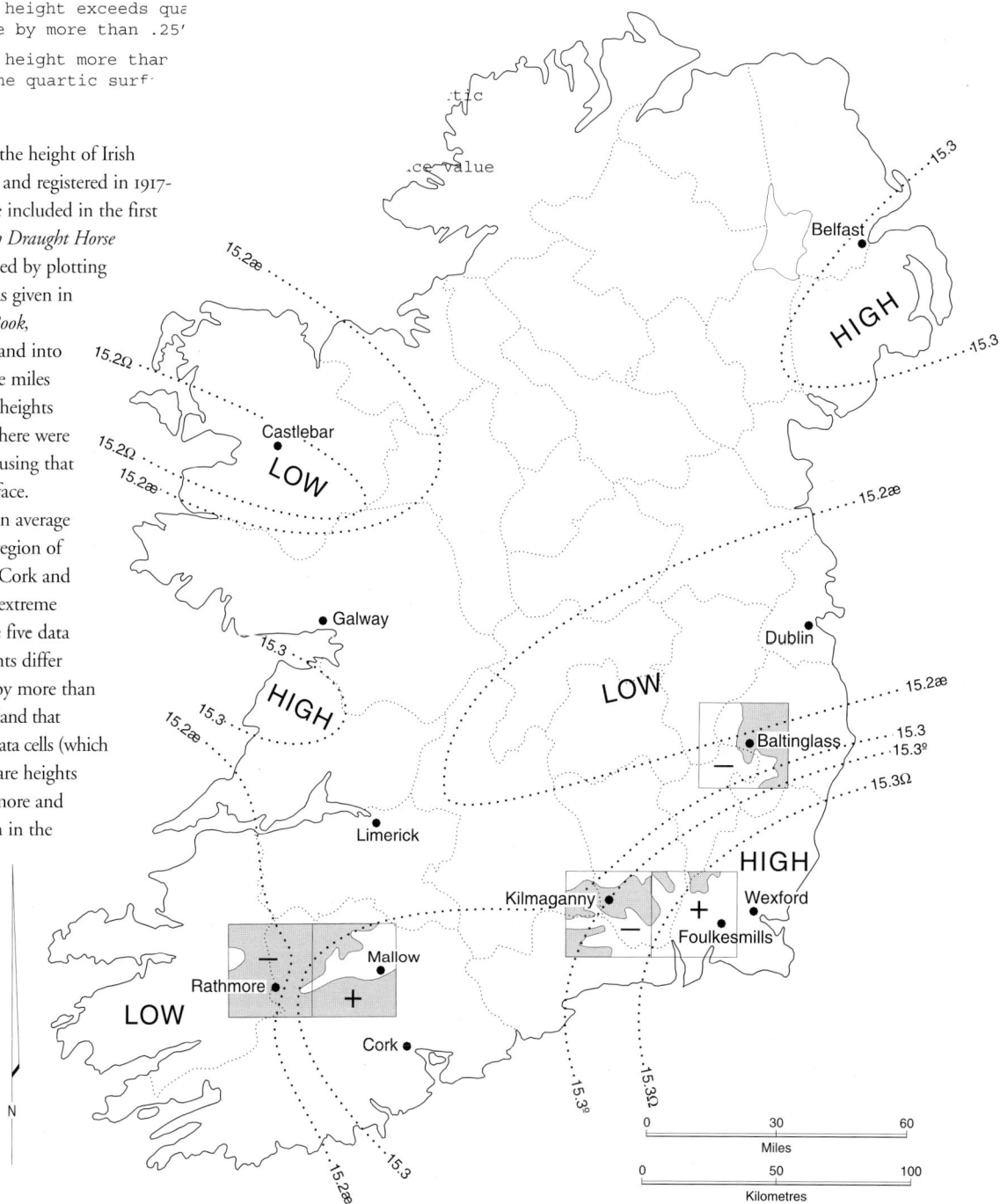

Land over 400'

+ Average mare height exceeds qua[rtic]
surface value by more than .25"

— Average mare height more than
.25" below the quartic surf[ace]

FIGURE 2

Trend-surface analysis of the height of Irish Draught mares inspected and registered in 1917-19 and whose details were included in the first three volumes of the *Irish Draught Horse Book*. This map was created by plotting the heights of all mares, as given in the *Irish Draught Horse Book*, volumes 1-3, dividing Ireland into grid squares of 400 square miles each, averaging the mare heights in each square in which there were eight or more mares and using that data to create a trend surface. Notice how mares were on average smaller in the Clew Bay region of Mayo and in the west of Cork and Kerry and highest in the extreme south east of Ireland. The five data areas in which mare heights differ from the quartic surface by more than .25 inches are shown, as is land that exceeds 400 feet in those data cells (which is shaded). Notice how mare heights were smaller in the Rathmore and Kilmaganny uplands than in the adjoining lower areas. Presumably, smaller mares were more suitable in the uplands than in the lowlands, and farmers bred accordingly. The height of the mares is shown in hands.

Map redrawn from Lewis, 1980

Rainbow (49) J. Dodd

Pride of Breffnin (46)
P.J. O'Keefe

Lucky Star (50) M. Dermody

North Kildare (42) P. Rourke

Sheldrake (72) P. Burke

Lughill (51) A. Conroy

Blue Garreth (36) L. Forde

Irishman (31) C. Bugler

Bantry Bay (63) T. P. Kehoe

Ossory (43) L. Campion

Kilcarty Boy (14) J. Kavanagh

Killanley (21) C. H. Reade

Irish Freedom (27) S. Leen

Satellite (30)T D'Arcy

Musheramore (32) W. Burke

Zeppelin(15)P .Hickey

Pirate Boy (45) M. Power

Discovery (19) W. Foley

Kildare (40) Fitzgerald

Black Harry (17) W. O'Donovan

Justice (26) E. M. Sweeney

All Moonshine (34)
D. Reardon

N

0   30   60
Miles

0   50   100
Kilometres

FIGURE 3
The location of registered Irish
Draught stallions standing at stud
in 1921. The lines connect points
at which stallions stood at
stud and therefore indicate some
of the spatial patterns in the
breeding industry. The exact
routes followed by stallions
between the points were,
unfortunately, not recorded.
Single dots with no radiating
lines attached indicate that the
stallion stood at stud only at that
locality. The names and Irish
Draught registered numbers are
shown for stallions that travelled
appreciable routes, as are the
names of their owners.
Map redrawn from Lewis, 1979

Vanderhum (as already noted), a Thoroughbred stallion that had first been listed in the Royal Dublin Society's *Register of Thoroughbred Stallions* in 1892. There was thus a strong infusion of Thoroughbred blood in Rainbow (49), and it was such infusions that caused many people to consider the Irish Draught as a type, rather than a breed.

County Kerry had more registered Irish Draught stallions in 1921 than any other county: nine, although only two of them travelled appreciable distances for their mares. Justice (26), owned by Edmond McSweeney of Gerahduveen, Kenmare, travelled to Kenmare on Wednesdays, Bantry (in County Cork) on Fridays, and Skibbereen (also in County Cork) on Saturdays. Justice (26) had been foaled in 1911 and stood 15.3 hands, was grey and was by Young J.P. (12), who also stood 15.3 hands and was grey, like *his* father, Young Sir Henry, who may or may not have been the registered stallion of the same name. The names Sir Henry, Young Sir Henry and Old Sir Henry seem to have been favourites among breeders in west Cork and adjacent Kerry, and it is by no means certain as to which was really which.

One of the most important stallions listed in 1921 was Kildare (40), who stood with Mrs Fitzgerald in the east-Cork/west-Waterford area (figure 4). Mrs Fitzgerald lived at Clonmult, in the hills between Midleton and Tallow. She was a renowned stallion owner, standing a Thoroughbred named Mount Edgar in addition to her Irish Draught sire.

Kildare (40) was a grey horse of 16.1 hands, foaled in 1913 and bred by Thomas O'Donnell of Buttevant. Kildare (40) was by Young J.P. (12), who was foaled in 1891 and was bred by C. Blackmore at Killenaule in County Tipperary. The dam of Kildare (40) was Molly Grey (321) by Young Arthur II (10), a sire who stood 16.1 hands, was foaled in 1895, was grey and was by the unregistered sire Home Rule. This latter horse was by one of the best-known hunter sires in the south of Ireland, Garret, who was mentioned in the report of

ABOVE: *The grey, 16.1-hand stallion Kildare (40), bred by Thomas O'Donnell of Buttevant in County Cork, stood at stud with Mrs Fitzgerald of Clonmult in 1921.*

Photo: *Irish Draught Horse Book*, 1918

the royal commission in 1897 as a draught.[15] Molly Grey (321) was grey, 16 hands high, foaled in 1905 and bred by Timothy O'Sullivan at Killinardrish in County Cork (figure 5).

Kildare (40) is one of the most influential Irish Draught sires. Fell (1991) has written that he is one of 'the two most important Irish Draught stallions since the start of formal registration'.[16] Kildare (40) was the sire of seventeen registered stallions. Among his progeny was Pride of Cork (88), who sired another sixteen stallions.[17]

In 1921 Kildare (40) travelled the area between Midleton, Youghal and Tallow in order to service mares. Three years later, in 1924, Kildare (40) was sold to the Larkin family of Woodlands, Killimer, in County Galway. While there the stallion was taken to serve mares during the breeding season at Loughreagh on Thursdays, Athenry on Fridays, Ballinasloe on Saturdays and home that night and all day Sunday, Borrisokane on Mondays and at home on Tuesdays and Wednesdays. All these journeys were made by train.[18]

ABOVE: *Molly Grey (321), the dam of Kildare (40), was bred by Timothy O'Sullivan of Killinardrish in County Cork in 1905. This 16-hand grey mare was sired by the grey 16.1-hand stallion Young Arthur II (10), who had been foaled in 1895. The grand-sire of Young Arthur II (10) was the famous hunter-getter Garret, who was mentioned in evidence to the Royal Commission on Horse Breeding of 1896.*

Photo: *Irish Draught Horse Book*, 1918

Denis Vaughan has pointed out that in the 1920s and 1930s

> the extensive train service helped farmers to be scientific in their breeding policies. People and stock could attend markets, fairs, race meetings and so on, with schedules arranged to fit in and running costs subsidised by the Government.

The County Galway owners of Kildare (40) certainly made good use of train services, to the great benefit of Irish Draught horse breeding in east Galway.[19] Vaughan has also stated that at the same period 'The main use … for draught was road work, taking a fair load at a good speed, which caused them to evolve into a nice type of carriage horse'.[20] In fact, Irish Draught had fulfilled the role of carriage horse for at least 200 years before then,

but Vaughan's comments confirm that, even in the early twentieth century, Irish Draught were regarded as carriage horses as well as workers on the land, and as horses that could be ridden and would hunt.

Licensing of All Stallions

The licensing of all stallions in Ireland, including Irish Draught, became mandatory in 1920. During that year there were 2,105 applications for licences, of which 1,718 were granted; 159 of these licences were for one year only because 'the horses were unsound or … unsuitable, but … for various reasons [the] Department considered it inadvisable to refuse Licences'. The political partition of Ireland in 1922 resulted in licensing of stallions in what became Northern Ireland being taken over by the Ministry of Agriculture for that jurisdiction. In that and the following year 'The disturbed state of the country operated against rigid enforcement of [licensing], and it is feared that in some cases unlicensed horses were used for stud purposes'.[21] As far as the Department of Agriculture in the newly independent 26 counties was concerned, however,

> There is … every reason to hope that it will be possible to take steps to ensure that no stallion will be serving without a licence during the 1924 service season.[22]

Conditions in Ireland in 1922-23 are reflected by statements in the annual general report of the Department of Agriculture for those years.

> The period covered by this Report corresponds generally to the year beginning with the 1st October, 1922, and ending on 30th September, 1923. It was a year of anxiety and struggle. The post-war depression … continued to weigh down Irish agriculture … During the greater portion of the time

large areas of the country were in a disturbed condition. Railway and other travelling and transit facilities were frequently interrupted and in some cases suspended for considerable periods.

Under those conditions it was remarkable that efforts were maintained to ensure that stallions were registered and no surprise that publication of volume 5 of the *Irish Draught Horse Book* did not take place in 1922.

Between 1924 and 1926 it appears that no register of stallions was produced. The grand total of registered stallions printed for that period in the general reports of the Minister for Agriculture of the 26 counties included 'stallions entered in the *Irish Draught Horse Book*' – suggestive of the difficulties of proper administration and of the need for cosmetic statistics in the official returns.

Irish Draught Stallions in 1939

The *Register of Stallions* for 1939, immediately preceding the outbreak of the Second World War, provides sufficient information to map the distribution of registered Irish Draught stallions and to show the routes they followed in search of trade of mares to serve. The pattern of distribution of Irish Draught sires was markedly different from that of 1921.[23] Virtually no Irish Draughts travelled in east Cork/west Waterford, although they remained popular in west Cork and in Kerry. Further north they concentrated in a great belt extending westwards from Arklow, through south Wicklow, across Carlow, north Kilkenny, central and north Tipperary, and across Clare to the shores of the Atlantic Ocean. From the north-Clare/Tipperary area a secondary concentration extended north through the fertile lands of east Galway and into the plains of Mayo. A subsidiary concentration existed, extending from the Killala area of north Mayo eastwards to the western edge of Longford.

Although there had been a number of Irish Draught stallions that travelled appreciable distances for their mares in 1921, the networks of travelling stallions were far better developed in 1939. Some, like Richard Barton's Irish Champion (87), almost certainly travelled at least some of their route by train. Even J. Dillon's Carrigeen Lad (123) may have used the rails, for the Dingle light railway led almost from his home stable in Tralee all the way to Dingle town, with convenient stops at stations such as Anascaul along the route. This 16-hand bay horse had been foaled in 1925 and was by the 16-hand bay horse Irish Mail (60) who was, in turn, the son of the same size, same colour sire, Irish Guard (13). That horse was by the 16.1-hand grey Prince Henry (5), who was by the unregistered King Henry by the equally unregistered Sir Henry and his father, 'Old Sir Henry'.

What the map for 1939 really shows is that, by that year, the farming community had come to rely almost entirely upon the Irish Draught for motive power. Truly heavy horses, such as Clydesdales and Shires, were only needed in the major areas of tillage where the soils were of sticky heavy clays, as in parts of Counties Dublin and Louth and in much of Ulster. They were also needed for traction in the major cities of Dublin and Cork. Elsewhere, the need was for a horse that could cope with mainly light farm work and only a limited amount of ploughing, that could trot with the trap to market, and that could take its master hunting when the chance arose. The horse that filled this role was the Irish Draught. MacLysaght wrote in 1939 that:

Nowadays a good ploughman, with a pair of lively Irish Draught horses, will plough nearly a statute acre in a day – a matter for surprise to farmers accustomed to the heavy, slow-moving Shires and Clydesdales of England and Scotland.

Dunmanus Bay
Inishbeg
Muinebeg
Brian Boru
April Dandy
Gay Venture
Erris Hero
Galway Blazer
Knock Down
Newtime
Irish Paddy
Grey Dawn
Wild Rover
Lough Allen
Prince of Mayo
Cahirmee
Lough Gara
Ballybane Star
Irish Rebel
Glengarriff
Irish Boy
Farmer's Delight
Kildare Guardian
Kildare Duke
Irish Pride
Lord Clare
Irish Pat
Western Rover
Pride of Connaught
Black Diamond
Royal Chief
Shannon Boy
Corofin
Shannon King
Dalcassion
Duhallow
Tallyho
Ballingarry
Prouder Still
Ardsallagh
Silver Star
Hackett's Freedom
Arandora
Irish Champion
Black Comet
Clontarf
Dublin Gaurd
Bright Star
Perfect Boy
Fenian
Konturk
Jack Steel
Golden Orb
Creeping Star
Kilclough
Rory O'More
Prince Rupert
O'Donnell's Son
Perfection
Lough Derg
Brian Og
Bright Boy
Castlehill Boy
Ranger
Ballyquirke
Shannon Bridge
Mountain Boy
Rising Sun
Galty Boy
Tipperary Boy
Garryowen
Kilfera
Kildare Artist
Banner County
Cloondara
Irish Hermit
Silver Prince
White Heather
Glandore
Night Mail
Carrigeen Lad
Grey Plover
Grainey
Gossoon
Speck
Taoiseach
Irish Life
Danny Boy
Proud Billy
Bright Light
Headford
Clonmult
Pride of Bantry
Brightnet
Irish Pearl

N

0   30   60
Miles

0   50   100
Kilometres

Figure 4

The location of registered Irish Draught stallions standing at stud in 1939. The lines connect points at which stallions stood at stud. Single dots with no radiating lines indicate that the stallions stood at stud only at that location. Notice the great increase in stallions as compared with 1921 (figure 3), and the way in which they concentrate in a broad zone from Carlow through Kilkenny, central and north Tipperary, and into Clare and east Galway. These were all areas of mixed farming with appreciable tillage. The major dairying areas, such as the Golden Vale, needed fewer draught horses because of the nature of their agriculture, and it is noticeable that there were fewer Irish Draught stallions there than in the region further north.

Map redrawn from Lewis, 1979

The Second World War

The Irish Draught increased in popularity during the difficult days of the Second World War (1939-45), when petrol and diesel were in very short supply, new motor vehicles were almost impossible to obtain and spare parts for vehicles a rarity. In July 1942 the Emergency Powers (Control of Export) Order came into effect in the Republic of Ireland, prohibiting the export of horses except under licence. During 1942 'Licences were only issued for the export, through the ports, of old and useless horses and of Thoroughbreds'.[24] Horses were too valuable for working purposes to be exported unless their working days were completely over. In 1943,

> Owing to the increased tillage operations and further deterioration in the transport position, it was found necessary to retain in the country any horses which could be utilised as workers or vanners, and licences have only been issued for the export of old and useless horses, unfit for working purposes, and of Thoroughbreds.[25]

In the Republic that same year the registration of Irish Draught sires reached a peak that was not surpassed during the twentieth century, even though the total number of Clydesdales and Shires was three below the peak of 81 that they had reached in 1940. During the 1939-43 period, and for a further three years, working horses played an essential, almost dominant, role in maintaining the economy of the Republic of Ireland.

By 1 December 1944 conditions had eased sufficiently in the Republic 'to relax the restrictions so as to permit the export of geldings of all types'. The floodgates had opened and the demise of the horse as a work animal in Ireland was at hand, even though that might not have been immediately apparent, for 'The total number of horses in the country [Republic of Ireland] in June, 1945, was 464,520, an increase of 5,654 on the preceding year'.[26]

Post-war Exports

In 1945, following the end of the Second World War, exports of horses were allowed subject to quotas on the numbers that could be sent to various states. Under the Scheme for Relief of Distress in Europe, 300 horses were also shipped to the Netherlands. An important feature of these exports was that they included not only geldings but also mares standing under 15.1 hands in their shoes, the idea being that larger and supposedly better breeding stock should be retained in Ireland. Significantly, only nine mares under 15.1 hands had been registered as Irish Draught by the inspectors who decided on entrants to the first three volumes of the *Irish Draught Horse Book*.

The Beginning of the End

By June 1946 the number of horses in the Republic was just over 12,000 less than it had been a year before. In the same period the number of unbroken horses under one year of age was more than 7,000 less than in the previous year, indicating a general reduction in horse breeding.

The number of horses used 'for traffic and manufactures' was 10.3 per cent less than in the previous year and, according to the annual general report for the Department of Agriculture for 1946-47, 'trade in horses was generally dull during the year'. Heavy draught horses rapidly became a rarity, at least in the Republic of Ireland. The last Shire to be listed in the *Register of Stallions* appeared in 1954, the last Clydesdale in 1967. The situation was not so dramatic in Northern Ireland, where Clydesdales were listed as 'currently earning premiums' in the 1970s, and where some still exist. Nevertheless, the number of horses in Northern Ireland declined even during the years of the Second World War so that, twenty years after the outbreak of that war, they had reduced by over one-third compared with 1939 numbers.

The greatest number of Irish Draught stallions

registered for breeding purposes in the twentieth century was in 1943, when 197 were listed. Thereafter, through the remainder of the 1940s, there was a gradual and steady decline, to 165 in 1950. Numbers declined rapidly in the years that followed – 125 in 1952, 94 in 1956 – but then increased in the economically difficult years of the 1960s when numbers throughout Ireland rose to just over 100, peaking at around 110 in 1964. In 1971 there were 119 registered Irish Draught stallions, but numbers then declined rapidly, to 62 in 1978.

Unfortunately, for the years after 1939, there is insufficient evidence to map the distribution and routes followed by Irish Draught stallions in Ireland. In any case, the days of the travelling stallions soon came to an end and it is doubtful whether any Irish Draught travelled for their mares after the 1960s.

For the post-1939 years there is photographic and verbal evidence to suggest that the Irish Draught underwent considerable changes as market forces demanded different sorts of horses at different times. Immediately after the end of the Second World War the demand was for a heavier-type horse suited to an increase in tillage and, when its working days were over, for the booming meat trade. According to Fell[27] this was met by the selection for registration as Irish Draught of heavier animals than hitherto: 'In selecting these heavier draughts there was an inevitable contamination from the Clydesdale.'[28] Ultimate responsibility for registering horses as Irish Draught in the immediate post-war years rested with the Department of Agriculture's inspector, Cooper. He appears to have taken the attitude that a marketable horse was more important than carriage-cum-riding animals, for which there was little trade. Consequently, the Irish Draught seem to have become heavier draught animals in the immediate post war years.

By the 1960s it was obvious there was little future for any horse as a draught animal, and attempts were made to make Irish Draught more suitable for the riding and Sport Horse market. This coincided with the appointment of Sheehy and then R.P. Jennings as the veterinarians who guided the horse-breeding programmes of the Department of Agriculture and, later (in the case of Jennings), Bord na gCapall (the Horse Board), in the Republic. It also coincided with the appointment of Charles J. Haughey – a noted horseman – as minister for agriculture in the Republic.

Mechanisation and Slaughter

Throughout the 1960s popular emphasis was placed on mechanisation, as if there was no role for the horse as a working animal. Even the production of pleasure horses seems to have been initially regarded as of little value. Within the Republic there was little attempt even to ensure the registration of more than a few (60 to one 100) Thoroughbred sires. An unknown hand has written on the copy of the *Register of Stallions* for 1965 in the library of the Royal Dublin Society, the sad words 'dead' or 'sold for slaughter' across the names of many of the draught stallions listed in that document. Seven of the 105 Irish Draught sires were so marked, as was the only halfbred listed in the register. The situation was even worse for heavy draught stallions. Of the nine Clydesdales registered, five have their names struck through, two are stated as 'dead', two as 'sold for slaughter' and one as 'exported to N.I.'. Within Northern Ireland, only three Irish Draught stallions were registered in 1960, plus three Clydesdales, four Thoroughbreds and one 'Other'. The day of the heavy horse had obviously ended.[29]

The number of horses in Ireland had shown remarkable consistency from 1861 until just before 1951, as table 1 shows.

Table 1: Irish horse population of Ireland, 1861–1980 (In 1,000s)

1861	1901	1940	1951	1960	1980
475	435	458	367	223	68

Between the end of the Second World War and 1951 there was a rapid decrease in the number of working horses, and the rate of decrease accelerated during the decade of the 1950s and in the early 1960s. This caused considerable consternation among a number of politically influential horsemen, including C.J. Haughey.

Survey Team on Horse Breeding, 1965

In January 1965, as minister for agriculture in the Republic, Haughey appointed a Survey Team on the Horse Breeding Industry. The team reported in August 1966, stating that

> the basis of the Irish halfbred industry is the crossing of Irish Draught mares and Thoroughbred sires. With the decline in the number of horses on the land there is a real danger that the foundation stock of Irish Draught mares will disappear … and the bone and substance of the world famous Irish hunter will disappear.

The report of the survey team led to a change in departmental policy on horse breeding and, later, to the establishment of Bord na gCapall to cater for the needs of the non-thoroughbred horse industry.

A National Horse-breeding Scheme, 1968

In 1968 the Department of Agriculture and Fisheries in the Republic 'implemented a national horse-breeding incentive scheme … divided into three sections: mare nominations, foaling premiums, and the provision of suitable stallions'.[30] This led to a marked increase in the number of mare nominations, from 3,242 in 1968 to 9,810 in 1974, although many of the mares were neither Irish Draught nor Irish Draught in type. There was also a major increase in the number of Thoroughbred stallions registered for service under the scheme, from 97 in 1968

to 232 in 1974, although the number of Irish Draught stallions registered declined from 96 in 1968 to 73 in 1974.

During the 1968-74 period there was an influx of Thoroughbred blood into the Irish Draught herd.[31] This may have been due to an appreciation of market needs by breeders and by R.P. Jennings, the veterinarian overseeing the breeding programmes of the department who was subsequently the initial manager of the breeding division of Bord na gCapall. The market now required lighter horses than had previously been the case, and these could be produced by crossing Thoroughbred sires on Irish-draught-type mares, rather than by using heavier, Irish Draught sires on Irish Draught mares.

Richard (Dick) Jennings MRCVS

Richard (Dick) Jennings was reared on a farm near Skibbereen in west Cork, and had a great love of horses from an early age: 'as a boy, growing up, I knew the pedigree of every animal at the horse fairs in Skibbereen.' After qualifying as a veterinary surgeon in 1948 Jennings initially worked in Professor Martin Byrne's large animal practice in and around Dublin, which handled large numbers of horses. Subsequently Jennings joined the Department of Agriculture as chief veterinary officer. 'He was assigned responsibility for the inspection of mares and stallions, and for the purchase of stallions.'[32] Jennings travelled Ireland up to five times a year, inspecting and registering Irish Draught, Thoroughbred, halfbred and pony stallions and mares. 'Mares without papers which were good enough, moved well and were good types were given papers. We had to start somewhere.'

One of the major problems confronting Jennings was the existence of heavy draught stallions in the Republic, whose influence resulted in the production of 'hairy, inferior mares'.

> Dick would visit these stallion owners and offer to lease them one of several stallions owned by the

Department of Agriculture … Thoroughbred, Irish Draught and Sporthorse [halfbred] stallions, depending on what the stallion owner favoured, were leased at a reasonable fee.

Jennings also purchased Thoroughbred stallions for the Department of Agriculture, mainly at the Newmarket and Doncaster sales in England.

> The first thing I looked for [when selecting stallions] was a well-proportioned horse with good-quality flat bone, good hocks and free of congenital defects. I had a preference for smaller stallions … Small horses often have very correct conformation and can improve the progeny of big mares that themselves are not so correct.[33]

Jennings also maintained that

> Breeders should not be afraid to use mares of 15.1 hands or 15.2 hands for breeding … in the fall of the year … the foals were often nearly as big as their dams.

Among the Irish Draught stallions that Jennings registered was the 15.3-hand grey, Blue Peter (536), who had many good offspring in the Galway–Mayo region. This stallion traced back in the male line via his sire, Kylemore (459), to Irish Pearl (193), Pride of Cork (88), Kildare (40) and Young J.P. (12). All these stallions were grey, 15.3 to 16.1 hands high and came essentially from County Cork, although Young J.P. (12) stood with C. Blackmore at Killenaule in County Tipperary when registered.[34]

Bord na gCapall (Horse Board)

Bord na gCapall was founded on 8 February 1971. Under the 'Bord na gCapall (Assignment of Additional Functions) Order, 1975', the board became responsible for administering foaling premiums, mare nominations, the registration of Irish Draught mares, and the purchase and location of Thoroughbred sires for hunter breeding. The board also had certain responsibilities for developing markets for non-Thoroughbred horses.

In 1975 the board included a list of stallions 'registered with the Department of Agriculture and Fisheries [in 1974] and thus eligible for the service of nominated mares' in its *Yearbook*. From the following year the board issued its own publication: *Approved Stallions*. This publication, from 1979 onwards, included stallions standing in Northern Ireland, as the board and the Ministry of Agriculture in Northern Ireland co-operated on horse breeding and registration. The 1975 *Yearbook* list stated that 'The Register is confined to stallions of the Irish-draught type, to Thoroughbreds and halfbreds'. This suggests that even the board was unsure as to whether Irish Draughts were a breed or a type, although the Irish Draught horse registered numbers were given for all 66 stallions listed as Irish Draught. The list of Bord na gCapall approved stallions compiled in December 1976 and printed in the 1977 *Yearbook* indicated no such uncertainty: the stallions were shown as Irish Draughts.

Irish Draught Horse Society

In 1976 the Irish Draught Horse Society was founded after exploratory meetings had been held at various venues in County Cork. The first exploratory meeting was held at Mary Quinlan's house at Farran, in County Cork. Quinlan had trained as a veterinary surgeon at the Royal Veterinary College in London, but suffered severe injuries in a car crash while a final-year student, and could not complete her studies. In 1937 Mary married Maurice Quinlan, who was born in Ballydesmond in County Cork. Initially, the couple lived in Sussex, but after Maurice had undertaken war service they bought a small farm at Farran and moved to Ireland. While in Ireland Mary Quinlan became fascinated by Irish Draught. Her interest in horses went back to her pre-student days. She had trained her own horse, the son of a Derby winner, and ran him in hurdle races while she was a student.

During the late 1940s and the 1950s Mary Quinlan dealt in horses and ponies, many of which she exported to England. As her business developed so she made contacts with many owners and breeders in Ireland, especially in County Cork. She also became conversant with the pedigrees of many of the horses that she sold and with those of stallions that stood at stud in the county.

The 1970s were a sad period for both heavy and light draught horses in County Cork, as in the rest of Ireland. With increased mechanisation, the market for heavy draught animals, which had previously dominated transport in the city of Cork, came to an end. Since 1904 the Department of Agriculture had licensed Shire stallions within a 10-mile radius of the city in order to sire horses for the urban transport market. Light draught horses, which were essentially Irish Draught or Irish-draught-type animals, dominated the remainder of the county and were used on the farms and as vanners in the larger towns and in Cork city. They had also been exported in large numbers to Britain and the European continent until they were ousted by the spread of motor vehicles, especially in the 1950s.

By the 1970s motor dealers were importing many second-hand tractors into Ireland, mainly from Britain, and they rapidly replaced the use of horses on the farms. The market for light draught horses in Irish towns had also been ended by increased mechanisation and there was little economic reason for farmers to retain their light draught broodmares. Consequently, in the later 1960s and the early 1970s 'It was a common sight at fairs to see lovely broodmares going for meat, to the distress of the men who were obliged to sell them'.[35]

There was a great danger that the Irish Draught would soon become extinct. Mary Quinlan decided otherwise and, with the aid of a small but dedicated group of supporters, particularly William Cotter, she inspired people to found the Irish Draught Horse Society. William Cotter was the first chairman and Mary Quinlan was the first secretary.

The formation of the society has been of great importance for the development of the Irish Draught as a breed. In March 1976 committee members of the new Society met representatives of Bord na gCapall and requested recognition of the Society, subsidies for pure-bred Irish Draught colts, and that registered Irish Draught mares have their Irish Draught registration numbers shown on their Irish-horse-register passports.[36] The board was then in the process of establishing a register of all non-Thoroughbred horses in Ireland and of issuing identity documents (passports) for all Irish horses and ponies. In 1979, by agreement between Bord na gCapall and the Northern Ireland Ministry of Agriculture, the *Irish Horse Register* was extended to include animals in Northern Ireland. Documents issued under the register were officially approved by the International Equestrian Federation.[37]

Breed Standard and Guideline

In 1982 the Irish Draught Horse Society published the *Breed Standard and Guideline*.[38] The standard states that

> The Irish Draught Horse is an active, short-shinned powerful horse with substance and quality. Standing over a lot of ground he is proud of bearing, deep of girth, strong of back, loins and quarters. He has exceptionally strong and sound constitution and is known for his intelligence and gentle nature and good sense. Height at 3 years old, stallions 16 hh [hands high] and over, mares from 15.2 hh with 9 inches or more of clean flat bone.

Number of Mares per unit area

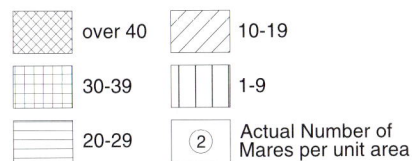

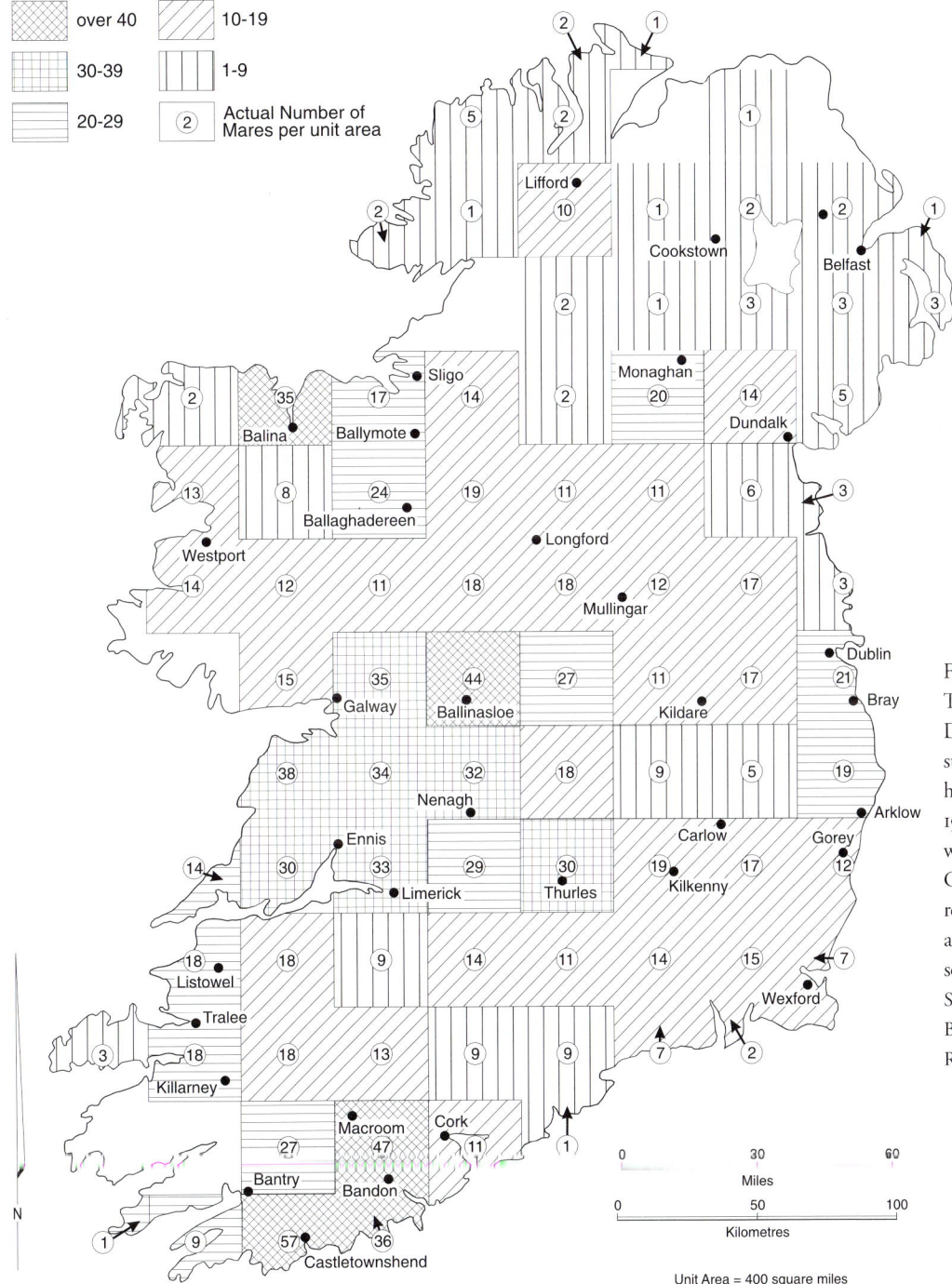

Pattern	Range	Pattern	Range
(cross-hatch)	over 40	(diagonal)	10-19
(vertical grid)	30-39	(vertical lines)	1-9
(horizontal lines)	20-29	②	Actual Number of Mares per unit area

FIGURE 5
The location of registered Irish Draught mares that visited a stallion under the official horse-breeding schemes of 1978. Notice how most mares were concentrated in the east-Galway/Clare/north-Tipperary region and in the fertile lands around Ballina, as well as in south-west County Cork.
Source: Breeding records of An Bord na gCapall.
Redrawn from Lewis, 1983

Unit Area = 400 square miles

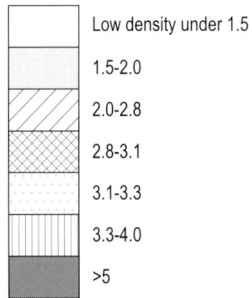

Low density under 1.5

1.5-2.0

2.0-2.8

2.8-3.1

3.1-3.3

3.3-4.0

>5

NORTHERN IRELAND

FIGURE 6

The number of non-thoroughbred horses and ponies per 1,000 acres of crops and pasture in the Republic of Ireland in 1975. The unorthodox intervals used for shading are those given on the original map. The map shows that horse and pony numbers per crop and pasture area were greatest in an arc from County Louth through County Dublin and then swinging westward to end on the west coast of County Clare, and in areas south east of this arc. Numbers per crop and pasture area were understandably much lower in the boggy and mountainous regions of County Kerry and west County Cork. Numbers, similarly defined, were also low in the main drumlin belt and in rugged County Donegal.

Redrawn from O'Neill et al., 1979

N

0   30   60
Miles

0   50   100
Kilometres

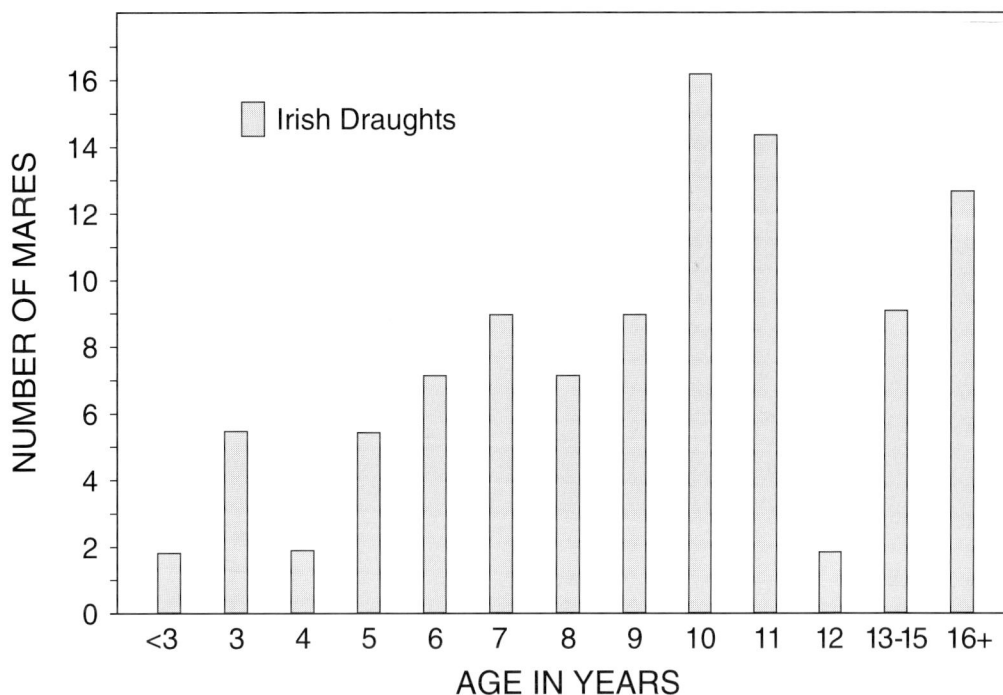

FIGURE 7: *The age of registered Irish Draught mares according to a sample survey of farms in the Republic of Ireland was undertaken in the mid-1970s by An Foras Taluntais. Notice how the majority of mares were over eight years old, indicating that farmers were using few young Irish Draughts on their farms at that time, and that unless there was government intervention and support for the non-thoroughbred breeding industry, few Irish Draughts were likely to be bred in future, especially as the available mares increased in age.*

Redrawn from O'Neill et al., 1979

The standard then stipulates the desired Irish Draught characteristics for head, shoulders, neck and front, back, hindquarters, body and legs, action and colour. This was the first time that an official standard had been published for Irish Draught.

The Year of the Breeder

Bord na gCapall designated 1978 as the Year of the Breeder and, through the Mare Replacement Scheme introduced that year, offered 'good breeding mares to approved breeders in certain selected areas who might wish to replace an existing barren or aged mare'. Although this scheme was not specifically aimed at Irish

Draught mares, it was of value to the breed, as was the Mare Purchase Scheme. Under the latter scheme 'Persons interested in acquiring a non-Thoroughbred broodmare for the first time will be eligible for a grant of £100 providing the mare is suitable and approved by the Bord'. Both these schemes were introduced 'on a pilot basis' in Donegal/Leitrim, north west Mayo, Kerry, Clare, Roscommon and Galway (excluding Connemara).

In 1979 Bord na gCapall collected details of all mares that visited stallions under the breeding schemes of 1978 in the Republic and in Northern Ireland; 1,269 registered Irish Draught mares visited stallions. These mares came from three main regions: east Galway-Clare-north Tipperary, west Cork, and the Ballina area of Sligo. Hardly any Irish Draught mares from Northern Ireland went to a stallion.[39]

Non-thoroughbred Horse Industry Study, 1979

In December 1979 a study of the non-thoroughbred industry was published; it had been commissioned by Bord na gCapall and carried out by An Foras Taluntais (the Agricultural Institute). This study included geographical information proving that, in 1975, expressed in terms of numbers per 1,000 acres of crops and pasture, non-thoroughbred horses were most common east of a line from Drogheda to Cork, with secondary concentrations in Clare, west Cork, Limerick and east Galway (figure 6).

These (with the exception of County Dublin, which was a heavy draught horse area), were essentially the regions in which Irish Draught stallions had been most common in 1939, the last year for which information on stallions that travelled for their mares is available. The study also showed an increase in the number of non-working and non-thoroughbred horses during the 1970s and concluded that 'The size of the non-thoroughbred herd is increasing at a satisfactory rate'. Less satisfactory, however, was the discovery that Irish Draught mares, on average, were four or five years older than halfbred mares.[40]

Pedigrees

The late 1970s and the 1980s were years in which increasing interest was focused on the pedigrees of Irish Draught. In 1978 Bord na gCapall, which was by then the body responsible for registering horses as Irish Draught and for maintaining the records, decided to close the *Irish Draught Horse Book* to all but the progeny of registered parents. According to Cotter (2003) the board 'reserved the right to introduce Thoroughbred blood from time to time'.[41] As Lewis wrote: 'Effectively, therefore, the Irish Draught is at last being transformed from a type into a breed.'[42]

In 1979 Begg traced the pedigrees of all 64 Irish Draught stallions that were 'currently on the Irish Horse Board Register of Approved Stallions'. In a potentially libellous article she claimed that six of those stallions were by a horse that had been sired by a Clydesdale out of a Thoroughbred mare. Her claims do not appear to have been refuted. Begg also drew attention to the four registered Irish Draught stallions that had been sired by Thoroughbreds and the two who had a Thoroughbred grandsire: 'no fewer than a further nine can claim that their dams are by a Thoroughbred.' In other words, 21 of the 64 registered Irish Draught stallions were certainly not Irish Draught by pedigree. In fact, Begg wrote, there was only a 'handful of sires descended from old strains of Irish Draught, once regarded as the Irish farmer's work-horse; some say this was the traditional Irish Draught.'

Begg also traced the pedigrees of registered stallions tracing back in the male line to certain foundation sires: the Comet (1) line; the Prince Henry (5) line, and the Young J.P. (12) line. Significantly, Begg ended her article:

> If Irish Draught are to be regarded as a breed, then under E.E.C. legislation the Stud Book would have to be closed in the near future to all except the progeny of animals already recorded on the existing Register, i.e. of traditional Irish Draught bloodlines providing they measure up to minimum standards (height and bone measurement).

Begg expressed the hope that

> the breed society will be in unison with the Horse Board on these minimum standards. Perhaps a grading system might be introduced for show

stock and working strains. This would obviate any further dilution of the remaining gene pool, small though it may be.

Begg concluded:

> The whole idea of fostering the Irish Draught is to retain the inherent genetic factors responsible for abundant resilient bone … a horse that will go on working relentlessly day after day, and show no signs of wear either in his temperament or physical make-up; a stamp of horse whose size and appearance is easily recognised as Irish Draught. It is these genes that the breeder should be trying to preserve within his Irish stock.

Three years later, in 1982, Lewis discussed breeding and the Irish Draught and regretted that 'few breeders know much about the lineage of individual Irish Draught', which he blamed on the fact that few volumes of the *Irish Draught Horse Book* had been published. He pointed out that, by using the manuscript records lodged in the Bord na gCapall archives, it was possible 'to trace the pedigrees of many sires'. Lewis then discussed the same families that Begg had traced in 1979, but added that:

> just because a horse traces back in direct male descent to one of the Irish Draught foundation sires, does not necessarily mean that the horse is a true-blue Irish Draught. King of Diamonds [547], for instance, is out of a mare believed to have been sired by the halfbred, True Boy. Admittedly, True Boy had a line back to Kildare (40), but he was nevertheless not wholly Irish Draught

Lewis concluded that

> given the present state of the Irish Draught

'breed', direct male descent is probably the best indication that one is breeding a 'genuine' Irish Draught.

Inspections and Resurgence of the Irish Draught

The published report of the Bord na gCapall team that inspected horses in 1982 encouragingly stated that there was 'discernible improvement in Irish Draught young stock'. The team expressed the opinion that credit was due to breeders 'and to the tireless workers from Bord na gCapall, particularly the breeding manager Dermot Forde'. The report noted that 'There are still far too many unsuitable animals' brought for inspection, and that 'The types and variations of animals brought out for registration throughout the country are sometimes remarkable'. The inspectors concluded that

> it must not be forgotten that Bord na gCapall has played an important role in the campaign to save the Irish Draught and the resurgence of the breed and its newly re-emerging quality has been in no small part due to the efforts of the officials and the volunteers [who helped in assessing animals submitted for registration] who have given unsparingly of their services over the past few years.[43]

Perhaps the self-praise was a reaction to the controversy that in 1982 surrounded Bord na gCapall and its registration of stallions. In 1987 the board was disbanded and, two years later, officially dissolved.

Society Registers Irish Draughts

Responsibility for inspecting and registering horses as Irish Draught was handed over by the board to the Irish Draught Horse Society in 1983. The Northern Ireland branch of the society had already been formed in 1978, and the first Irish Draught mare inspections in

Northern Ireland had been held in 1980. A sister society, the Irish Draught Horse Society of Great Britain, had been founded in 1979 and already organised its own breeding-incentive schemes. In 1988 the Northern Ireland branch of the Irish Draught Horse Society inaugurated its own foal-incentive scheme.

Appendix Irish Draught Scheme

In 1982 an Appendix Irish Draught Scheme was introduced in order to increase the very low number of registered Irish Draught mares and to improve the quality of the Irish Draught horse population. In 1986, for example, there were only 748 live registered and Appendix Irish Draught mares, but numbers increased to a peak of 1,755 in 1993.[44] Mares of suitable type, with at least three registered Irish Draught grandparents and no foreign blood, were eligible for registration as Appendix Irish Draught mares as long as they passed inspection. The last Appendix Irish Draught mares were registered in 1992, and just over 1,260 mares were registered under the scheme. Filly foals by registered Irish Draught stallions out of Appendix Irish Draught mares were eligible for full Irish Draught registration. Between 1990 and 1997, 337 mares registered as Irish Draught were out of Appendix mares, accounting for almost 37 per cent of all Irish Draught mares registered in those years.[45]

Irish Draught Horse Incentive Scheme, 1990-94

The disbanding of Bord na gCapall in 1987 was followed in November 1989 by the nomination, by the minister for agriculture in the Republic, of a fourteen-member Horse Advisory Committee.[46] This was followed in 1990 by the initiation of the Irish Draught Horse Incentive Scheme, which operated from 1990-94. Under this scheme a grant of £400 was offered for every live pure-bred foal by a registered Irish Draught stallion out of an Appendix or fully-registered Irish Draught mare. This scheme proved beneficial in that the percentage of Irish Draught and Appendix mares covered by registered Irish Draught stallions rose from 44 per cent in 1988 (before the scheme was introduced) to 65 per cent during the time covered by the scheme. Once the scheme ended the percentage fell again to approximately 43 per cent.[47]

Quality Mare Retention Scheme, 1994-99

In 1994 the Irish Horse Board Co-operative Society Limited (which is the successor of Bord na gCapall and was founded in 1993 as a joint venture between the minister for agriculture and the breeders) initiated a scheme to support non-thoroughbred horse breeding. The scheme was part-funded by the European Union's Operational Programme for Agriculture, Rural Development and Forestry.[48] Mares, selected on the basis of conformation, soundness and performance, qualified for two payments of £500 each for two foals sired by approved stallions. A total of £1.5 million was allocated to the scheme, which operated until 1999, but only two-thirds of the money was utilised. The rest had to be returned.[49] 1,172 mares qualified for the scheme, of which 327 were descended from King of Diamonds (547), who was a noted progenitor of show-jumping stock.[50] Not all of these mares were Irish Draught. Although the scheme was of value to Irish Draught breeders it was not aimed specifically at them and its effect on the breed is difficult to evaluate.

An Endangered Breed

During the 1990s there was a decrease in the percentage of foals sired by Irish Draught stallions and entered in the *Irish Horse Register*, from 38 per cent in 1990 to 21 per cent in 1999. During the same period there was an increase in popularity as sires of what are now called Irish Sport Horses. These are halfbreds with varying amounts of Thoroughbred and Irish Draught in their pedigrees. O'Toole wrote in 2001 that 'The Irish Draught Horse is numerically a small breed'. She then stated that 'There are approximately 900 mares and 90 stallions in the current population'. The market for Irish Draught has declined almost continuously since the end of the Second World War so that, no matter how important they are as foundation stock for hunter and Irish Sport Horse breeding, few breeders can afford the luxury of producing them. In 1999 only 45 per cent of registered Irish Draught and Appendix mares were covered by registered Irish Draught stallions.

According to the Food and Agriculture Organisation of the United Nations, a population with less than 1,000 females and twenty males is endangered. The American Livestock Breeds Conservancy considers any breed with less than 1,000 annual registrations to be endangered. The Irish Draught horse is thus, at the beginning of the twenty-first century, one of the world's endangered breeds.

The new millennium opened with research into the genetics of the Irish Draught[51] and with a genetic eval-uation of the sires of show jumpers.[52] There were also calls for a change in the nature of Irish Draught, so as to turn the breed into competitive equine sports animals.[53] At the same time there were other calls for the retention of the Irish Draught as part of the equine genetic heritage of Ireland.

In 2003 O'Flynn, the chairman of the Irish Horse Board, stated that 'The Irish Draught horse is our native breed and forms the foundation of our Sport Horse industry'. He considered that 'we need more emphasis on "blood" in our present sports stock [and should there-fore] make more use of the Thoroughbred for our crosses'. At the same time O'Flynn argued that 'we must keep the Irish Draught as our foundation'. In the same year the minister for agriculture and food in the Republic of Ireland wrote that 'it is essential that an adequate number of Irish Draught mares continue to breed pure … the Irish Draught horse [is] a very valu-able national asset'.[54]

The future of the Irish Draught horse is thus by no means certain in the early years of the new millennium although the statements of the minister for agriculture seem to imply that government support may be forth-

TOP: *Champion mare, Enniskeane Flash.* ABOVE LEFT: *The judges.* ABOVE RIGHT: *View of the show ring.*   Photos: Joan C. Griffith

ABOVE: *Champion stallion, Welcome Diamond.*
LEFT: *Reserve champion stallion Crosstown Dancer.*

Photos: Joan C. Griffith

10

Genetic Aspects
of the Irish Draught Horse

John Flynn

Perhaps the next most intriguing question after where we go when we die is where we actually came from, and how we evolved to form what we know as the modern human race. While the concept of 'from underneath the proverbial head of cabbage' no longer satisfies most prying minds, it may well in the end offer as good an explanation as what may emerge from extensive and elaborate population studies. The Adam and Eve theory provides a plausible biblical record, but it does not explain the origin, coexistence and interdependence of human, animal and plant life. The alternative and more heuristic approach in explaining the evolution of all three species is in accordance with Darwin's theory of evolution, which embraces the idea that all living organisms evolved from a basic primitive molecular make-up that existed billions of years ago. This structure provided the essential blueprint for self-replication, which set in motion the theory of evolution of life. As this process

progressed, living organisms began to differentiate and diverge through changes in molecular structures by mutation events from one generation to the next, a process that eventually brought into existence present-day plant, animal and human life.

Regardless of whatever was responsible for the existence of life, the presence on earth of so many different species, both plant and animal, would inevitably promote and urge the quest to determine the identity of different species, and how to embark on an investigation process to establish what it is that differentiates one species from the next. At the beginning of the last century scientists started to investigate human population; these studies were based on race and geographical distribution. It was not until the latter part of the last century, however, that significant progress was made in identifying differences in genetic markers within and between the human population and animal breeds. The principle of identifying genetic markers among population and the more recent advancement in marker identification through DNA technology has led to an explosion in investigative studies in what is now generally known as population genetic studies.

The commercial world of animal breeding did not take long to realise the potential in genetic-marker identification, and it was not long before stud-book registrations from horse and cattle-breed societies introduced blood typing and, more recently, DNA profiling into registration as a back-up in pedigree assurance. Genetic markers are also extremely useful in screening for inherited diseases, and for the production of quality milk and meat in the livestock industry.

The animal kingdom of the domestic equine species, known as *equus caballus*, is comprised of many different breeds, or sub populations, which are dispersed throughout the world. Some equine breeds are considered native to a particular country, while other populations migrated to or were imported from other parts of the world. Some populations may not necessarily be all from the same breed, but are made up of a heterogeneous group of horses of different breeds. Due to confinement within regions by geographical barriers and generations of interbreeding, a particular type of horse evolved, resulting in the formation of a new breed with characteristic features indigenous to that population.

Irish history is steeped in a tradition of horse breeding. While the origin of our largest population, the Thoroughbred, is well documented, perhaps the biggest mystery surrounds the origin of our world-renowned Irish Draught horse. With the prospect of being able to assess the origin of the draught horse at genetic level now on the horizon, a totally new approach can be entered into whereby scientific data from identified genetic markers can be compared through genomic analysis and mitochondrial DNA sequencing. Data from all population studies carried out in the past and in the future can be downloaded onto a gene-bank website, offering a wonderful opportunity for direct comparisons to be made on all horse breeds throughout the world.

In animal-population investigations, the first approach is to be sure that the breed of interest is selected on the basis that each individual within that breed satisfies the necessary criteria. This procedure is standard practice for any authority controlling the registration of a particular breed, such as the Irish Draught Horse Society. The bigger the number of animals included in the investigation, the more reliable the results. Due to financial constraints, it is unusual for a study to exceed 100 animals, though as little as twenty animals can suffice. Animals should be randomly selected without any bias towards gender, age or family relationships. In the past, blood samples were usually tested, but more recently, hair follicles and mouth swabs have been used. The next and most important factor in population studies is the type and number of genetic sites being investigated. Again, the greater the number of markers tested, the more accurate a reflection it will be of the breed.

During the last 50 years the major problem in population studies was the restricted number of genetic markers available for testing. Immunogenetic and electrophoretic techniques provided the main source of blood-group biochemical protein markers. These markers are encoding, or class 1 – that is, they are the product of particular genes that are inherited from one generation to the next. These markers were responsible for a major advancement in population genetics in the latter half of the last century. From about 1975 a new and unlimited source of genetic markers emerged with the advent of DNA and its vast potential in producing various types of genetic markers depending on which technology was used. These type of genetic markers revealed many characteristics based on fragment analysis, which displayed great variation from one individual to the next, culminating in the production of DNA profiles unique to each individual in human and animal species. With such an abundance of markers available, there was inevitably a massive increase in population studies in the last ten years throughout the world.

The general approach to population genetics is to establish the frequency of the markers identified in each individual at each genetic site. This parameter gives the first indication of differences at genetic level between one horse breed and the next. Some breeds can have a high frequency value for a particular marker, whilst another breed can have a low frequency value for the same marker. Indeed, some breeds display what are known as breed-specific markers that are unique to that particular breed. For example, in a population study on Irish horse breeds that I carried out in 2000, Thoroughbreds displayed 88 markers, Sport Horses 136, Irish Draughts 137 and Connemaras 130 markers. An interesting finding in this study was the presence of one marker that was unique to the Sport Horse breed at a significant level. As we know, this breed evolved mainly from the Irish Draught, and we must conclude that the Sport Horse is influenced by another breed – possibly the Clydesdale, which was used extensively as a workhorse in the past. The Sport Horse shared 136 markers with the Irish Draught, which you would expect. The possible explanation for the absence of this marker in the Irish Draught population may be that this breed went into a severe population decline about 40 years ago and produced an evolutionary 'bottleneck' that resulted in the loss of the particular bloodline that possessed this marker in the Irish Draught population, but was retained in the Sport Horse breed due to cross mating with the Clydesdale. Based on this reasoning, it would be prudent to assume that the Clydesdale had a significant influence in the Irish Draught breed, particularly as I have established from my British colleagues that this marker is prevalent in the Clydesdale population in the UK. Three-dimensional displays of frequency distributions between different horse breeds can give good

visual differences at a glance, and are displayed in this section.

The next important parameter to be measured from genetic data is heterozygosity. This is the estimation of the percentage of different marker combinations at genetic sites (heretozygous) against the percentage of similar marker combinations (homozygous) that are the result of mating within the breed, and are inherited in what is referred to in normal Mendelian fashion. Mendel, a Czech monk, had an interest in investigating obvious difference in similar plant species, and was the first person to discover in plants the genetic patterns of inheritance responsible for appearance, such as size, shape and colour. He was able to establish that some genetic components – now called genes – were inherited from one generation to the next, and were responsible for any differences in appearances from its previous generation. This concept led to the idea of varying degrees of gene expression, from dominance to recessive, and must be taken into consideration with inherited genetic markers.

In any population study the basic principle of Mendelian inheritance must prevail against systematic evolutionary forces such as mutation, migration and random mating, so that the balance between genetic markers and their subsequent combination through inheritance should remain constant from one generation to the next. This phenomenon – known as the Hardy-Weinberg principle – is derived from the two population geneticists, Hardy and Weinberg. Heterozygosity gives a good reflection of the genetic balance within a population, such as inbreeding, by comparing the actual or observed heterozygosity against the expected heterozygosity using the Hardy-Weinberg principle. In my study, using inbreeding coefficient estimations, the Irish Draught population did not appear to be excessively inbred when compared with its more genetically diverse cousin, the Sport Horse.

A number of software packages have been developed

CLOCKWISE FROM TOP LEFT:
Old Vic, a Thoroughbred stallion; Cruising, an Irish Sport Horse stallion; Crosstown Dancer, an Irish Draught stallion; Tulira Roebuck, a Connemara-Pony stallion.

Photos: supplied by owners

for calculating parameters in population genetics, such as DISPAN, PHYLIP and ARLEQUIN. Once the genetic data is downloaded onto these programs, gene frequency, heterozygosity, genetic diversity, genetic distance and ancestral family-tree investigations can be carried out. Typical examples are illustrated in this section. The data compiled from my study is included in a gene bank website and will, in conjunction with all other relevant data carried out worldwide, help to determine common lineages that will hopefully throw some light on where exactly the true origin of the Irish Draught lies. In the last five years, maternal mitochondrial DNA, which is inherited independently of recombinant genomic DNA, is beginning to show enormous potential in determining ancestral lineages. An investigation using mitochondrial DNA is currently being carried out in University College, Dublin; Weatherby's blood-typing laboratory (which is part of the Irish Equine Centre) is assisting by supplying samples from the Irish Draught population that should provide some interesting findings in the not-too-distant future. It is perhaps disappointing to be unable to report more information about the origins of the well-known horse breed at this time, but at least it is encouraging to relate that the foundation had been laid upon which a network of genetic information can build an indelible blueprint of the identity and origin of the Irish Draught horse.

Allele Frequency Locus A

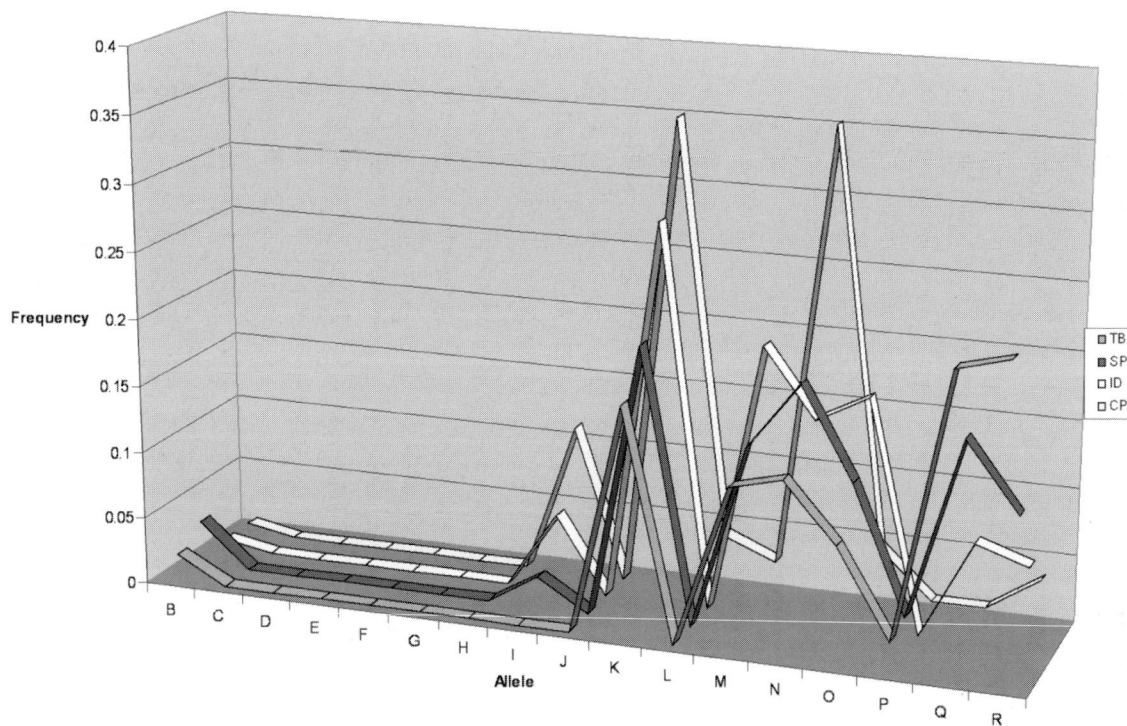

ABOVE: *The above graphics represent three dimensional patterns of gene frequency distributions at two genetic sites, illustrating good visual differences at genetic level between four Irish horse breeds.*

Allele Frequency Locus B

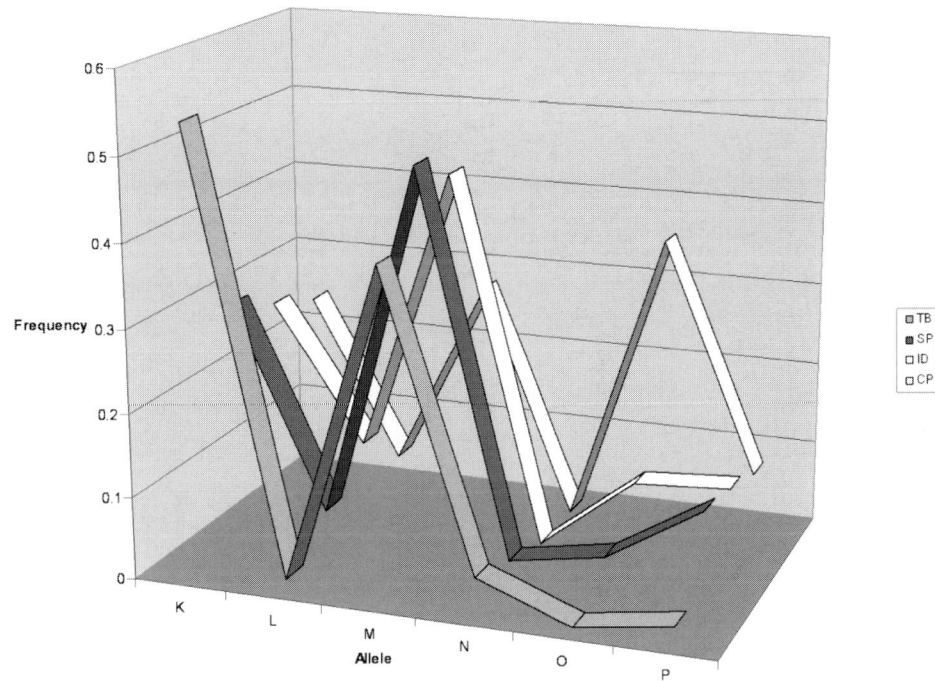

Allele Frequency Locus C

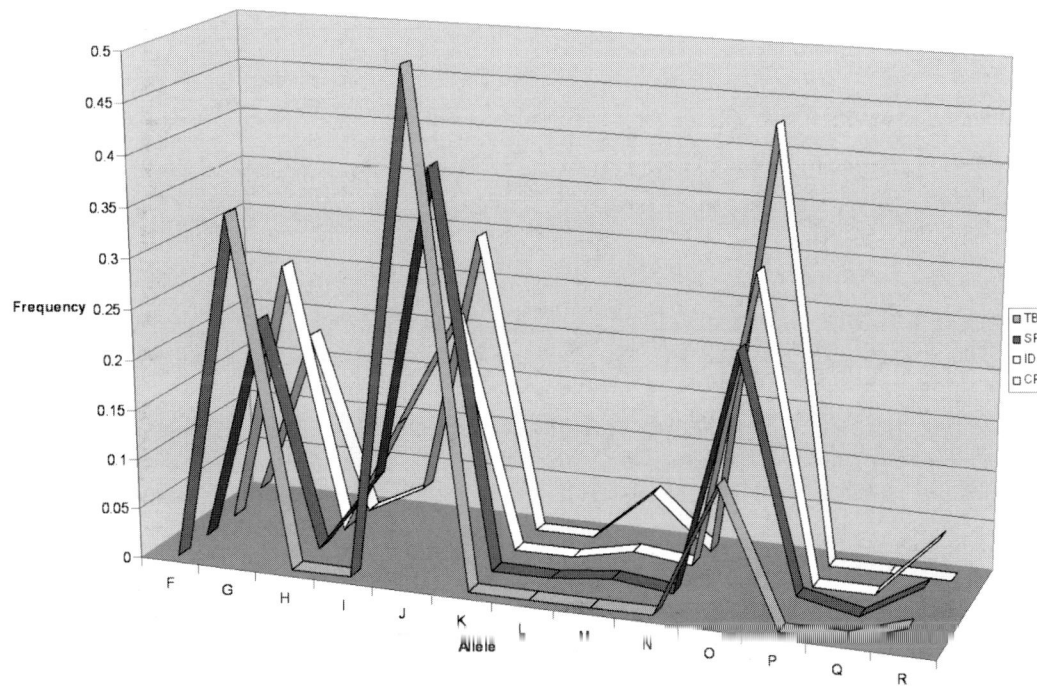

ABOVE: *A three-dimensional graphic display of the observed and expected heterozygosities on twelve DNA and seven blood-group genetic markers showing reasonable agreement suggesting the Irish Draught population is not excessively inbred.*

11

Present-day
Competition Horse

NORMAN STOREY

Since the advent of showjumping in Ireland – and its subsequent development as an international sport at the end of the nineteenth century – the Irish Draught horse has played a major role. The temperament, durability and athleticism of the Irish Draught, so important in crosses with the Thoroughbred, has created a potent mix that is suitable for the demands of modern-day showjumping. Numerous crosses with Irish Draught breeding are competing successfully on the international circuit. The Irish Draught-Thoroughbred-cross is famous throughout the world as the Irish Sport Horse, a much-wanted competition horse.[1]

From the earliest times riders have used horses for work and for pleasure. The first recorded competition to identify the horse that could jump the highest took place in Dublin in 1868.[2] Eventing began as a military discipline: army riders with fit horses had to be disciplined for parades yet ready for battle, and to fill their spare time riders developed dressage tests and rode across country. From these humble beginnings competing with horses continues to develop. There are so many different types of competitions available today that different breeds and types of horses are required for many of them. Nevertheless, the Irish Draught breed is to be found in many sports as either the pure breed or as a cross with other breeds.

Traditionally, horse breeding in Ireland has been a farm-based enterprise, involving the production of work and military horses. The advent of farm machinery and the decline of the horse in the military changed the emphasis of horse breeding, and it is now part of the international entertainment and leisure industry. The demand now is for sport and general leisure horses. Increased affluence and more leisure time have led to a greater demand for the leisure horse. These changes are clearly summarised in table 1.[3]

ABOVE: *Leaping competition on Leinster Lawn, Dublin, 1871.*

Photo: Royal Dublin Society Archive

Table 1: Irish horse population, selected years

Year	Working horses and ponies	Thoroughbred horses	Other horses and ponies*	Total
1889				450,000
1950				390,614
1960	176,000	13,281	34,402	223,774
1988	4,600 **	14,700	33,700	53,000
2003***		50,000	60–70,000?	110,000

* Other horses and ponies refer to the number of horses involved in sport and leisure
** Many of these would be draught types that would no longer be involved in farm work
*** Source: 'The Horse Industry', Dermot Ryan, IRH to WBFSH general assembly, Dublin, 5 December 2003
? = estimated

There was little change in the total number of horses in Ireland from the late 1800s to 1950. In the decade from 1950 to 1960 the number halved, and halved again in each of the decades to 1980. Since then the numbers have increased in the Thoroughbred and leisure industries.

Sport Horse breeding in Ireland has remained a farm-based enterprise; the 1985 Farm Structure Survey[4] showed that 24,000 farm holdings kept horses. Just under 20,000 (10 per cent of all farm holdings) kept non-Thoroughbred horses (at that time Sport Horses were more generally referred to as non-thoroughbred horses). While half of these kept only one horse, 1,100 kept five or more non-thoroughbreds.

A study carried out in 1979[5] showed that only 11 per cent of the holdings keeping horses cited commercial reasons for doing so. Over 50 per cent said they 'just liked horses' or described the enterprise as a hobby. Since the mid-1980s, production quotas and levies have become the norm in Irish farming, and many farmers began to keep horses as an alternative farm enterprise in the hope of making an economic return. In the early 1990s the broodmare population increased and foal production rose to over 6,000 per year. The expected returns did not materialise, and numbers have declined to less than 5,000 foals annually. In 1994, the average number of broodmares on farms that kept horses in counties Sligo and Tyrone was just over two.[6]

The Irish Draught horse was Ireland's and farming's workhorse. It was developed over the centuries into a suitable horse for use on small farms. As most farms could only afford one or two horses, the need was for a utility horse. Accordingly, the Irish Draught was used for farm work, to pull the trap and was saddled up for hunting and riding. This accounts for the fact that it has a variety of qualities and does not fit into the usual categories. It is certainly not a cold-blooded horse, being much lighter and faster than the Shire or Clydesdale, but also more powerful than the Thoroughbred. Traditionally, the Irish Draught mare was bred pure and crossed with the Thoroughbred stallion. This cross produced the world-famous Irish hunter or show jumpers of yesteryear, such as Bellvue, Goodbye and The Rock. Hybrid vigour would appear to play an important role here. These and others like them were the horses that made Ireland famous as a sport-horse-breeding nation.

ABOVE: *Goodbye by Renwood (Thoroughbred) ridden by Seamus Hayes. Winner of the Hickstead Derby in 1961 and 1964 and many international grands prix. The only horse to come down the Hickstead Bank (seen here) during the first running of the Derby. The angle of the bank was subsequently altered to make the descent easier.* Photo: Will Hayes

Beethoven in 1970 is the only horse to date to win a world championship for Great Britain. He was by the Thoroughbred stallion Roi D'Egypte and out of an RID (Registered Irish Draught) mare – 'the classic formula for an Irish hunter at its best'.[7] In the 1970s and early 1980s the great Ryan's Son flew the flag for traditional Irish breeding; by the Thoroughbred Ozymandias and out of an Irish Draught mare, Ryan's Son won a team silver medal at the Los Angeles Olympics for Great Britain.

Unfortunately, this halfbred horse was not good enough to meet the changes taking place in show-jumping competitions. It is generally agreed that it is not athletic enough to compete against the clock or to negotiate the much more technically designed courses. A lighter, more athletic animal is required – one with more Thoroughbred blood. So the halfbred mare is crossed again with the Thoroughbred stallion to produce a three-quarter-Thoroughbred horse. A further cross with the Thoroughbred stallion will produce a seven-eighths-bred animal. These 'blood' horses can cope better with modern competitions. The word 'blood' is loosely used to denote a horse with more Thoroughbred breeding in its pedigree.

Today's market requires 'athletic' horses regardless of their breed, type or pedigree. The amount of Thoroughbred breeding in the pedigree is immaterial. In fact, many top European-bred horses have little or no Thoroughbred blood in their first or second-generation pedigrees.

Summary of Traditional Irish Breeding

An RID mare covered by a Thoroughbred stallion produces the halfbred. The halfbred mare covered by the Thoroughbred stallion produces the three-quarter-bred horse. The three-quarter-bred mare covered by a Thoroughbred stallion produces the seven-eighths-bred horse. The halfbred, three-quarter-bred and other such crosses are now collectively referred to as the Irish Sport Horse (ISH). The Irish Sport Horse does not exist as a breed as such. Traditionally, it was a mixture of Irish Draught and Thoroughbred with some Connemara Pony bloodlines. In recent years the introduction of different European breeds into the country means that the pedigrees of Irish competition horses of the future will contain many different breeds.

The Irish Sport Horse pedigrees, breeding and performance details are recorded in the *Irish Horse Register* (IHR) or studbook. The Irish Horse Board (IHB) is responsible for the maintenance and development of the *Irish Horse Register*. The Irish Sport Horse is now recognised by the World Breeding Federation of Sport Horses as a breed in its own right.

The Irish Draught breed is renowned for its placid attitude. A good temperament was essential in horses used for farm work, and this placid temperament is one of the breed's strengths today. Modern competition horses travel the world by land, sea and air. Their training programmes are intense and many continue to compete at international level in a number of different and often intimidating environments until they are fifteen to twenty years of age. To maintain this level of performance for many years, horses must have a good temperament.

The leisure rider also requires a horse with a good temperament, as in many cases their training and ability is limited and temperamental animals are not suitable. This good temperament is not only transmitted to the crossbred offspring but also to the second-generation progeny.

Another essential characteristic of modern competition horses is veterinary soundness. Most horses will have to undergo a veterinary examination at least once in their lifetime. Top horses will be vetted at every competition and will be subjected to blood tests for prohibited substances. Again, the Irish Draught is a very sound breed. Only horses that remained sound over a long period of time were of any use to the farmer. Horses that were regularly off work due to unsoundness were no use for the rigours of ploughing, tilling, sowing, mowing the hay, and reaping and binding the corn. Unsound animals were moved on and never entered the breeding herd.

In an effort to maintain soundness, all mares and stallions approved for breeding by the Irish Draught Horse Society and the Irish Horse Board must pass a veterinary examination. Due to the decline in the Irish Draught mare population and the increase in availability of Thoroughbred mares, the use of the RID stallion on Thoroughbred mares has increased in popularity. This is generally referred to as the 'reverse cross' in Irish Sport Horse breeding. Examples of such breeding include the international show jumpers Special Envoy and Mill Pearl.

Changes in breeding objectives have, of course, been influenced by the developments in the competitions. Showjumping is an example of how they have changed through the years and why the type of horse required also had to change. The competition rules can be changed overnight, but to breed a horse that can cope with these developments may take up to ten or more years. The original concept was to jump as high as possible to win a competition. Whichever rider-and-horse combination could jump the highest, regardless of the number of rounds necessary to achieve a result, was the winner. With the introduction of the clock, time became the determining factor in establishing the winner; whoever had the least number of faults in the shortest time was declared the winner.

With the introduction of indoor arenas came jumping in confined spaces compared to the big expanse of the outdoor fields. Tighter turns and fences closer together called for more accurate riding and more athletic horses; the plainer type could not cope with these situations. Indoor arenas also meant showjumping could be an all-year-round sport. The introduction in recent years of machine-cut poles – much lighter than traditional forest poles, combined with shallower cups to support them – also required more accurate riding and athleticism.

Properly designed, safe courses are a very important feature of modern competitions. As well as lighter poles and shallower cups, course designers include related distances and very sharp turns in order to get a result. The fences are often at the maximum height allowed, so riders have to be at their best to succeed.

Equestrian sports are currently in the process of developing competitions that meet the demands of television. This will bring further changes and development in the future.

Those wishing to and who enjoy competing with horses have a huge range of equestrian sports to choose from. Within each discipline one can compete at many different levels, from the international professional rider to the leisure or hobby competitor. The various professional disciplines – Olympic and world championship – include showjumping, eventing, dressage, long-distance endurance riding, driving and vaulting. The non-professional side of the industry consists of in-hand and ridden-hunter showing, and leisure riding such as riding clubs, riding schools, trekking, hunter trials, le trec and hunting. Again, within each area, many different standards of competition, riding and horses are catered for.

The breeding sector is, of course, the primary activity in the industry, and is best documented and recorded. It does, however, need clear breeding goals, defined with reference to market requirements.[8]

Despite all the changes, the Irish Draught breed remains in demand, especially in the crossbred horse. Both the pure-bred and crossbreds are to be seen in many of our present-day competition animals, both at national and international levels, and at professional and amateur-rider levels.

In recent years breeders have turned away from traditional breeding. The success of European breeds in international competitions, especially showjumping and dressage, has influenced the thinking of breeders. Successful Irish Sport Horse stallions, such as Cruising by Sea Crest RID, have also had a major impact on breeding trends.

The number of Irish Draught mares available for breeding has declined and is now classified as a rare breed. In 1900 there were 250,000 Irish Draught horses in Ireland. One hundred years later – in 2,000 – this dropped to approximately 1,000 breeding mares and 100 approved stallions.

In 1986 over 90 per cent of the foals registered with Bord na gCapall were sired by Thoroughbred and registered Irish Draught stallions. Only 8.4 per cent were by Irish Sport Horse and foreign-bred Sport Horse stallions (FBSH). In 2002 only 45 per cent of the registered foals were by Thoroughbred and RID stallions; 53 per cent were by ISH and FBSH stallions. These trends can also be seen in the changes in the number of approved stallions.

The average age of the current crop of international competition horse is eleven to thirteen years. The average age of jumpers at Jerez in 2002 was eleven years, eventers twelve years and dressage horses thirteen years. Put another way, they were foals in the years 1989-91.

In the late 1980s and early 1990s 38-40 per cent of the registered foal crop was sired by RID stallions. Furthermore, the early 1990s witnessed the highest number of Irish Draught mares at stud for many years – both Appendix Irish Draught (AID) and RID – and the largest proportion covered by RID stallions. The result of this high usage of RID stallions can be seen in the large number of current show jumpers with Irish Draught breeding.

Table 2: Foals registered, total number and per cent by breed of sire

Year	Number of foals	Per cent by RID registered stallions	Per cent by Thoroughbred stallions	Per cent by ISH stallions	Per cent by FBSH stallions
2002	4826	17.3	28.0	28.6	24.5
1996	4933	24.5	38.0	23.1	10.3
1991	5053	37.9	41.8	15.8	1.1
1986	2613	24.6	65.9	8.8	0.0

Table 3: Number of approved stallions by breed

Year	RID Stallions	Thoroughbred stallions	ISH stallions	FBSH stallions
2001	97	122	66	88
1996	97	163	61	25
1991	94	141	49	4
1986	84	160	32	2

With the big drop in the use of Irish RID stallions in recent years, the question arises as to whether there will be as many international show jumpers by RID stallions in the next eleven or twelve years (2012-13).

The influence of the Irish Draught continues to dominate the Sport Horse broodmare population. The international market is very competitive. The collapse of communism in Eastern Europe has seen many of these countries restructuring their breeding programmes and organising more international shows. The 2002 and 2003 World Breeding Federation of Sport Horses (WBFSH) leading dressage horse was the Latvian-bred Rusty (47).

Table 4: Number of AID and RID mares at stud and the proportion covered by RID stallions

Year	At stud	Covered by RID (per cent)	At stud	Covered by RID (per cent)	At stud	Covered by RID (per cent)
1986	184	79 (43%)	564	255 (40%)	748	304 (41%)
1989	457	280 (61%)	645	455 (71%)	1102	735 (67%)
1992	743	461 (62%)	715	489 (68%)	1450	950 (66%)
1996	455	137 (30%)	694	341 (49%)	1149	478 (42%)
1999	315	82 (26%)	677	360 (53%)	992	442 (45%)
2001	250	86 (34%)	777	478 (62%)	1027	564 (55%)

Irish Horse Board's Quality Broodmare Retention Scheme (1995-99) accepted 1,172 mares for two grants of £500 on the production of two foals. Of these, 290 (24.74 per cent) were pure-bred Irish Draught. Almost 50 per cent (572) of the total number of mares accepted were by RID stallions.

The international market continues to expand and the demand for international horses remains very strong. Only 17 per cent of the jumping horses competing at the Olympic Games in Sydney in 2000 competed again at the World Championships in Jerez, Spain in 2002. In event and dressage, a similar picture emerges: only 20 per cent of the Olympic eventers and 23 per cent of the dressage horses competed in Jerez.[9]

Table 5: Breed of mare accepted for Quality Broodmare Retention Scheme

Breed	Number	Per cent of total		
RID	179	15.27	290	24.74 per cent
AID	59	5.03		
ID	52	4.44		
ISH	847	72.27		
Other breeds	35	2.99		
Total	1172	100.00		

Table 6: Breed of sire of mares accepted for Quality Broodmare Retention Scheme

Breed	Number	Per cent
RID	572	48.8
Thoroughbred	405	34.56
ISH	154	13.14
Other Breeds	41	3.5

Current Competition Horses

The Irish Horse Board's *Summary of Achievements of Irish Sport Horses in 2003* identifies the achievements of 36 jumpers and fifteen eventers at major shows and events worldwide (table 7 compares the breed of sire of each group). Despite the demand for more blood horses, the Irish Draught is the dominant breed sire of jumpers. The Thoroughbred dominates the eventers.

The sires and dam sires of the jumpers are all well known as sires, showing once again that jumping ability is a heritable characteristic. If breeders wish to breed jumpers they must breed from established pedigrees.

The great King of Diamonds RID appears in the pedigree of fourteen jumpers as either the grandsire (ten horses) or great-grandsire. Clover Hill is the sire of nine jumpers (25 per cent), Cruising ISH and Cavalier FBSH have six each, Furisto FBSH has three, while Errigal Flight and Master Imp – the only Thoroughbred represented – have two each. The dam sires include Regular Guy, Chairlift, Diamond Serpent, Ginger Dick, Holmacre, Diamond Lad, Diamonds are Trumps, Smooth Stepper, Sky Boy, Bahrain and Clover Hill.

The breeding of eventers does not appear to be as organised, as only one stallion has more than one representative competing: Stan the Man has two; interestingly, they are full brothers – Shear H2O and Shear L'Eau. Cavalier, Cruising and Master Imp are also sires of eventers; others include Highland King, Blue Laser, Western Promise, Glenagyle Rebel RID, I'm a Star, Hallo, Peacock,

Table 7: Per cent by breed of sires of IHB-listed competition horses, August 2003

Breed	Jumpers Per cent by breed of sire	Eventers Per cent by breed of sire
XX*	5.5	60.0
ISH	33.4	20.0
RID	36.1	6.7
FBSH	25.0	13.3

*XX is the notation for Thoroughbred

Edmund Burke, Fine Blade and Salluceva. The full brothers by Stan the Man – the jumper Sails Away and the eventer Sailing – are also full brothers by Cruising out of Victoria Plum by Bahrain. The jumpers Killossery by Clover Hill and Killossery Kruisette by Cruising are half-brothers out of the ISH mare Jeannie.

An analysis of the current younger crop of competition horses again shows the breeding changes that are taking place. Taking the finals of the four-, five- and six-year-old jumping classes at the RDS and the Future Event Horse League as 'national championships', a comparison of the information in table 7 ('Per cent by breed of sires of IHB-listed competition horses') with that of table 8 ('Per cent by breed of sires of young horses') is interesting.

In eventing the breed sires have changed very little, with the Thoroughbred influence dominating. Somewhat surprisingly, the proportion by European breeds has increased and, more surprisingly, has decreased slightly in jumpers. In the breeding of jumpers there has been a significant shift away from the Irish Draught in favour of Sport Horse sires.

The Future

The trends of the past ten to fifteen years raise many questions. How many competition horses will have Irish Draught breeding? Is the traditional cross of Irish Draught and Thoroughbred a thing of the past? The trends suggest that in the future Irish Draught bloodlines

Table 8: Per cent by breed of sires of young horses, 2003

Breed	Jumpers Per cent by breed of sire	Eventers Per cent by breed of sire
XX	5.0	61.0
ISH	50.0	11.0
RID	15.0	6.0
FBSH	20.0	22.0

will be seen more in the second and third generations of the pedigree. Will the cross of Irish Draught and European breeds be successful? In 2001 106 (10.3 per cent) of the total number of AID and RID mares at stud were covered by FBSH stallions. Will hybrid vigour with these other breeds be as successful as with the Thoroughbred? What effect will the competition developments have on the type of horse required? What will be the main criteria for selecting breeding stock? Will pedigree selection become a more dominant feature of event horse breeding? Will there be an increased use by breeders of scientific analyses such as 'relative breeding indices' in selecting breeding stock for the future?

The following list is of pure and part-bred Irish Draught horses that competed internationally in the year 2003. This year has been chosen as a sample year with a view to illustrating the presence of Irish Draught horses in international competition. All results are from 2003 unless stated.

Showjumping

The pure-bred and part-bred Irish Draught horses can be seen in many of the pedigrees of current international show jumpers. The majority are part-bred but there are a number of excellent examples of what can be achieved by the pure-breds.

Pure-breds in Showjumping

Carlow Clover

Carlow Clover, ridden by Robin Sweely of the US, finished fourth in the $25,000 WEF Challenge Cup at Palm Beach during March. They came tenth in the $100,000 US Open Jumper Grand Prix CSIO at the same venue, and in May finished eighth in the Pan-American Games selection trials. This 1994 gelding was bred by Joseph Delaney, Mountrath, County Laois, and is by Clover Hill out of Clonard Diamond AID by Diamonds are Trumps.

ABOVE: *Clover Hill.* Photo: Irish Horse Board

Coille Mór Hill

Coille Mór Hill (1987) is an RID stallion by Clover Hill and had his most successful season in 2001. He won both the national Isuzu Trooper outdoor and the Horsepower indoor leagues for rider Tom Slattery and breeder and owner Michael McKeigue, Ballinasloe, County Galway. Coille Mór Hill is out of Lawrencetown Lassy RID.

Gelvin Clover

Gelvin Clover is a 1993 Irish Draught stallion by Clover Hill RID out of Culdberg RID by Ginger Dick RID. He was bred by Kieran Rowley, Swinford, County Mayo, and is ridden by Clement McMahon for Ireland. Gelvin Clover was a member of the Irish team that won the Nations Cup in Hamina, and of the fourth-placed team in the Samsung Nations Cup at Falsterbo, CSIO 5 in Sweden. The combination was one of only three double-clears in the final top-four teams.

Ginger Watt

A 1992 Irish Draught gelding, Ginger Watt is by Ginger Dick RID out of Cecelia's Dream AID by Atlantic

Boy RID. He was bred by Walter Hughes, Claremorris, County Mayo. Ridden by world champion Dermot Lennon, Ginger Watt won the Christmas Cake Accumulator (1m30-1m50) at the CSI W at Olympia, London in December 2002. Interestingly, another Ginger Dick gelding finished fourth in the same event. This horse was ridden by Esben Johannessen for Norway.

Part-breds in Showjumping

At the European Showjumping Championships in Donaueschingen, Germany, there were three part-bred Irish Draught horses competing – two for Ireland and one for Great Britain. The Irish representatives were Carling King and the approved stallion Coolcorron Cool Diamond. Mister Springfield represented Great Britain and was ridden by Robert Smith. Two part-bred Irish Draught horses helped Ireland's Nations Cup team take second place in the Samsung Nations Cup Superleague at the Rome CSIO 5 in May. They were Carling King and the 1998 gelding by Kildalton King, Windgate King Koal.

The following are examples of horses of 50 per cent Irish Draught from the year 2003.

Ballayser Twilight
Ballayser Twilight won the Grand Prix at the Eindhoven CSI 1 in the Netherlands. By Clover Hill RID out of a Prince Reza mare, he was bred by Betty Parker, Dunganstown, County Wicklow, and ridden by V. Voorn of the Netherlands.

Bohemio
By Mister Lord out of the AID mare Blackwater Beauty, Bohemio was on the Mexican silver-medal-winning team and finished fifth overall in the individual placing at the Santo Domingo (DOM) Pan-American Games during August. Bred by Judith McGinn,

Mallow, County Cork, the gelding was ridden by Frederico Fernandez.

Boherdeal Clover
Ridden by David O'Brien for Ireland, Boherdeal Clover is an approved ISH stallion by Clover Hill out of Virginia Wolf by Regular Guy. He was bred in 1991 by Pamela Miller, Mount Cashel Stud, County Roscommon.

Carling King
A 1991 Irish Sport Horse gelding by Clover Hill RID out of Gortnagager Star which is by the Thoroughbred stallion Chairlift. Carling King was bred by Pat Geraghty, Glenamaddy, County Galway. He was a member of the winning Nations Cup teams at Aachen and at St Gallen, and on the runner-up teams at Rome, Wellington and Hickstead. Carling King is ridden for Ireland by Kevin Babington, and was ranked twenty-fourth in the world by the WBFSH in the 2003 world breeding rankings for jumping horses.

ABOVE: *Boherdeal Clover.*　　　Photo: Irish Horse Board

King in sixth place. He has been a regular member of the Irish Nations Cup teams during the past couple of years, and was on the winning team at St Gallen.

Cruise Hill

Another Irish Sport Horse mare containing some of the best bloodlines available, Cruise Hill by Cruising out of the AID mare Breffni Clover by Clover Hill RID won the Reporanka Trophy Puissance during October. Competing at the Helsinki CSI W and ridden by David O'Brien for Ireland, she was bred by Tony Murtagh, Virginia, County Cavan in 1991.

Cullohill Clover

Cullohill Clover finished fifth in the Massazza Grand Prix in Italy during October. This 1987 gelding is by Clover Hill out of Queen of Hearts.

Double O Seven

Double O Seven is a three-quarter-bred Irish Draught. He is a 1989 ISH gelding by Clover Hill out of Craven A ISH who is by King of Diamonds RID – a combination of the world's best jumping bloodlines. This horse is bred by Kieran Horan, Carrowmore, County Sligo, and is ridden by Philippe Lejeune. Double O Seven competes for Belgium.

Frisky IV

Frisky is a 1990 Irish Sport Horse gelding by Clover Hill RID out of Fiddlers Field xx (xx denotes Thoroughbred) by Skyliner xx. Frisky is an example of reverse cross-breeding and was bred by T.R. Hogan, Oola, County Limerick. Frisky is ridden by Geir Gulliksen of Norway.

Flurry D

Flurry D won the Grand Prix for O. Baldo of Italy at the Napoli CSI 2 show in May. Flurry D is by Flagmount King RID and was bred by Mick McGuigan, Dungannon, County Tyrone.

ABOVE: *Coolcorron Cool Diamond.*   Photo: Irish Horse Board

Clover Brigade

A 1990 Irish Sport Horse stallion by Clover Hill, it was bred by William Walsh, Borrisokane, County Tipperary. Clover Brigade won the Preis der Kolher and Stoffers Ohg 1m40 class at the Neustadt Dosse CSI 2 show in January 2003. He was ridden by Daniel Etter of Switzerland.

Coolcorron Cool Diamond

A 1989 stallion by Glidawn Diamond RID, Coolcorron Cool Diamond is owned and ridden by Robert Splaine, Belgooley, County Cork. He was bred by Francis Fitzgerald, Bonmahon, County Waterford. Coolcorron Cool Diamond won the St Gallen Generali Grand Prix at the Swiss CSIO 5 show in May 2003, with Carling

Gerry Maguire

Gerry Maguire is a 1994 Irish Sport Horse gelding by Clover Hill RID. This gelding is ridden by Robert Smith for Great Britain.

Hopes Are High

Ridden by Mathew Broom, Hopes Are High took fourth place in the 1m30 class at the CSI A show in Vejer De La Frontera, Spain during February. At the same venue during March they finished fifth in the 1m40 class. By Flagmount Diamond, this 1998 gelding was bred by Michael Hughes in County Armagh.

Katie Riddle

Katie Riddle is a 1994 mare by Flagmount Diamond RID and is ridden by Lars Nieberg for Germany.

Killossery

Killossery is a 1992 gelding by Clover Hill RID out of Jeannie ISH by the Thoroughbred stallion Radical. He was bred by Killossery Lodge Stud, Kilsallaghan, County Dublin. He is ridden for Ireland by Shane Carey from the Army Equitation School. He was a member of the Nations Cup winning team at Hamina, Finland in June.

Lismore Clover

Lismore Clover is a 1994 Irish Sport Horse mare by Clover Hill RID out of Lismore Lyric by Holmacre, and was bred in Donegal by Patrick O'Neill. She is ridden by David O'Brien for the Irish Army Equitation School.

Loughtown Atlanta

This 1989 gelding by Clover Hill RID out of Northern Rose by Northern Value xx was fifth in the MCR Cup (1m45) and second in the BJ Trophy (1m40) with Cristino Torres Garcia at the Falsterbo CSIO 5 show.

Midnight Call

Midnight Call is a 1992 gelding by Duca di Busted out of the RID mare Lady Glen by Flagmount Diamond. He was bred by the McLoughlin Brothers of Dundonald County Down. Ridden by Edward Doyle for Ireland, he shared joint second place in the Puissance at the five-star Belfast show in December.

Mister Springfield

Bred by Robert Gallagher, Derry, Mister Springfield was a member of Great Britain's Nations Cup winning team at Hickstead. Mister Springfield is a 1993 gelding by Western Promise ISH out of Glebe Bess RID.

Ringwood MCD

Ringwood MCD is a 1993 Irish Sport Horse gelding by the Thoroughbred stallion Rich Rebel out of the RID mare Killea Hunter by Silver Hunter. This horse is an example of the traditional breeding of Irish competition horses. The gelding was bred by Michael Ryan, Templemore, County Tipperary, and is ridden by C. Torres Garcia for Spain.

Sea Wolf

Sea Wolf is a 1991 gelding by Ginger Dick. In February he took fifth place in the Grand Prix FEI World Cup qualifier for Norway's Esben Johannessen at Bordeaux CSI W.

Tomgar Rocky

This is a 1991 gelding by Diamond Lad RID. Tomgar Rocky was bred by Charles Pigeon, Kilbeggan, County Westmeath. In June he won a 1m40 class at the Drammen CSIO 5 show for Germany when ridden by H.D. Dreher.

Windgate Illusion

The pedigree of Windgate Illusion is one of the new generation of jumpers. Foaled in 1995, his pedigree combines the Irish Draught and European breed of Holstein. He is by Cavalier out of the mare Ginger Rose by Ginger Dick RID. During August he was placed fourth with a double clear in the Grand Prix at the Italian show of Cervia CSI 1. He was bred in Dunboyne, County Meath, by Edward Cawley.

Windgate King Koal

Out of a Prince Rois mare, this horse was bred by Laurence Pender, Enniscorthy, County Wexford. He was a member of the second-placed team in the Nations Cup in Rome.

World Breeding Showjumping Championships

At the FEI World Breeding Showjumping Championships for young horses in Lanaken, Belgium, Irish Draught breeding is to the fore in the five-, six- and seven-year-old horses.

Welcome Captain by the Irish Sport Horse stallion Captain Clover out of the RID mare Welcome represented the *Irish Horse Register* in the five-year-old class.

In the six-year-old championship four horses had Irish Draught breeding: Suir Clover out of Rathlin Pride AID, Cnoc na Seimhre by Clover Hill RID, Carnhill Surprise by Crosstown Dancer RID and Early Days, also by Clover Hill. These three finished first, second and third respectively in the Canada Life six-year-old championships at the RDS horse show.

Suir Clover and Carnhill Surprise are three-quarters Irish Draught, as Suir Clover is by the Clover Hill stallion White Clover and Carnhill Surprise is out of the AID mare Carnhill.

In the seven-year-old class the Irish Draught breed was represented by the pure-bred stallion Welcome Flagmount. Welcome Flagmount is by Flagmount King out of Welcome RID. This pedigree makes Welcome Flagmount a half-brother to Welcome Captain. It is not often two horses out of the same mare represent Ireland in the same championships.

Millstreet show is Ireland's leading show for finding potential young jumpers, and 2003 was no different with two of the important championships going to part-bred Irish Draught.

World Breeding Record

At the 2002 international CSI B in Genoa, a world breeding record was set. The grand prix was won by Conor Swail with Windgate King Koal, with Robert Splaine on Coolcorron Cool Diamond in second place. What makes this a unique record is that both these horses are sired by full brothers. Windgate King Koal is by Kildalton King RID and Coolcorron Cool Diamond by Glidawn Diamond RID. Kildalton King and Glidawn Diamond were bred in Kildalton College out of the great RID mare Kildalton Countess, and are by the King of Diamonds. Never before were the winner and the second-placed horse in an international grand prix sired by full brothers bred on the same farm.

One-quarter-bred Irish Draught

There are many examples of competition horses that contain Irish Draught breeding in their second generation pedigree.

Ado Annie

Ado Annie is a 1993 Irish Sport Horse mare by Errigal Flight ISH out of the ISH mare Coolrain Princess, who is by the RID stallion Blue Henry. In fact, she has Irish Draught blood on both sides of the pedigree as Errigal Flight is by the world-famous King of Diamonds. Ado Annie is ridden by Will Simpson for the US.

Killossery Kruisette

A 1993 mare, Killossery Kruisette is by the great Cruising, who is by the Irish Draught stallion Sea Crest. Ridden by David O'Brien for Ireland, she won the MCR cup (1.45m) at the CSIO 5 Falsterbo show in Sweden ahead of Loughtown Atlanta, who was fifth.

ABOVE: *Ado Annie.*   Photo: Irish Horse Board

Richmont Park

A grandson of the RID stallion Diamond Lad, Richmont Park was a member of the winning Swedish team in the Samsung Nations Cup at the Falsterbo CSIO 5 show in July. By the stallion Coevers Diamond Boy, he was ridden by Royne Zetterman.

Other examples are Lismakin, Andy and Shannondale (grandsons of King of Diamonds RID), Quick Flash (a grandson of Diamonds Are Trumps RID), Touch of Clover and Say You Will (grandsons of Clover Hill RID), Windgate Mystique (a grandson of Sea Crest RID), Eezy (a grandson of Flagmount Diamond RID), Cullawn Diamond (a grandson of Diamond Prince RID), Point Blank (a grandson of Diamond Lad RID) and Rincoola Abu (who has both Sea Crest RID and Clover Hill RID as grandsires).

Eventing

The Irish-bred event horses have been very successful. For the past eight years Ireland was ranked number one in the world by the WBFSH for breeding eventers.

There are currently ten Irish eventers listed in the world's top 40, and include Supreme Rock by Edmund Burke, Shear L'Eau and Shear H2O by Stan the Man, Custom Made by Bassompierre, Moon Man by I'm a Star, Gormley by Sandalay, Ringwood Cockatoo by Peacock, McKinlaigh by Highland King, Nicky Henley and The Wexford Lady by Fine Blade.

Irish Draught breeding appears very little in the first generation of pedigrees of international event horses. The Irish Draught does not have the speed required. Nevertheless, there are many examples of eventers' pedigrees with Irish Draught in blood in the second generation.

At the European Eventing Championships in Punchestown, Moon Man was on the Great Britain gold-medal-winning team. Ridden by William Fox Pitt, Moon Man is by I'm a Star xx out of Stopford Eddy by the Irish Draught stallion Prince Edward.

Once again, Irish-bred horses did very well at Badminton CCI 4 event. Supreme Rock won the event, and – for the second year running – seventeen Irish-bred horses finished in the top 44.

Winning the intermediate section at Sorton Hall event was a son of the Irish Draught stallion, Carrabawn View. Pebbly White Stuff was exported from Cavan in 2002 and accumulated 44 points in just eight events.

Grange Bouncer

The most successful pure-bred Irish Draught in national competition in recent years is the registered stallion Grange Bouncer RID, who competes regularly at CCI 2 level, and has competed at Blarney and Punchestown international events. He is a 1992 grey stallion by Prospect Pride out of Grange Heather RID by Kilmore Heather RID, and is owned and bred by Jack Lambert, Killinick, County Wexford.

Dressage

Dressage has never been a very popular sport in Ireland. The better movement of the European breeds usually makes them more-suited to dressage than Irish-bred horses. In the past couple of years, however, membership has increased and it is not uncommon to see 50 to 100 horses at a regional competition. Most of the international horses are of European breeding. There are, however, some examples of both pure and part-bred draught competing. O'Leary's Irish Diamond – who competes in the US regularly – is an approved RID stallion by Glidawn Diamond.

The RID mare Beezies Sue competes on the national circuit with much success. A 1993 grey mare by Sea Crest out of Princess of Woodlands by Pride of Toames, she was bred by the Hession family of Woodlands Equestrian Centre, County Sligo. Simone Hession has produced and ridden her to this level.

In 2000 Beezies Sue represented Ireland in the novice young-riders dressage team that won at Blarney. In England, she won or was placed in all her classes. In 2001 she won the dressage class at the Irish Draught national show, and she was a member of the winning riding-club team championship. At the national dressage championship she won the riding club open and elementary freestyle championship.

Beezies Sue won the open riding-club championship again in 2002, as well as many novice and elementary competitions. She won the Irish Draught trophy for the best pure-bred Irish Draught at Dressage Ireland's national championships and repeated it in 2003.

In 2003 Beezies Sue won the medium championships at Blarney dressage festival. In England, she won two medium competitions.

Part-breds

Claggan Roxy Music
Another part-bred dressage by Rakish Paddy RID. Ridden by Laragh Hamilton, she represented Ireland in the junior European championship team at Samur in France. At the national dressage championship in

Cavan, the partnership finished fourth in the Intermediare 1 final and sixth in the Prix St George.

Kildalton Rainbow
This unusual cross of the Arab and the Irish Draught was novice and elementary champion at Dressage Ireland's south-east regional finals in 2003. Owned and bred by Kildalton College, she was ridden by Ms Rosemary Gaffney. She is by Kildalton Gold RID out of the Arab mare Mimis Orana.

Tonka Wakkan
A 1998 gelding by White Clover ISH out of Rhue Lady RID by Corran King RID. At the national dressage championship she was placed second in the potential dressage horse class and won the Lady Cliodhna Trophy for the highest-placed Irish-bred horse.

In-hand Showing

During the spring and summer season over 120 agricultural and horse shows are held throughout the country. They are organised by local committees with the support of the Irish Shows Association (ISA).

The ISA is a 32-county association that organises all-Ireland championships for the various age categories of young Sport Horses. They aim to identify horses with excellent conformation and movement. Many go on to become competition horses, especially eventers. Exhibitors must qualify their animals for the finals which are held late in the season. The prize fund varies from €1,500 to €9,000. In each championship there are approximately 25 opportunities to qualify for the finals. These qualifiers are held at various shows prior to the final. An example of a championship is the €6,350 Tullamore Dew Broodmare and Foal Championship. Sponsored by Tullamorre Dew, the final is held at the Iverk Show, Piltown, County Kilkenny. Each mare and foal is judged as a unit, with slightly more emphasis put

ABOVE: *Mister Springfield.*   Photo: Irish Horse Board

The Royal Dublin Society's annual horse show is the premier horse show. Breeders and producers of young horses, mares and foals, as well as ridden hunter, all descend on the hallowed turf of Ballsbridge in the first week in August. Standards are set and measured as exhibitors aim for the various supreme championship titles. The continued influence of the Irish Draught in Irish Sport Horse breeding can be seen in the results from the RDS and other shows.

The Limerick show hosts the Aughinish Alumina Limerick Lady Championship for two-year-old fillies deemed to be suitable for producing hunters, show jumpers and eventers. Down through the years it has been dominated by Irish Draught fillies.

on the conformation and movement of the mare. Each entry must be registered with the IHB, and only one may qualify for the final from each qualifier. The champion receives the Tullamore Dew Trophy and €2,540 in prize money. There are all-Ireland championships for colt and filly foals, yearling and two and three-year-old colts/geldings and fillies. The ISA also organises the following all-Ireland championships for pure-bred Irish Draught horses:

> The Irish Draught Horse Society Yearling Colt or
>   Gelding Championship
> The RID Mare Championship
> The Roscommon Yearling Championship
> The Irish Draught Mare of the Future
> The Leitrim Breeders' Championship

Showing Horses Under Saddle

Many champion young horses go on to have successful careers in ridden show classes. Most compete in one of the three hunter classes based on the estimated weight they can carry. There are light, medium and heavy-weight classes.

Many champion riding horses are part-bred Irish Draught, especially those in the medium and heavy-weight divisions. Again, results from the RDS highlight their influence.

The show-hunter scene in Great Britain offers a great opportunity for Irish-bred horses to come to the fore. Down through the years there have been many examples of Irish horses winning classes and championships. For example, Thomastown won the supreme hunter championship at Whitchurch and North Shropshire Show. This five-year-old heavyweight horse is by Kildalton Gold RID.

12

The Irish Draught
in the Twenty-first Century

JOAN C. GRIFFITH AND MARY MCGRATH

The Irish Draught Today and Tomorrow

Historically, the Irish Draught has evolved over the centuries with or, as some might say, without a plan. In recent times, much more careful consideration has gone into the selection and breeding programmes of Irish breeders. We would like to take a moment here to emphasise the work of those responsible for the future of the Irish Draught horse. The task falls primarily on the members of the Irish Draught Horse Society in Ireland, its affiliated groups around the world, and the Irish Horse Board. Secondarily, it rests with breeders, buyers, promoters and riders of the breed. Ireland has long been an important player in exporting sound, sane, and reliable riding horses, and will continue to be for the foreseeable future.

The Irish Draught Horse Society (IDHS)

The IDHS has members in branches at national and local level. The society organises mare inspections and awards registered Irish Draught (RID) status to those mares whose conformation, breed type and appropriate pedigree meet the specified criteria. Geldings are eligible for RID status. The society also runs a national breed show, offers training courses for judges and an international training course for affiliated groups. The branches organise their own local shows, meetings and promotional efforts. Participation at the local level enables owners and their horses to move on to the national level competitions, culminating each year in August with the National Irish Draught Horse Show and the Royal Dublin Society Show.

In conjunction with the Cavan Equestrian Centre, the society co-ordinates the National Registered Irish

Draught Sale in October of each year. In conjunction with the Irish Horse Board, IDHS judges and inspectors participate in stallion inspections for the *Irish Sport Horse Studbook*, which include the registered Irish Draught. It also works hand in hand with Weatherby's blood typing at the Irish Equine Centre to co-ordinate DNA testing of Irish Draught animals.

In 2002, as the number of RID mares was declining dramatically, the society decided to re-open the Appendix Irish Draught (AID) Mare Scheme in order to register those halfbred mares with one RID parent and three RID grandparents, no warm blood or foreign bloodlines, and with both parents and grandparents registered in the *Irish Horse Register*. The Appendix helps to retain some Thoroughbred blood in the breed. The society also offered an amnesty registration for mares with ID (Irish Draught) dams and two full generations of Irish Draught breeding. This scheme was organised to bring into the register animals whose dams were eligible

but never inspected, which otherwise would have prevented their offspring from being put up for full inspection.

The Irish Horse Board (IHB)

The IHB operates the *Irish Horse Register* and assigns IHR (*Irish Horse Register*) numbers to all horses in Ireland, including the Irish Thoroughbred, the Irish Draught, the Irish Sport Horse, the Connemara Pony, and foreign-bred stallions standing in Ireland. The IHB assists the IDHS in financial terms with breeding-incentive schemes, promotional monies for their publications, computers, equipment, and sometimes salary considerations. The Irish Horse Board, in co-operation with the society and the Northern Ireland Horse Board, runs the inspection and performance testing of stallions, and awards the RID, as well as S1 and S2 statuses. Approved RID stallions have full pedigree, have passed a veterinary exam and have also passed performance testing. S1 stallions have passed a veterinary exam and have full pedigree but have not passed or been put forward for performance testing. S2 stallions have a full pedigree but have not passed the veterinary exam nor have they been put up for performance testing.

The Horse Board administers funds, including the 2000-06 National Development Programme, which helps to provide the incentive schemes for the Premier Mare Scheme and Quality Broodmare Retention Scheme. These premiums are awarded to breeders for breeding 'pure-bred' Irish Draught that pass inspections for quality and soundness.

In terms of its rarity, the Irish Draught has been listed as an endangered breed in Ireland, but if one looks at the number of registered Irish Draught stallions at home, as well as those standing abroad, a more encouraging picture emerges. What may yet save the breed is its growing popularity abroad. For the total population of Irish Draught stallions, one must also add in the figures

Table 1: Irish Draught mare population, 2004

Irish Draught mares in Ireland	Breeding herd population
RID	1525
ID	612
AID	573
Total	**2710**

Table 2: Irish Draught foals born 2003

Filly	201
Colts	176
Total	**377**

Data supplied by the Irish Horse Board, April 2004

Table 3: Irish Draught stallions worldwide

Country	RID	S1	S2	in Ireland	Total
Ireland	97	109	18		224
Great Britain	50				50 (approximately)
North America	30				30 (approximately)
Other countries, includes Australia, New Zealand, South Africa, Switzerland	10				10 (approximately)
Grand Total	**187**	**109**	**18**		**314**

for the S1 and S2 stallions. The RID stallions to have had the most influence in RID stallions now standing abroad are Pride of Shaunlara, King of Diamonds, Ben Purple, Clover Hill, Lahinch, Laughton, and are to a lesser degree the lines of Glenside and Blue Peter. These lines have progeny in Britain, New Zealand, Australia, US, Canada and South Africa.

While the total herd size is small, approximately – 314 stallions and approximately 2,710 mares – this may in fact be a sustainable number for a special breed if one considers the fact that in the year 1918 – with the opening of the original *Irish Draught Horse Book* – there were 51 stallions and 375 mares approved to form the basis of the foundation lines, and that newly-approved stallions are listed with numbers starting in the 860-plus range, and newly-approved mares are listed starting in the 12,000-plus range. Clearly, the

Table 4: Stallions selected for performance testing

Breed	Inspected	Selected for performance test
Irish Sport Horse foreign bred	21	7
Sport Horse	13	4
Irish Draught	21	9

breed shows slow growth over time, and while some consider it a rare breed, it is not a vanishing breed.

With the most recent round of stallion inspections (March 2004), of the stallions presented, twenty were selected for performance testing. The table below (Table 4) provides a breakdown that shows the Irish Draught is favourably represented, including five of the seven Irish Sport Horses that had at least one RID parent or grandparent.

As recently as spring 2004, the Irish Horse Board reviewed its practice of excluding S1 and S2 from the register. This review was largely due to falling in line with European Union legislation for inclusion of all stallions of a breed into the official register of that breed. These changes mean that S1 and S2 stallions will no longer be put into the supplemental stallions list but will be added into the official studbook as a separate section. According to the IHB, the changes are already in place.

Breeders, Buyers, Promoters and Riders of Irish Draught Horses

The decision made every spring by breeders as to which stallion they will use with which mare plays a vital role in determining the number of animals to be added to the register as Irish Draught, thus making them eligible

ABOVE: *Buttermilk for sale.*

Pen, ink and wash drawing by Hugh Douglas Hamilton

for RID. Buyers and promoters need to be aware of the pedigree of the animals they are buying, selling and promoting to be sure they are indeed RID and not just ID. This holds true for stallions to ensure they are approved RID, not S1 or S2. While it is true that S1 and S2 stallions on the register cover a number of mares annually, these progeny are added to the Irish Sport Horse ranks. One must also remember that the always-in-demand Irish hunter is the progeny of the Irish Draught and the Thoroughbred-cross, and in order to

have the Irish hunter/Irish Sport Horse, there must be a pure-bred Irish Draught in the background.

Conclusion: A Horse for All Seasons

We have shown in the foregoing chapters the efforts made to improve the working draught horse and to provide an animal of quality to meet the transport requirements in towns and cities, and the demands of the newly-emerging small farmers in the late nineteenth

ABOVE: *Island Rambler, the Irish Draught mare that aroused the greatest interest at the Dublin Horse Show in 1967. Bred in County Westmeath by the sixteen-year-old stallion Merrion. The mare cost £35 as a yearling, and bred the supreme hunter champion at the RDS show.* Photo: Private collection

and early twentieth centuries. In each period, there were horses of different kinds to carry out different work. The type and quality of horse was in direct relation to the wealth and influence of the owner. Illustrations show us that in every generation there were some good horses but even more bad horses. The better horses belonged to professional people, landlords and their agents, and the richer farmers. They were often a status symbol, much as a good car is today.

For brief periods, particularly in times of war, sporadic attempts were made to breed better horses by importing fine stallions to cross with the native mares. Each time, the best animals were sold abroad and the remaining animals were left in limbo. Our romantic notion of Irish peasants with wonderful working horses is simply incorrect. The majority of horses in Ireland were small, hungry, worm-ridden and seriously overworked. People living one step away from starvation did not own good horses. This included the vast majority of the population

in the years leading up to and immediately following the Famine. Horses were owned by the wealthy and symbolised money, power and land ownership. In the late nineteenth century the increase in trade and industry demanded a greater supply of sound working horses. The large estates, the improving landlords and – more recently – the Department of Agriculture and the Royal Dublin Society carried out their own breeding programmes to produce a type of draught horse with an influx of Thoroughbred blood – a horse better suited to the Irish environment and labour requirements.

In 1967 the first Irish Draught mare classes were held at the Royal Dublin Society Horse Show. The entrants were on the whole neat – 15.3 or 16.0 hands high. Their movement was active but not exaggerated. They were calm and very easy to handle. They and their parents were probably the last generation to have worked in the fields and the towns. Since then, breeding programmes have continued. The horses have become considerably bigger than those used around the farm, and a large foal will usually beat a smaller one in the show ring. In order

ABOVE: *In recent years riding cross-country has become a major form of equitourism in Ireland. There are many opportunities to relax and admire the spectacular views.* Photo: Bord Fáilte

for the breed to maintain the characteristics for which it was first chosen, it is vital that we make use of the horses, and that breeding programmes should be based not just on conformation but on proven temperament and ability. Big is not necessarily best, and the show horse is not necessarily the best performer. If we do not make use of the Irish Draught horse it will eventually be reduced to simply an exhibit in the show ring.

Many people return to riding later in life when they have more time on their hands, and this is the horse for them. Others wish to take part in le trek or riding-club events, in showjumping, showing, driving, hunting, hunter trials or breeding; the Irish Draught is ideally suited to all these pursuits. It can carry heavy weights and it can carry children with the same ease and sure-footedness. Its ability to cross-country is legendary.

In the Irish Draught we have inherited a horse eminently suited for today's leisure rider. Every Irish Draught horse can jump, do dressage and perform cross-country, but rarely at international level. We should ask ourselves, how many of us actually want to perform internationally? The honest answer is very few. What most of us really want is a horse that is safe and user-friendly. With the Irish Draught, generations of careful breeding have resulted in a calm, sound, careful horse that loves people. The Irish Draught, once the traditional Irish *capall oibre*, is now the horse for today.

ABOVE: *Trekking, one of Ireland's fastest growing tourist attractions.*

Photos: Bord Fáilte

ABOVE: *Competition driving; Ben Good driving his team of grey Irish Draught geldings.*

Photo: *The Irish Times*

LEFT: *Breeding; mare and foal.*

Photo: Gay Keogh

OPPOSITE PAGE:
(top) *Showing mare, Sumas Folklore.* Photo: Gay Keogh
(bottom left) *Stallion, Silver Granite.* Photo: Tony Parkes
(bottom right) *Showjumping; Crosstown Dancer at IDHS event.*
Photo: Mary Davies

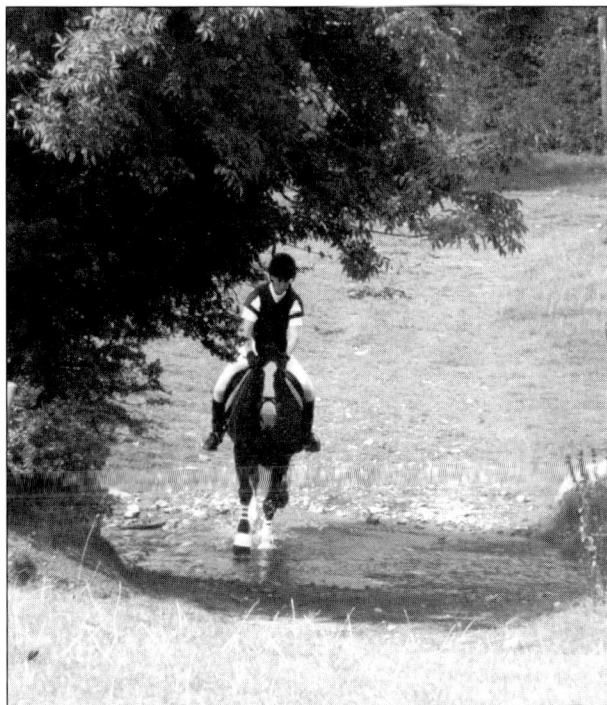

OPPOSITE PAGE: *Ceremonial; Joseph McGrath driving his pair of grey mares at Punchestown.* Photo: Caroline Norris

ABOVE: *Dressage; extended trot; Beezies Sue.* Photo: Tony Hessian

LEFT: *Cross-country events; Irish Draught and rider negotiating a river.* Photo: Mary McGrath

An Garda Síochána

The Garda Mounted Unit recognises the value of the Irish Draught horse. They will soon have a full complement of fifteen Irish Draught geldings on their force. Draughts have been chosen because of their temperament, soundness and calmness under difficult conditions. Other police forces in Canada, Australia and New Zealand are showing interest in recruiting these Irish horses for their own mounted units. Their endorsement confirms qualities that are eminently suitable for the ordinary rider.

ABOVE: *Two members of the Royal Canadian Mounted Police (pictured with two Garda Mounted Unit members prior to the parade) rode garda horses in the 2004 St Patrick's Day Parade in Dublin; (left to right) Garda Den Burns on Western Rajah (sire Blue Rajah, dam Western Starlight), Constable Nilu Singh on Realt Ban, Garda Lorraine Gibbons on Boru (sire Huntingfield Rebel, dam Teach Mhic Chonaill) and Constable Corey Carlisle on Macha.* Photos: Garda Mounted Unit

CLOCKWISE FROM TOP LEFT:

Garda mount Macha (sire Silver Granite, dam Boston Princess) with Garda Peter Woods at the St Patrick's Day Parade in Dublin, 2003.

Garda mounts on duty at a demonstration outside Dáil Éireann, 2002. Photo: *Sunday Tribune*

Garda mount Ferdia is pictured here with Commissioner Pat Byrne and Garda Peter Woods at his official handover ceremony, Tallaght, February 2003.

PART 3

Resources

The Irish Draught Horse in Publications

Joan C. Griffith

In order to fully understand the Irish Draught horse and its place in written texts, one must also understand its relationship to the present-day Irish Sport Horse, formerly known as the Irish halfbred or Irish hunter. It is also important to consider the history of Ireland itself and especially Irish farming practices. Nearly every farm in Ireland had a horse and that horse was the Irish Draught. The search for materials on the Irish Draught horse must go beyond the traditional research venues such as the library; one must also seek out more general and popular information in horse magazines, auction catalogues, show programmes and photographic collections; from local farmers and horse dealers; and at old-time traditional Irish fairs. Access to private records is also important; without it, it would not have been possible to compile much of this resource guide.

Terminology used to identify what we know today as the Irish Draught horse has varied widely throughout the generations; for the various purposes for which it was used, the following terms must be considered: working horse, creamery cob, tram horse, farm horse, farmer's horse, carthorse, vanner, omnibus horse, trooper's horse, non-thoroughbred horse, halfbred horse, Irish Sport Horse, pure-bred Irish Draught, part-bred Irish Draught, Irish hunter, heavyweight hunter, mediumweight hunter, lightweight hunter, high-class hunter, registered Irish Draught horse, Appendix Irish Draught mare, and – simply – draught horse.

Historically, there have been few books published covering exclusively the Irish Draught horse; those that have are all recent publications. This bibliography endeavours to document whatever information is or was available about the Irish Draught horse. This bibliography started with one article from *Horse and Hound* magazine, published in 1998, which piqued my interest in the breed but left many unanswered questions.

The search for information was on, a search that quickly lead me to *The Irish Draught Horse* by Alex Fell, published as part of the J.A. Allen Breed Series in 1991. At about the same time – in the early 1990s – Dr Charlotte Moore published two works, *Irish Draught Mares 1918-1992* and *Irish Draught Stallions 1911-1993*. For almost a decade these were the only publications available.

Though not readily available, Helen O'Toole has brought together a great deal of new information in her 2001 master's thesis, *The Characterisation of the Irish Draught Horse Population in Ireland*. In early 2002 Nicholas O'Hare published a sort of trilogy: a revised edition of his 1978 publication, *The King of Diamonds*, and first editions of *The Modern Irish Draught* and *The Irish Sport Horse*. Two of these books deal primarily with the draught, while the other is concerned with its halfbred relations. In 2003 both the IDHS and one of its branches, the Irish Draught Horse Society, Northern Ireland (IDHS-NI), both published twenty-fifth anniversary books, *IDHS 25 Years* and *Solid Silver*. Prior to these publications, it appears that only the IDHS yearbooks and promotional flyers addressed the Irish Draught horse directly.

A number of author names crop up again and again in the IDHS yearbooks, including those of Sally Begg, Colin A. Lewis, Nicholas O'Hare, Charlotte and Nigel Moore, Norman Storey, Michael Slavin, to name but a few. A number of equine correspondents also published in provincial and national newspapers, including Michael Slavin, Nicholas O'Hare, Grania Willis and others.

In many other Irish horse-related publications, the Irish Draught horse is mentioned in a few paragraphs, and oftentimes the Irish Draught is not recognised or inaccurately cited, especially in relation to the identification of the breed, which is all too often stated as 'not recorded' or 'unknown', when in truth the dam or sire, granddam or grandsire was an Irish Draught. On the other hand, if one knows where to look, it is not impossible to find a wealth of information about the Irish Draught. Granted, this may mean that the reader must possess a broad knowledge of pedigrees and breeders in order to ascertain the parentage of the animal in question, but to a large degree the Irish Horse Board publications – *Irish Sport Horse Studbook Approved Stallions, Supplemental Stallions, Registered Irish Draught Mares, Irish Sport Horse Marebook*, and *Registered Foals* – provide the needed data if one is willing to take the time to understand the arrangement of the information. The scope of this annotated bibliography is intended to be inclusive rather than exclusive, so as to bring together useful sources that tell the story of the Irish Draught horse in Ireland. It is hoped that this resource guide will allow future scholars to further study the Irish Draught horse. It does not, however, purport to include specific information on breeders or the pedigree of individual animals; that information can usually be found in various directories and websites.

As far as this author has been able to determine, there is no archive or library collection in Ireland, or anywhere else in the world for that matter, which collects the materials necessary to do scholarly research on the Irish Draught horse. Irish university libraries do not begin to have basic collections; the Irish Horse Board, and even the Irish Draught Horse Society itself, do not have complete records or complete archives of the activities of the horses that they are charged with fostering. This is in part due to the fact that the Irish Draught horse was, for such a long time, part of the fabric of life of the Irish farmer; it was what would be termed today as part of 'popular culture', and that meant much information, including photographs of the day, being discarded as having little value. To some extent, record keeping was rather poor and incomplete. This is regrettable, as the historical materials about this breed will surely be lost if not collected and maintained properly. As the Irish Draught horse can now be classified as an endangered breed by the most standard definition, it is hoped that this book, and this chapter in particular, will stimulate interest in learning more about the Irish Draught and encourage those who care about the breed to collect and maintain the materials: the books, journal articles, yearbooks, newspaper articles, show videos and auction catalogues needed for further research. A future goal might be to start an oral-history project to record the living memory of the people who kept and bred these animals, and to amass a documented collection worthy of donating to an appropriate library or archive.

The following information is included for each item reviewed: author, title, publisher and date of publication, followed by a brief descriptive and evaluative paragraph. The purpose of the annotation is to inform the reader of the relevance, accuracy and quality of the source cited. In some cases, due to the nature of the material, only a summary is provided. The coverage of this resource bibliography includes selective primary and secondary materials, such as trade books, vanity publications, university publications, society publications, government publications, sale catalogues, show programmes, articles from journals, magazines and newspapers, chapters and pages in books, internet resources, websites, databases and List Servs.

The bibliography is divided into seven sections:

1. Early Works
2. Books and Journal Articles
3. Irish Draught Horse Society Publications
4. Irish Horse Board Publications
5. Show and Sale Catalogues
6. Newspapers
7. Electronic and Multimedia Publications

Within the sections items are listed alphabetically by author's last name, or otherwise by title. For authors with more than one publication, works have been listed together to show a more comprehensive arrangement of the scope of their work.

The generous assistance of Irish horse breeders, Irish libraries and museums, Irish societies, Irish government records and the owners of various private collections in Ireland is gratefully acknowledged. With the exception of information available on websites related to the Irish Draught horse, this resource bibliography concentrates on publications of the nineteenth through to the twenty-first centuries, from the Republic of Ireland and Northern Ireland, where the vast majority of primary materials were originally produced.

1. Early Works

The early works set the stage for the horse in general terms and to some degree describe the framework and environment from which the Irish Draught horse evolved. There is little else published on the topic remaining; some titles listed in library catalogues are misplaced or lost, or are at least not to be found at the time of writing.

There is a sentence in several of the books listed in this bibliography that reads, 'The first authentic reference to the Irish Draught horse dates from the close of the eighteenth century'; however, no actual reference is included in these publications to identify the source of this information. These writers may, in fact, be drawing from the report of the Commission on Horse Breeding, where it is mentioned that Dr Cox prepared an interesting treatise on Irish horses that shows that from 1740 both racehorses and draught horses alike were constantly imported and scattered over the country. In his *Notes on the History of the Irish Horse*, Cox states that draught horses were mentioned as early as 1565 in official state papers, although we can only assume he meant Irish Draught horses, and not a more general term for working horses.

Carden, R.G., 'The Irish Hunter', pp. 228-38, in *The Horses of the British Empire*, vol. 1, edited by Sir Humphrey F. De Trafford (Walter Southwood and Co. Ltd., London, undated, *c.* 1907).

This is the often-quoted article by Carden that relates information he collected on the origin and history of Irish horse breeding and particularly the makings of the 'hunter'. In common with others, he quotes the words of Sir William Temple: 'Horses in Ireland are a drug, but might be made a commodity, not alone of greater use at home, but also fit for exportation into other countries'. A couple of the reports refer to the Irish horses as being 'shy' due to growing up in the fields until of ridden age, thereby having little human handling. It also includes newspaper reports of horses being imported from Morocco (1742). 'We are told that, prior to about the year 1850, there was a breed of horse in Ireland known as the "Irish cart or draught horse"', and 'Irish Draught horses proved to be the best hunters of their time'. There are many quotable phrases in this excellent piece on the Irish hunter. Carden also reviews the work of the royal commission of 1896 under Earl Cadogan, the work of the Department of Agriculture and Technical Instruction of Ireland, the Royal Dublin Society. In addition, he comments on horse shows, fairs and hunting, and draws reasonable conclusions as to the way forward in Irish horse breeding.

Commission on Horse Breeding, Ireland, *Reports by the Commissioners Appointed to Inquire into the Horse Breeding Industry in Ireland* (Dublin, printed for Her Majesty's Stationery Office by Alexander Thom and Co., 19 July 1897, C–8561). 'The report of the Chairman and Others, Wyndham Thomas, Earl of Dunraven KP to his Excellency George Henry, Earl of Cadogan KG, Lord Lieutenant-General and General Governor of Ireland'. The commission formulated questions that were sent out to interested individuals all over the country. Key figures of the day were invited to testify, and Dr Cox

was invited to give historical information on Irish horse breeding. He cited a number of sources, including Mr Kenny who describes 'the old Irish mares', and Maxwell's *Wild Sports of the West*, published in 1838, in which he says, 'during the last century the West of Ireland was celebrated for its well-boned and enduring animal, that without any pretension to extraordinary speed, was sufficiently fast for fox hounds and an excellent weight carrier, and, better still, able to live with any dogs, and in any country'. Cox also cited Sir William Temple's much-quoted 'Horses in Ireland are a drug'. Cox speaks of the 'draft' horse and 'cart' horse, while some witnesses referred to the Irish 'draft' or 'carthorse' of the 'old-established type'. The committee reviewed the Congested Districts and have reports on horse breeding practices in each. There is also much discussion of the hackney stallion.

The Earl of Enniskillen reported on various horse types: agricultural, hunters, cavalry, jobmasters, halfbred as hunter sires, Thoroughbred stallions, ponies and hackneys. Some of the members seemed to favour using the hackney to improve other breeds, while a dissenting group headed by Enniskillen thought it would be better to financially encourage all breeds and registration, and he publicly disagreed with Dunraven's report.

Cox, Michael, F., *Notes on the History of the Irish Horse* (Sealy, Bryers and Walker, Dublin, 1897).

Compiled by Cox, a member of the senate of the Royal University of Ireland, from various sources including sales notices and other books of the day, such as the Brehon Laws and the Archives of Modena (Italy). There are wonderful references to the exportation of Irish horses as well as the importation of other breeds into Ireland – for example, the 'Spanish wanted to buy Irish horses, not sell Spanish horses, in 1601' – and a reference to state papers of 1565: 'We find draught horses occasionally referred to in the State Papers as caballi, always; Irish, *capal*'. There is mention of the Irish hobby in a series of state papers dealing with Irish horses, and reference to the Archives of Venice and Modena from the period 1480-1534. This a totally obscure reference work but a joy to read and re-read.

Department of Agriculture and Technical Instruction, Ireland, *Irish Draught Horse Book* (HM Stationery Office, 1918-32), vols. 1-4.

Volume 1 covers stallions number 1 to 51, mares 1 to 375; volume 2 covers stallions 1 to 59, mares 1 to 543, and so on. Each time a new volume was produced the introductory information was reprinted and original lists were recorded and added to from the last edition. Volume 1, at 60 pages and 21 centimetres in size is more like a pamphlet than a book. The volumes consist of an alphabetical listing of stallions with their registry number, owner, breeder and pedigree, an A–Z list of owners, and an A–Z list of mares with owner, breeder, pedigree and progeny. As far as can be determined, the Irish Horse Board does not have original copies of these books; volumes can only be found in libraries or in private collections. Interesting to note is that in addition to the copies at the National Library of Ireland there are only three libraries in the world with volumes: there is a compete run at Cambridge University library, and partial runs at the National Library of Scotland (vols. 1, 2, 4, and 5) and New York Public Library (vols. 1 and 4).

Scharff, Robert Francis, 'On the Irish horse and its early history', proceedings of the Royal Irish Academy, vol. xxvii, section b, no. 6, March 1909 (Hodges, Figgis, and Co. Ltd., Dublin, 1909).

This article describes the historical remains of the '*Crannóg* skulls' and the information about Arabian and Libyan horse influences in Irish breeding. He notes that the Irish horse differs markedly from the heavy races of England and the Continent in that it resembles in certain aspects the Arab horse. While some say this influence came with the importation of Spanish horses,

he maintains that this Arab blood dates back to the tenth century, whereas the Spanish blood did not arrive until the 1600s. Scharff's work is often quoted in historical studies of the introduction and development of horses in Ireland.

Youatt, William, *The horse, with a treatise on draught; and a copious index,* published under the superintendence of the society for the diffusion of useful knowledge (Library of Useful Knowledge, Baldwin and Cradock, London, 1831).

An interesting work as it outlines the various horse breeds in the history of the horse and lastly mentions the Irish horse. The treatise on draught in the subtitle is an essay about the power of the horse: how it is calculated, the difference of opinion as to wheels, the act of drawing and the resistance to the power employed, the moving power, etc. Breeds described include horses from pre-Christian times in Egypt and Greece, wild horses of the plains of Great Tartary, Arabs, Dongola, east Indian, Chinese, Persian, Toorkoman, Tartar, Calmuck, Turkish, German, Swedish, Finish, Norwegian, Icelandic, French, Spanish, Italian and American. There is also a long section on the history of the English horse, including the road horse, farmer's horse, coach horse, heavy draught, cavalry horse, racehorse, Arabians, the hunter, Galloway and ponies.

There are three sections of this work which help us understand the background of the Irish horse: the farmer's horse, the hunter and the Irish horse. Of the farmer's horse he writes:

> The Farmer's horse is an animal of all-work; to be ridden occasionally to market or for pleasure, but to be principally employed for draught … A farmer, and, more particularly, a small farmer, will prefer a mare to a gelding, both for riding and driving. She will not cost him so much at first; and he will get a great deal more out of her. There can be no doubt

that, taking bulk for bulk, a mare is stronger and more lasting than a gelding; and, in addition to this, the farmer has her to breed from.

Of the hunter he writes,

> The hunter, however, or the hunting horse, i.e. the horse on which a farmer, if he be not a professed sportsman may occasionally with pleasure, and without disgrace, follow the hounds, is in value and beauty next to the racer …

Of the Irish horse he writes,

> For leaping the Irish horse is unrivalled. It is not, however, the leaping of the English horse, striding as it were over a low fence, and stretched at his full length over a higher one; it is the proper jump of the deer, beautiful to look at, difficult to sit, and, both in height and extent, unequalled by the English horse.

2. Books and Journal Articles

Books and journal articles in this section were primarily found in private collections. Some information was found in Irish libraries, primarily the National Library of Ireland in Dublin. Many of these titles are difficult if not impossible to find, for they did not receive wide distribution at the time of publication. A few critical *IDHS Yearbook* articles have been selectively described as they add enormous insights into the body of knowledge about the Irish Draught.

Begg, Sally, 'The Thoroughbred influence and traditional working strains', *IDH Yearbook*, 1979, pp. 31-37.
In this *Yearbook* article, Begg – a noted breeder and owner of Irish Draught – traces the pedigree of 64 RID stallions back to the original foundation lines, and details those with Thoroughbred sires and those whose dams are by Thoroughbred sires. Additionally, she looks at those RID stallions whose dams were sired by registered halfbred sires, as well as the contribution made by a Clydesdale stallion who was bred to a Thoroughbred mare but whose progeny was registered as an RID stallion. She debunks some traditional pedigree myths, and to date these seem not to have been challenged. Useful pedigree charts are included.

Begg, Sally, 'A study of the development within the breed over the past five years', *IDH Yearbook*, 1983, pp. 27-33.
In this article, Begg updates her work of 1979 with reference to various stallion lines alive at the time in Ireland and England (totalling 71). Top stallion sire lines go back to Young J.P., with 56 – due in part to the progeny of two stallions, King of Diamonds (eight sons on the register) and Pride of Shaunlara (ten sons on the register). The rarest lines were Woodranger, Prince Henry, Young Authur (represented by Timohoe Heather, England), Glenside and Rusheen Lad (both of Ireland) respectively with one each. Begg maintains that stallions exported to the UK were the more traditional, heavy type, and that those in Ireland were becoming the modern competition type. Pedigree charts are included and updated.

Browne, Noel Phillips, *The Horse in Ireland* (Pelham Books Ltd., 1967).
This book is a collection of essays about the horse in Ireland. The Irish Draught horse is mentioned in the introductory chapter as an important part of Irish horse breeding. Browne, a racing commentator and breeder, rightly believes that the fate of the Irish Draught is in the hands of the Department of Agriculture and its breeding-incentive schemes. He goes on to suggest in 1967 that unless a breed society is formed the Irish Draught horse as a separate breed will become a part

of history. (The breed society was not formed until 1976.) An excellent all-round history on Irish horse breeding.

Clayton, Michael, *The Hunter: Horse, Cob and Pony* (Country Life Books, Surrey, 1980).
Clayton was at one time the editor of *Horse & Hound* and wrote extensively on hunting. In a chapter on hunter breeding, the Irish Draught is identified as the foundation stock for the hunter-type horse: the draught mare put to a Thoroughbred stallion producing a wonderful hunter type. Clayton believes that the reverse cross – Thoroughbred mare to Irish Draught stallion – is not as suitable. This book is perfect for the uninitiated in hunting classes as it describes clearly the different classes in which the hunter type is shown: heavyweight (to carry 14 stones); middleweight (12½-14 stones); lightweight (12½ stones); small hunters (by height, up to 15.2 hands); ladies' hunter (ridden side-saddle), novice hunter and working hunter. Informative to read with a number of good photographs from both Irish and English venues.

Cotter, Billy and Powell, Jack, 'The great debate: a breed or a type', *IDHS Yearbook*, 1981, pp. 17-22.
In this *Yearbook* article, Billy Cotter, life president of the Irish Draught Horse Society, maintains that the Irish Draught is in itself a breed and that he can trace the breeding of his horses for centuries. Jack Powell, Irish Draught horse judge, says it is a type and that the closing of the Irish Draught book was wrong. This debate has been conducted for many years by many people. The final answer probably depends on more DNA research.

Duggan, Eugene, *Horse and Hand: Farming practices of the parish of Lackagh during the first half of the twentieth century* (Athenry, County Galway, 2000).
A book about farming life in a small parish that includes information and customs about stock kept on farms and a chapter on the horse. Duggan describes how farmers borrowed other horses to make up teams for ploughing (locally they called this 'in-co', meaning 'in co-operation'). Duggan recalls that though Shires, Clydesdales and Irish Draught were used to do work on the farm, the farmer favoured the Irish Draught, a multi-purpose animal able to pull a plough, to till, sow, mow, reap and cart, as well as being used to drive to town and to Mass with a sidecar (jaunting car) or trap. The book includes photographs of many farm machines pulled by horses.

Edwards, Elwyn Hartley, *Horses: Their Role in the History of Man* (Willow Books, London, 1987).
Based on a Scottish television series, the author has edited over 30 books on horses and horsemanship, and was also an editor of *Horse & Hound*. One interesting photograph in this book is of Irish-draught-type horses that had been abandoned by the British in Cairo during the 1930s, where the Brooke Hospital for Old Warhorses was founded (now the Brooke Hospital for Animals). Otherwise, the Irish Draught is mentioned for use as an 'omnibus' horse or 'tram' horse, often a mare, doing work of the most severe kind with two out of three dying in service. An excellent overall book about the horse.

Fell, Alex, *The Irish Draught Horse* (Allen Breed Series, J.A. Allen and Company Ltd., London, 1991).
This has been the 'book of record' for the Irish Draught horse. As part of the Allen Breed Series, Fell did in-depth research and pulled together in detail an introduction to the breed, its history and the pedigree of foundation stallion lines. She interviewed a number of breeders of the day for this little book that is packed with lots of useful information. The book includes many photographs not seen in other publications, including some by Ruth Rogers, a photographer for the Irish Horse

Board during the 1980s. The author is a lifelong enthusiast of the breed, as well as a judge in the UK. Sadly, this book is out of print, though it can sometimes be found on websites selling second-hand books. This publication may have caused a revolution in books about the breed as it seems to have been the first published exclusively on the topic.

Flanagan, James, 'The role of the horse in rural policies from an Irish perspective', EU Equus 2001 Conference, Skara, Sweden, 12-13 June 2001, available at www.euequus 2001.nu/matierla/flanagan.doc James Flanagan is the chief inspector at the Department of Agriculture, Food and Rural Development, Ireland. His report outlines the financing of the Thoroughbred and non-thoroughbred or Sport Horse sectors. Information regarding the Irish Horse Board states that is was established in 1994 as a breeders'/producers' organisation. This paper outlines monetary aspects of the Irish horse industry. Includes information on the percentages of foals registered in the *Irish Horse Register* from 1982–2000.

Holden, Bryan, *The Long Haul: the life and times of the railway horse* (J.A. Allen, London, 1985).
While most of the photographs in this book are certainly not of the Irish Draught, there are a few that are to the greatest probability Irish Draught type, including a two-horse omnibus, express parcel and delivery vans. There are also examples of heavy and light harnesses for working horses, and a wide range of horse breeds used in work, from pit ponies in the mines to Clydesdales in train yards. Interesting, though not totally related to the Irish Draught; it does, however, present a view on the life of working horses of a bygone era.

Holdstock, Mark, *The Great Fair: horse dealing at Ballinasloe* (Souvenir Press, 1993).
This book describes the Ballinasloe fair in great detail, and includes chapters on farmers' and travellers' horses.

Holdstock believes the Irish Draught to be a cross of the Irish hobby and the larger Norman horses that came to Ireland during the invasions. Other working horses which may have played a part are the Shire, Clydesdale and Suffolk Punch. Good photographs of the fair and historic practices of how the deal was done. Holdstock notes that horses at the fair are either half-bred or three-quarter-bred Irish Draught, with very few Thoroughbred. A horse may change hands three or four times during the day, with the price going up with each deal.

Horse & Hound, publishes a sport-horse-breeding special in March of every year. The issue for 26 March 1998 includes a profile of Irish-draught-stud owner, Moira McKenna.

Irish Field Directory, an annual publication of the *Irish Field*. Includes directories of studs, stallions, trainers, jockeys, hunting ogransations, riding centres, riding clubs, pony clubs, polo clubs, etc. Irish Draught breeders and sellers can be found in the listings.

Kelly, Fergus (ed.), *Early Irish Farming: a study based mainly on the law texts of the 7th and 8th centuries* AD (School of Celtic Studies, Dublin Institute for Advanced Studies, 1997), Early Irish Law Series iv.
This work, based on law texts of the seventh and eighth centuries, is a massive volume (751 pages) covering aspects of law in relation to all types of farm livestock, and includes translations from early manuscripts detailing laws against offences by domestic animals, offences against domestic animals, accidents, diseases, horse qualities, etc. There are two types of horses mentioned: the workhorse and the riding horse. Interesting information about how early Irish riders rode with a saddle cloth, not a saddle, which were introduced by the Norsemen. A scholarly work that should not be overlooked.

Lewis, Colin A., *Horse Breeding in Ireland and the Role of the Royal Dublin Society's Horse Breeding Schemes 1886-1903* (J.A. Allen Company Ltd., London, 1980); 'Irish horse breeding and the Irish Draught, 1917-1978', *Agricultural History Review*, vol. 31, 1983, part 1, pp. 37-49; 'The horse breeding industry in Ireland', with Mary E. McCarthy, *Irish Geography*, vol. 10 (1977), pp. 72-89; *From Hobby to Irish Draft* (forthcoming: working title, to be published by Geography Publishers, Dublin, 2004).

Professor Lewis has published widely on the Irish horse and the Irish Draught. Being one of the early authors in the *Irish Draught Horse Yearbook*, he contributed a series of articles on the height of mares, the distribution of stallions, etc., later published as 'Irish horse breeding and the Irish Draught horse, 1917-1978', in the *Agricultural History Review*, vol. 31, 1983, part 1. With his geographer's hat on, he provides a unique perspective on the Irish Draught horse, and plots out the data in map format. His best work, by far, is his award-winning title, *Horse Breeding in Ireland*, which won the National University of Ireland's prize for Irish historical research. The book deals primarily with the halfbred horse and the Royal Dublin Society breeding schemes of 1886-1903, and includes some details and distribution maps on the Irish Draught. This book is out of print. Professor Lewis also published a series of articles in the *Irish Draught Horse Yearbook* about the development and distribution of the Irish Draught.

Maguire, Desmond, *Horses Are My Life: the story of Ned Cash King of the horse dealers.*

A fun read with reminiscences about the life and dealing of Ned Cash, who was, by all accounts, a real character in the world of horse buying and selling. Irish Draught were prominent in his early trading. It includes interesting photographs taken at the fairs and on farms. Maguire was a news editor for the *Irish Farmers' Journal*, and by way of interviews and conversations was able to assemble a collection of short pieces that conjure up what it must have been like to walk in Ned's shoes. Ned Cash's second wife, the successful rider Frances Cash, is also mentioned.

Moore, Charlotte, *Irish Draught Mares 1918-1992* (C. Moore, July 1993); *Irish Draught Stallions 1911-1993* (C. Moore, 1993).

Moore has created a valuable pedigree-research tool, assembled over a number of years and from a number of sources. In these two volumes, she has compiled relevant data on the RID stallions of Ireland and the UK, as well as the Irish RID and AID mares. Using these indices it is possible to trace the 'back breeding' of an animal by using its *Irish Horse Register* number and registered Irish Draught (RID) number. She records the animal name, sire, dam, year of birth, colour, height, county of breeder and owner. Moore is a life-long enthusiast of the breed, as well as a breeder. These publications are available from the author.

Ó Dochartaigh, Niamh, *The Galway Show: the story 1892–2000* (Galway County Show Society).

Adorned with mostly black-and-white photographs, this special publication includes some information about the Galway Show and its history, together with photographs of Irish Draught winners, such as RID stallion Coille Mór Hill, John Shorten with his champion mare with foal at foot, and the best young ID mare, Drimcong Pride.

O'Hare, Nicholas, *The Irish Sport Horse: the 21st century performance horse* (Harkaway, 2002); *King of Diamonds: an Irish showjumping dynasty* (Harkaway, 1997, revised 2002); *The Modern Irish Draught: a special breed for a special purpose* (Harkaway, 2002); 'Origin of the Irish Draught', *Irish Draught Horse Yearbook*, 1978, pp. 6-14, (reprinted in 1983 *Yearbook*).

Nicholas O'Hare is probably better qualified than most to author this trilogy of books on the Irish

Draught/Irish Sport Horse, having been an equine correspondent and journalist for many decades as well as the editor of the *Irish Draught Horse Yearbook* (1978-85). He has also contributed numerous newspaper articles over the years. In each of these books, O'Hare points out the significance of Thoroughbred blood in the back breeding of the draught, and clearly has a viewpoint on the way forward for the breed. Books are available from the author. Only disappointment here is the lack of photographs.

The Irish Sport Horse: the 21st century performance horse
In terms of providing an overview of the political landscape related to the Irish Sport Horse and Irish horse breeding in general, this book really hits the mark. Unlike the *King of Diamonds* and *Modern Irish Draught*, O'Hare digs deep in his knowledge to ponder the horses that have made their names in Irish horse breeding in the twentieth century, and sets the stage for the twenty-first century. He brings together his vast knowledge of the Thoroughbred, the halfbred horse, the Irish Draught, and the newcomer on the scene, the European warm-blood.

King of Diamonds: an Irish showjumping dynasty
O'Hare details the role of the RID stallion, King of Diamonds, said to be one of the key sires and grandsire of show jumpers. Although this stallion was essentially a halfbred horse himself, he was nevertheless RID. He sired more than 40 registered sons, both pure-bred and halfbred. The book details all of his progeny, first, second, third and fourth generations – primarily the stallion lines – and a few special mares that bred some of his best sons. Although some of the entries only list the pedigree (which can be found elsewhere), other entries have much commentary from O'Hare, and these are most interesting as his insights go a long way to describe these animals.

The Modern Irish Draught: a special breed for a special purpose
The breeding of the modern Irish Draught is traced in what O'Hare considers to be the most influential draught lines: King of Diamonds, Clover Hill, Pride of Shaunlara, Ben Purple, Laughton and Slievenamon. He provides brief sketches on the offspring of these stallions as well as his usual commentary on the horses and some of the owners. He also includes a section on mares, and reports on a number of them from the last quarter of the twentieth century.

'Origin of the Irish Draught'
O'Hare considers critical information about the possible origins of the Irish Draught horse in this early work from the 1978 *IDHS Yearbook*, drawing from Scharff, the Brehon Laws, Irish horse mythology, Blundenville, Duke of Ormonde, Sir William Temple, Carden, Department of Agriculture, *Irish Draught Horse Book*, up to and including the missing registers which supposedly disappeared in 1972.

O'Molloy, Desmond Art, 'Power unit of the future: the Irishmen who stick by their native draught breed', *Heavy Horse World*, 12, 1, 1998, p. 18.
A one-page commentary on two Irishmen who continue to use Irish Draught as their 'power units' on the farm. This article is certainly in support of the 'green dream' farming profile to reduce reliance on fuel consumption and stop environmental damage by utilising horse power. There is a trend in Ireland and indeed in Europe to use the horse instead of the tractor to do small jobs and, increasingly, work related to forestry.

O'Toole, Helen, 'The characterisation of the Irish Draught horse population in Ireland', thesis submitted in fulfilment of the degree of Master of Agricultural Science, Faculty of Agriculture, Department of Animal

Science and Production, National University of Ireland, Dublin, November 2001.

Since completing this masters degree in agricultural science, Helen O'Toole is now working for the Department of Agriculture. She studied the decline in the number of pure-bred foals from 1990-99 as well as past breeding practices and their effects on the genetic composition of the breed. The study looks at data from 1997-2000. It is interesting that the study showed an increase in foals by RID parents but a decrease in foals by AID parents. However, the statistics clearly show that RID mares do not reproduce themselves with enough 'pure-bred filly foals' in their breeding life span. A conservation plan is proposed. The thesis is available at University College Dublin library.

Quarton, Marjorie, *Breakfast the Night Before: recollections of an Irish horse dealer* (Andre Deutsch, 1989; revised and incorporating material from *Saturday's Child*, Lilliput Press, 1993).

A tear jerker for anyone who likes to read horse stories. Quarton writes with clarity and recollects her life of horse dealing and farm life in County Tipperary. Untypical as she was – a woman in a man's world – she brings her experiences to life with vivid and interesting accounts. Irish Draught and halfbred horses played a large role in her buying and selling of horses. A book not to be missed. A bestseller when first published, one of a rarity of horse books to be reprinted.

Sheedy, Larry (ed.), *Sixty-five years of ploughing for progress, 1931-1996,* (National Ploughing Association of Ireland, Athy, first edn. 1981, second edn 1996). This publication includes substantial contributions from Professor Seamus Sheehy, Sean McConnell, Charlotte Brenner and Denis Murphy. There have been national ploughing championships in Ireland since 1931. Originally with horse and plough, today it is mainly undertaken with tractor and plough. The competitions

have 21 classes, three of which are horse ploughing, including a prize for the 'best presented pair of Irish Draught horses'. An interesting view on a popular farmers' event, the book is available from the association.

Slavin, Michael, *Showjumping Legends Ireland 1868-1998* (Wolfhound Press, 1998).

Slavin has until recently been the voice of the Irish equine on RTÉ radio, and has also written and spoken widely on the Irish horse and Irish Draught. He brings his vast knowledge of the sporting world to this book which follows the showjumping world for over 100 years. Primarily speaking about the halfbred horse, he brings the legendary animals and riders to life. The Irish Draught is mentioned, but only slightly – rather as the sire or dam of a famous showjumper. Well written, well researched, the book provides an excellent historical perspective. Slavin also owns and operates the Tara Hill Bookshop where some of the books in this bibliography were found. Well worth the visit. Slavin still contributes articles to local newspapers on equine topics.

Smith, Brian, *The Horse in Ireland* (Wolfhound Press, 1991).

A truly wonderful book about Irish horses. Smith, a former education officer with the Horse Board, writes on every aspect of the Irish horse from the earliest times to the present day. Topics include sporting horses of the eighteenth and nineteenth century, treatment in folklore, and the development of racing, showjumping and eventing. The Irish Draught horse is mentioned, but only on a few pages in the section about native horses and current uses. The book contains many photographs, some full-page colour, others black and white. Nothing new here about the Irish Draught, but a good book (366 pages) on the Irish horse.

Storey, Norman, *Irish Draught Broodmare Report 2001* prepared by the IDHS Breeding Committee, available

on the IDHS website:
www.irishdraught.ie/rid-broodmarereport2001-01.asp

Teagasc, *Sport Horse Production, Alternative Enterprise Booklet,* no. 4, 1997, revised edition; published *c.* 1990 as *Non-thoroughbred Horse Production.*
A resource for the small farmer. Teagasc provides a number of useful booklets on horse breeding. This booklet is a generalists' view on selection of type of horse to breed (show jumper, show horse, event horse, Irish Draught or riding), management of the yearling, grassland management, nutrition and financial aspects. Especially useful for those who see horse breeding as a secondary activity on the farm.

Watson, Mervyn, 'The role of the horse on Irish farms', *From Corrib to Cultra* (Institute of Irish Studies, Queen's University, Belfast, *c.* 2000), pp. 122-135.
Watson gives an overview of the various horse breeds native to Ireland: Celtic pony, hobby, Connemaras, Cushendall pony, Kerry bog pony, Irish Draught, and the the UK imports, Shire and Clydesdales. Interesting that the Connemara, Kerry bog and Irish Draught were all used as multi-purpose animals for riding, carting, ploughing, hauling, and so on. But the Irish Draught had the unique role of serving as the foundation breed for the Irish hunter.

3. Irish Draught Horse Society Publications

The IDHS has, over the years, produced a number of publications relating to its annual events, shows, sales and breeding statistics, as well as promotional information about the society and the Irish Draught horse itself. The following materials represent the hard work of a volunteer-based group dedicated to promotion and education about the breed. In recognition of their keen interest in the topic, these people have been termed both enthusiasts and propagandists.

The Irish Draught Horse Society (IDHS) is a membership-based group; contact:

Helen Kelly
IDHS Secretariat
Derrynagara
Collinstown
County Westmeath
Ireland

In general, the IDHS was created: (1) to preserve, promote and endeavour to improve all that is best the Irish Draught horse; (2) to encourage and assist those interested in the preservation, promotion and improvement of the Irish Draught horse, especially breeders and owners; (3) to establish a breed standard, definition and description for the Irish Draught horse and to update this as the society sees fit; (4) to protect the standard of the breed by ensuring that the only inspections carried out in any part of the world for acceptance onto the studbook and register are carried out by inspectors authorised by the society; (5) to appoint a panel of judges and inspectors selected for their interest and knowledge of the Irish Draught and its breeding standards, and to make amendments and deletion of this list from time to time; (6) to encourage the continued improvement and upgrading of the Irish Draught horse by advocating the careful selection of mares and stallions chosen from good lines of breeding that conform to the breed standards proclaimed by the society from time to time.

Irish Draught Horse Society Yearbook, 1988 to present; continues the *Irish Draught Horse Yearbook 1978-85.*
In 1988 the Irish Draught Horse Society took over publication duty for the *IDHS Yearbook,* and in successive years it was produced under the editorial direction of several active members including Charlotte and Nigel

Moore, Sally Begg, Anne Loughnane, Dan Moore and others. No publication of the *Yearbook* in 2002 and 2003 due to preparation of the society's *25 Years* book. In early 2004 the society announced an open call for contributions for the next publication of the *Yearbook*. No publication date was set at the time.

Irish Draught Horse Yearbook, 1978-85 (Agricultural Publications Ltd., Dún Laoghaire, County Dublin), continued as the *Irish Draught Horse Society Yearbook*, 1988 to present.

From 1978-83, the *Yearbook* was under the editorial direction of Nicholas O'Hare, and more or less in conjunction with the Irish Draught Horse Society and/or Bord na gCapall. It was published by various versions of Irish Agricultural Publications Ltd. and at least once as a supplement to the *Irish Farmers' Monthly*. The *Yearbook* had an annual marketing niche that included wide distribution to magazine subscribers. There seems to have been no *Yearbook* published in 1984 (*see* entry for *Irish Horse and Pony Yearbook*, 1984-85).

By 1985 it was produced by an editorial committee made up of Marily Power, Nigel Moore and Noel Cawley. During this period many well-written-and-researched articles appeared by O'Hare, Colin A. Lewis, Sally Begg, Marily Power and others, with topics covering the origin of the Irish Draught horse (first printed in 1978 *Yearbook*; reprinted in 1983 *Yearbook*). Hunting, articles on specific stallions, health-care topics – shoeing, worming, etc. – and highlights of the Greenvale awards and Bord na gCapall incentive schemes. Early society enthusiasts endeavoured to record background information on the breed, and provided promotional and marketing ideas that were lacking at the time.

Irish Horse and Pony Yearbook, 1984-85; includes the *Irish Draught Horse Journal,* 1984.

Could this be the missing information for the unpublished 1984 *IDHS Yearbook*? No other issues of the *Irish Draught Horse Journal* are known to have been published. This publication seems to have been funded in part by the Irish Horse Board.

IDHS Breed Standard and Guideline

First published in *Irish Draught Horse Yearbook*, 1979. During the period 1979-2004, revisions to the breed standard included only slight changes in height of stallions and mares, amount of bone and colour. Information can be found on the IDHS website: www.irishdraught.ie/rid-breedstandard.asp

IDHS

The Irish Draught Horse: from earliest times to the present day, edited by Nicholas O'Hare and Michael Slavin (Irish Draught Horse Society, Dublin); commonly known as the 'History Book'.

This publication – issued twice, though with different cover photographs – is a good reference book from the society. Nicholas O'Hare and Michael Slavin bring together relevant information about the Irish horse, including myths, early scientific data, the Irish hobby, historical information from various sources, government support, Department of Agriculture inspectors' report, Irish draught as hunter, remounts, wartime needs, the new IDHS, Irish Mare Championships, the Greenvale years, Kerrygold winners, early shows, era of show jumpers, prominent stallions, opening of the Appendix for mares, 1988 IDHS Ireland and IDHS Great Britain.

IDHS *Newsletter*, commenced February 1996 as a quarterly, later changed to three times a year; edited by Michael Swords.

Covers the highlights of annual general meetings, council meetings, national shows and results, inspections, annual sales statistics, etc. Additionally, some branches have their own newsletters distributed to branch members. Some issues also available on the IDHS website: www.irishdraught.ie/ne-newsletter2002.asp

Irish Draught Horse Society – 25 Years (IDHS, 2003). Edited by Elizabeth Deane and Anne Loughnane. A collection of pieces from owners and breeders, as well as interviews with some 'old-timers' in the Irish Draught world. A wonderful book, with many photographs not seen before. The interviews are of special interest as they capture the recollections of some noted figures. However, this is not the 25-year history of the society as the title implies: it also includes pieces from a few of the members of the 'daughter societies' in Northern Ireland, Great Britain, New Zealand, Australia, US and Canada, as well as enthusiasts in Germany, South Africa and France. It clearly shows how the interest in the Irish Draught has become international. Available as hardcover and paperback.

IDHS Information Brochures

IDHS, Captain Tommy Ryan, 1996.
The Irish Draught Horse, c. 1998 (brochure with Suma Stud mares on the cover).
The Irish Draught Horse: a horse for all seasons 2002; includes examples of promotional materials from the society, general breed history, membership information, pure-bred and halfbred performers' pictorials. Includes contact information; available as pdf on IDHS website:
www.irishdraught.ie/idhs_bkl.pdf

IDHS Northern Ireland

Solid Silver: celebrating the silver jubilee of the Irish Draught Horse Society NI 1978-2003, Moira McKenna (ed.) (Alder Press, 2003).
Edited by Moira McKenna, this is the 25-year history of the Northern Ireland branch of the Irish Draught Horse Society. Filled with information and photographs from its beginnings in 1978 through to 2002, it includes lists of winners over the years, as well as how to read a passport and how to understand the difference between ID and RID. It is very well organised

and documented. Published in limited-edition hardcover of 200; also available as paperback.

4. Irish Horse Board Publications

The Irish Horse Board (IHB) is a co-operative society with over 12,000 members and a board of thirteen directors; ten represent five electoral regions and three are appointed by the Minister for Agriculture, Food and Rural Development. The objectives of the board are to promote the Irish Sport Horse, to maintain the *Irish Sport Horse Studbook*, to operate schemes to improve quality, and to promote equestrian tourism and equestrian education.

Irish Horse Board publications are available in printed format, on CD-Rom, or as downloadable pdfs from the IHB website. Used in combination, the publications of the Irish Horse Board give full details of the current status of Irish Draught horses. The Irish Horse Board is also responsible for the issuing of Irish horse passports. Contact:

Irish Horse Board
Maynooth Business Campus
Maynooth
County Kildare
Ireland

Archival publications housed at the Irish Horse Board, Maynooth, County Kildare

Irish Draught Horse Book, Register of Mares
The earliest of these are large, handwritten ledger volumes, while more recent volumes are smaller and typeset. The older listings include page-by-page information on the mares that passed inspection, owner/breeder names, notes on breeding, stallions used, progeny, notes on whether they went to slaughter or died, etc. Some of these volumes are in very brittle condition. A

paper ledger no longer exists, as up-to-date register information for mares is today kept in computerised databases, although the Board does retain original copies of foal-marking charts.

Horse Breeding Act 1934, List of Exempted Stallions

Sample volume covering stallions from 1902-24. A listing of stallions bought and sold by the department and used in its breeding schemes. Many old Irish Draught stallions of the period are recorded in these volumes. Interesting to note that for many of the Clydesdale stallions listed, notation indicates they were castrated after their first stud season because they produced inferior stock. Irish Draught stallions, on the other hand, were bought and sold and never a mention of any kind, leading one to believe that they were good producers of quality stock.

Approved Stallion Books

Covering many decades; samples from the 1950s, 1960s, 1970s, 1980s and 1990s (1987 cover photograph is of Grey Macha RID). Supplements are published in between printings of the annual.

IHB recent and current publications

Irish Sport Horse Studbook: approved stallions 2002-2003 incorporating stallion progeny performance (IHB, 2000). *Irish Sport Horse Studbook* is maintained jointly by the Irish Horse Board and the Northern Ireland Horse Board. This directory includes indices covering stallions by breed, stallions available for artificial insemination and index by county. Breed categories include Thoroughbred, Irish Sport Horse, registered Irish Draught, foreign breed, stallions standing abroad and approved for use in the IHR through AI, Arab, Connemara, riding pony and Appendix, together with deceased, exported, retired or excluded stallions whose progeny gained points in showjumping, eventing or dressage. Stallion pedigrees are shown, as well as breeder contact information. Progeny to have won points is listed. There is statistical information on coverings and registrations by listed stallions as well as a genetic index. This book has a supplement sheet of approved stallions (approximately five pages added to the list since publication of the last published book). The book also includes the rules and procedures of the *Irish Horse Register* for registrations, inspections, the issuing of passports and information on blood typing. The Irish Horse Board's inward-buyer programme is described. This information is also available on CD-Rom and online on the IHB website. These stallions are in the main studbook and have established studbook pedigree, passed the official veterinary examination, passed the visual examination and passed a performance test.

Irish Horse Register Supplementary Stallions List 2003 (IHB, 2003).

Lists the various stallion breeds in S1 and S2 category that are not fully registered and listed in the *Irish Sport Horse Studbook*. S1 may also include stallions that have been selected for performance testing. S1 stallions have established pedigree and have passed the veterinary examination (this category may contain stallions selected for performance testing; upon passing they are moved to the approved list). S2 have established pedigree but did not pass the veterinary examination. There is also a listing of stallions that do not have established pedigrees but did pass the veterinary inspection.

The Irish Sport Horse Studbook Marebook: mares and their progeny (IHB, 1 June 2000).

Lists mares registered in the IHR after 1 January 1999 and all mares that had progeny recorded in the IHR after 1 January 1995. Includes mares which have been approved for IHB Quality Broodmare, Premier Broodmare and Premier Broodmare (NI) Retention Schemes. Breeds included are Thoroughbred, Irish

Sport Horse, registered Irish Draught, Appendix Irish Draught, Irish Draught, Weatherby's non-thorough-bred, foreign breed, Arab, pony and others, as well as index of owners and index of mares.

Irish Draught Horse Marebook (IHB, 1999).
Records the registered Irish Draught mares, Appendix Irish Draught mares and their progeny. Includes all RID and AID mares, but not the ID who have not yet been put forward or passed inspection. Includes a subset of the list of Quality and Premier Broodmare Retention Schemes which refer to RID and AID mares. Includes owner index.

The Irish Horse Register, incorporating *The Irish Sport Horse Studbook*; supplementary section: *Foals Registered in 2002*.
Alphabetical listing of stallions and their progeny by category, approved, S1 and S2, listing IHR number, breed code, date of birth, sex, colour, foal name (if breeder has registered a prefix), dam, sire of dam, and owner-breeder details. Owner index is at the back of the publication. An annual publication which, when used in conjunction with the stallion and mares books, makes it possible to trace the breeding record of Irish Draught horses. The foal book gives details on which breeders selected which stallions for the breeding season of the previous year.

Quality Broodmare Retention Scheme (IHB, 18 June 1998); *Premier Mare Scheme: Irish Draught foals* (IHB promotional brochure, 2002).
Quality Broodmare Retention Scheme lists names, pedigree and owners' contact information of 1,172 mares (18-6-98). Includes charts showing number of mares accepted by breed: RID, AID, ID, ISH, TB, WNTR, FB. Charts shows the sire of mares accepted: RID, TB, ISH and other breeds. Also indicates which Irish Draught stallions have been the most influential in the scheme.

Top ten sires of the 1,172 mares in the scheme: Clover Hill, Diamond Lad, Ballinvella, Glidawn Diamond, Flagmount Diamond, Carrabawn View, Grey Macha, I'm a Star, Kildalton Gold, Laughtons Flight. Also has chart with top ten sire of the 290 RID, AID and ID mares: Clover Hill, Diamond Lad, Pride of Shaunlara, Uibh Fhaili '81, Ginger Dick, Powerwood Purple, Glenagyle Rebel, Kildalton Gold, Flagmount Diamond, Grey Macha. Also includes chart with top ten sires of RID mares: Uibh Fhaili '81, Diamond Lad, Pride of Shaunlara, Clover Hill, Glenagyle Rebel, Ginger Dick, Holycross, Grey Macha, Pride of Toames and King Elvis.

Genetic Evaluations of Showjumping Horses in Ireland 2000 (IHB, 2000).
Includes statistical data for 1993-99. Appendix 4 is on breeding values for approved IHR stallions; appendix 7 on breeding values for females sorted by name; appendix 8 on breeding values for females sorted by breeding value – primarily ISH, as RID mares would be kept for breeding and not competition purposes.

Achievements of Irish Sport Horses and Ponies (IHB, 1999, 2000).
Lists achievements of Irish Sport Horses and ponies in showjumping and eventing latest information on top performers in Ireland and other countries. Includes photographs and competition highlights.

Newsletter (IHB, June 2001).
Short pieces about microchipping of foals and DNA testing, and statistical information on stallion inspections 1995-2000. Also included are *Irish Sport Horse Studbook* competitions and results, and photographs and highlights of some of the winners. Outlines the thirteen points of primary funding schemes and information on the National Development Plan for 2000-06.

Selection of Sellers and Suppliers of Sport Horses and Ponies in Ireland (IHB, 2003).

Listing of those breeders and sellers who chose to be included. Includes advertising, marketing and promotion of ISH and RID horses.

Irish Horse Yearbook (IHB, 1978-80)

Annual round up of horse activities: showjumping, breeding and eventing, with many photographs of prize winners. Primarily a directory with similar information as the *Irish Field Directory*.

Marketing publications

The Irish Horse Board publishes a number of marketing and promotion pieces about the Irish Sport Horse. Some of these include information about the Irish Draught horse and their pure-bred or part-bred progeny. Primarily promotional information. It appears some titles are published for a few years only, then other similar publications take their place.

5. Show and Sale Catalogues

National Irish Draught Show Programme (IDHS, 1985 to present).

Lists classes, schedules of events as well as the entries, owners and breeder's details in each class.

Royal Dublin Society Horse Show Programme (1967 to present).

From the 1967 programme:

Class 65 Irish Draught Mare in foal or having produced a foal in 1966 or 1967, entered in the *Irish Draught Horse Book* published by the Department of Agriculture and Fisheries. (This Class is confined to mares selected for competition and invited to compete by the Royal Dublin Society.)

18 Mares were entered, including Moral Code (6246), Lady Grey (6300), Springfield Dawn (5951), Enniskeane

Countess (5990), Twister (6168), Outer Limits (6263), Rosenamona (6438), Lislarkin Lassie (5937), Wild Rose (6305), Oriental (6264), My Girl (6211), Eurydice (6180), Rose Love (5929), Come On (6265), name missing, and Island Rambler (6274).

Class 65A Colt Foal: 2 colt foals were entered

Class 65B Filly Foal: 2 filly foals were entered

Class 66 exhibition class of selected registered Irish Draught stallions (no class adjudication): 6 stallions were exhibited: Merrion (477), Bantry Pearl (525), Golden Plover (537), Laughton (446), Armanda Star (566) and King of Diamonds (547).

IDHS National Sale

The national sales of Irish Draught horses have been held at a several venues over the years. Beginning in 1986 and continuing to the present day, the sales primarily include foals, yearlings, 2-3-year-olds, usually a few broodmares and occasionally stallions. The seller sets a reserve price, and if the bidding does not reach the seller's asking price the animal is not sold at auction. There are those who say many deals are made after the bidding has ended. First national sale included a 3-year-old stallion, Holycross, sold for 6,400 guineas; 56 lots for sale: foals, broodmares, geldings. IDHS, first national sale, 27 September 1986, was held at the Sale Yard, the Square, Rathdowney, County Laois.

Goresbridge

www.irishhorse.com

The second sale was held at Goresbridge in 1987 and again in 1988

Tattersalls

www.tattersalls.ie

Tattersalls held the sales in 1991, 1992, 1993, 1994, 1995, 1996, 1997, and 1998.

Cavan Equestrian Centre
www.cavanequestrian.com/home.asp
Commencing in 1999, Cavan hosts the Annual National Registered Irish Draught Sale, held in October of the year.

Annual Stallion Parade
Under the auspices of the Irish Draught Horse Society and the Halfbred Horse Breeders' Society; held at Ulster Lakeland Equestrian Park, Necarne Castle, on 23 February 2002.

Also held around the provinces and nationally are stallion parades at local venues. These parades help mare owners select a stallion for the coming breeding season.

6. Newspapers

A number of provincial and national newspapers in Ireland carry information about horse shows and show results. A number of them also publish more substantial pieces on the draught and Irish Sport Horse, especially regarding the National Show and the Royal Dublin Show. The newspapers also have long established archives and photographic collections, but these are difficult to search and retrieve information from unless the date for the piece in question is known. A number of equine journalists wrote for the newspapers over the years, including Michael Slavin, Nicholas O'Hare, Grania Willis, Ruth Loney, Helen McCullough and others.

Farming Life
www.farminglife.com
Include *Equestrian Life* section

Farm Week
RTÉ Radio 1 programme, *Farm Week* takes a look back at the big issues relating to farming and food matters each Friday night at 7.30pm (repeated on Saturday morning at 7.30am).
www.rte.ie/radio1/farmweek

The Irish Farmer's Journal
www.farmersjournal.ie

The Irish Field (and *The Irish Field Directory*)
www.irishfield.com

Irish Independent
www.unison.ie/irish_independent

Ireland's Horse Review
www.irelands-horsereview.com

Horse Week
horseweek@mortonnewspapers.com

7. Electronic and Multimedia Publications

Before the Internet, pedigree information and general information about the Irish Draught was hard if not impossible to find outside of Ireland. With the advent of websites and databases, it is now relatively easy to learn about pedigrees and the breed itself. The Irish Draught has had a revival abroad, and societies can be found in many countries outside Ireland, including Great Britain, Australia, New Zealand, US and Canada. Many breeders of Irish Draught, Irish Sport Horses, and/or Irish Draught Sport Horses (as they are referred to in a number of countries) have websites that advertise stallions, breeding mares and offspring for sale. There are two group List Servs open to anyone to communicate with enthusiasts around the world. Some show videos were made and are still available, though generally these are hard-to-find items.

Websites

Several websites serve as official society sites in various countries. These are all affiliated groups to the parent Irish Draught Horse Society based in Ireland. In general, society websites have sections on news, membership information, contact information, horses for sale, diary dates, breed information, show results, photographic gallery, related links, etc. There are also many websites of breeders and owners, and though these are not included in the resource guide they can be found from links on the society pages or by utilising an Internet search.

Irish Draught Horse Society, Ireland
www.irishdraught.ie

The Irish Horse Board
www.irishhorseboard.com
section on Irish Draught horse
www.irishhorseboard.com/irish.htm

Royal Dublin Society
www.rds.ie

Northern Ireland Horse Board and IDHS (NI)
www.nihorseboard.org
Irish Draught pages
www.nihorseboard.org/irishdraught.htm

The Irish Draught Horse Society (Great Britain)
www.irishdraughthorsesociety.com

Irish Draught and Sport Horse Society of Australia Inc.
www.idshs.com.au
New Zealand Irish Horse Society
www.irishhorse.org.nz

Irish Draught Horse Society of North America
www.irishdraught.com

The Irish Draught Horse Society of Canada
www.idhs.ca

Databases

Irish Horse Board Stallions online database
www.irishhorseboard.com/stallions/default.asp
then go to
www.irishhorseboard.com/Stalbook/St_fr_Hd.htm
(updated March 2003).
In the top left-hand box click on the breed for either current stallions or dead, exported or excluded stallions. A list of stallions will appear in the bottom left-hand box; click on the name you wish to view. The entry will be shown in the main window displaying the horse pedigree, owner, statistical and progeny information, and IHR and RID numbers for registered stallions. There are printable pedigrees. Site maintained by the IHB Ireland.

Del Mar ALL-Breeds Database
www.pedigreequery.com/allbreed

All-breed Pedigree Database
Although much of this site remains a free service, certain features of this site are subscription based. A subscription for unlimited access is $20 (US) for four months or $50 per year (credit card or cheque payment). If you initially signed up for the free trial period prior to 1 March 2004 you can renew your trial subscription to continue accessing the site (you do not need to re-register). All other users will have to create a new account to access this site in its entirety.

For those who choose not to subscribe, the database will still offer free pedigrees, progeny reports and the ability to add/edit horses in the database. Subscriber benefits will include access to hypothetical mating reports, line-breeding reports and more. It is also planned to improve the features offered to subscribers over time; see below for more information.

Free Service
- Simple 5 generation pedigrees (no detailed information)
- Progeny reports
- Photographs
- No hypo mating, line breeding or female family
- Limited adding and editing horses

Subscription Service
- 5-9 generation pedigrees (full information)
- Line-breeding reports
- Hypothetical mating
- Female family
- Improved features
- Full access

Internet List Servs

There are at present eleven Yahoo groups on the Internet for Irish-draught-related information. Some of them have very few members. The top three are listed below.

Irish Draught
www.groups.yahoo.com/group/IrishDraught
A mailing list for owners, breeders and fans of the Irish Draught horse and Irish Draught crossbreds. Discuss breeding, training, competing and life with these beautiful horses. Members of the list compete or participate in three-day eventing, dressage, hunter/jumpers, foxhunting, pleasure riding and, of course, breeding Sport Horses. This group is generally used by people in North America, Ireland and Australia. This site is the most active in terms of numbers of messages exchanged by its members, as well as photograph postings to the archive files.

IrishDraughtHorse
www.groups.yahoo.com/group/IrishDraughthorse
Dedicated to the promotion and preservation of the famous Irish Draught horse. This site is dedicated to positive insight on how to promote and enjoy this wonderful horse. Run by Jim Leary, owner of O'Leary's Irish Diamond RID stallion.

IDHS (North America)
www.groups.yahoo.com/group/IDHS
Exclusively for the members of the Irish Draught Horse Society of North America. It is a discussion forum for topics of interest to the members of this group. Only members in good standing of the IDHS (NA) may participate on this list. This organisation also has regional List Servs in some parts of North America.

Videos

National Irish Draught Show Video, 1985
There have from time to time been videos produced at the national show; however, the only one the author has seen to date is of the first show. It is not clear from what source show videos are available. If used in conjunction with the show's printed programme, one can envisage the entire event. Amazing to see in real life Pride of Shaunlara, a young Blue Rajah, a three-year-old Sea Crest and other famous names in the Irish Draught horse world.
Narrator: Michael Slavin
Place: Suma Stud, Navan, County Meath
Date: 1985

A number of other videos seem to have been produced or sponsored by the Irish Draught Horse Society, such as the *Lambertstown Show 1986*, *Kerry Gold Show 1985*, *National Draught Horse Shows*, *IDHS Dinner Dance*, and other special events. These videos are difficult to find and are primarily in private collections.

Ride On (December 2003)
During the European Eventing Championships held at Punchestown in September 2003 a unique celebration

and presentation of the Irish horse took place and is now available on video. Over 130 horses took part in a spectacular show combining live action, film, music and drama. *Ride On* reflects the spirit and special nature of Irish horses, from donkeys, Connemara, TB and ISH to Irish Draught horses. Representing some of the best Irish Draught were champion mares Millhollow Queen and foal, Ardattin Mandy and foal, Rosetown Annie and foal, the Garda geldings, a 24-year-old Sea Crest, Grange Bouncer, Beezies Sue, and international ISH stars, Cruising and Flo Jo, as well and many other world-famous Irish horses.

for more information, e-mail:
rideonvideo@hotmail.com

Image Collections and Photographic Archives

Most of the photographic images for this book were found in these collections. The search for images of Irish Draught horses was a time-consuming search, as these collections are arranged in some cases by place name or activity. Many of the photographs happen to include the Irish Draught horse as part of the picture, and in only a very few cases was the Irish Draught horse the subject of the composition.

National Library of Ireland, National Photographic Archive
www.nli.ie/new_coll.htm

Bord Fáilte (Tourist Board)
www.ireland.ie/home

Country Life Museum, County Mayo
www.museum.ie/countrylife

National Gallery of Ireland
www.nationalgallery.ie

Irish Picture Library
www.fatherbrowne.com/ipl

Glossary

Appendix Irish Draught (AID): Appendix Irish Draught refers to mares only. Mares inspected at two years of age or older and approved as AID by an official inspection panel must have one parent approved as RID and three grandparents as RID.

BJ Trophy: An international speed showjumping class at the CSIO Show in Falsterbo in Sweden.

Bord na gCapall: The body responsible for registering horses until the formation of the Irish Horse Board in 1993.

Cold-blood: Heavy horses, descendants of Europe's Diluvial horse, are termed cold-bloods as they are usually quite calm in temperament. Thoroughbred and Arab horses represent hot blood, and crosses between the two are thus called warm-bloods or, in Britain, halfbreds.

Colt: Entire young male horse up to the age of three years old.

Crossbreds: The crossbreeding of two pure-bred animals, to produce the traditional halfbred; 50 per cent one breed, 50 per cent another breed.

Filly: Young female horse up to the age of three years old.

Garda Siochana: Guardians of the peace. Ireland's national police force.

Gelding: Castrated male horse of any age.

Genomic: Study of genomes and gene products presenting data of biological significance.

Halfbred: A horse bred by a registered Thoroughbred out of a mare of unknown ancestry, or one other than Thoroughbred. Primarily, this is a British term and is extended to three-quarter-bred or even seven-eighths bred. A three-quarter-bred, for instance, would be by a Thoroughbred out of a halfbred mare; (see also Irish Sport Horse and warm-blood).

Hames: A metal fixing around a horse's collar to which the traces are attached.

Hand: 4 inches, originally based on a hand held sideways. Unit of measurement used for horses until recently e.g. 16.2 hh (hands high). Now expressed in centimetres: 4 inches equals 10 cms. Therefore 16.2 equals 162 cms.

In hand: Horse being led in the show ring by a person on foot.

Irish Draught (ID): Irish Draught refers to: 1. All pure-bred animals that are eligible for or have failed inspection; 2. Stallions that have been selected for and are awaiting performance testing prior to approval.

Irish Sport Horse (ISH): The traditionally bred Irish Sport Horse or halfbred was a cross between the Thoroughbred stallion and a registered Irish Draught mare. The halfbred mare when crossed again with a Thoroughbred stallion produced a three-quarter-bred. The modern Irish Sport Horse may contain bloodlines from many different breeds, including European breeds. The terms Irish Sport Horse, Sport Horse, Irish hunter, hunter, and non-thoroughbred are names used to describe the same animal.

Made hunter: An experienced hunting horse.

Mare: Female horse four years old and upwards.

MCR Cup: An international showjumping competition at the CSIO show in Falsterbo in Sweden.

Mitochondrial DNA: This type of DNA is passed down intact exclusively in the female line. The premise is that all horses can be traced to a single female approximately 200,000 years ago.

Pacer/Ambler: A horse with a lateral gait whereas a trotter has a diagonal gait. Very comfortable to ride.

Prix St Georges: Highest level of dressage competition.

Pure-bred: The idea of a 'pure-bred' animal developed during the nineteenth century.

Registered Irish Draught (RID): Registered Irish Draught refers to: 1. Mares and geldings inspected at two years of age or older and approved as RID by an official inspection panel; 2. Stallions inspected by a panel of judges and a veterinary surgeon and who pass a performance test for approval as RID at three years of age or older.

Stallion: Entire male horse four years old and upwards.

Stallions, Registered Irish Draught (RID): Registered Irish Draught stallions are inspected by a panel of judges and a veterinary surgeon and pass a performance test for approval as RID at three years of age or older.

Stallions, Irish Draught S1: Section 1 refers to stallions only. Stallions that do not qualify for RID status on inspection may achieve supplementary 1 stallion status provided they have established pedigree and have passed the veterinary examination. Animals that are being performance tested or not yet approved are in this category.

Stallions, Irish Draught S2: Section 2 refers to stallions only. Stallions with established pedigree but who do not pass the veterinary examination may be classified as section 2.

Straddle: The piece of harness that rests on the horse's back and carries the weight of the shafts.

Sport Horse (see Irish Sport Horse)

Teagasc: (Training) the Irish Agriculture and Food Development Authority.

Thoroughbred (TB): Thoroughbred and Arabs are known as hot-blood, full-blood or blood horses 'for their fiery temperaments' (see also halfbred, warm-blood, cold-blood); the amount of Thoroughbred blood in the animal is a key factor when stating per cent, ie. ½ bred (50 per cent crossbred animal), ¾ bred (three-parts Thoroughbred, one-part other bred), ⅞ bred (seven-parts Thoroughbred, one-part other bred), and so on.

Warm-blood: The European term for halfbred horses. Hot-blood, or full-blood, is recognised as being either Arab or Thoroughbred. Cold-blood horses are the heavy horses descended from the Diluvial horse of Europe. The European warm-blood (nowadays termed Sport Horse) is a mixture of other breeds.

Notes and References

Introduction

1   From www.iol.ie/~edmo/famine.htm *Irish Famine & Castlemagner.*
2   Seamus MacPhilib, 'Country Life Museum Curator of Agriculture' in *Irish Examiner*, Farming section,) 18 December 2003 p. 8-9.
3   Alex Fell, *The Irish Draught Horse, p.* 1, 1991.
4   Quote by Earl of Enniskillen 23 *July*, 1897, part of the Reports by the Commissioners, Commission on Horse Breeding, Ireland.
5   Scharff, Robert Francis, 'On the Irish Horse and Its Early History', *Proceedings of the Royal Irish Academy* Volume XXVII, Section B, No. 6 March, 1909
6   Department of Agriculture and Technical Instruction for Ireland, *Irish Draught Horse Book* Vol. 1, His Majesty's Stationery Office, 1918, p, 1 Introduction.
7   Carden, R. G. 'The Irish Hunter', p. 228-238 in *The Horses of the British Empire, Vol. 1* edited by Sir Humphrey F. De Trafford, London: Walter Southwood & Co. Limited, (undated, *c.* 1907),
8   Lewis, Colin A., *Horse Breeding in Ireland and the role of the Royal Dublin Society's Horse Breeding Schemes 1886-1903*, J.A. Allen & Co. Ltd. London. 1980, p. 11 Introduction.
9   *Irish Draught Horse Book*, Vol. 1, 1918, p. 5.
10 Lord Derby, quoted in Department of Agriculture and Technical Instruction for Ireland, *Irish Draught Horse Book* Vol. 1, His Majesty's Stationery Office, 1918, p, 7 Introduction.
11 *Bord na gCapall* (IHB) Report and Accounts July/September 1978.
12 *Irish Draught Horse Book* Vol. 1, 1918, *p.* 9.
13 Holdstock, Mark, *Great Fair Horse Dealing at Ballinasloe, p. 68.*
14 Fell, op cit. *p. 3.*
15 Quote by Pat Gleeson, in Alex Fell, *The Irish Draught Horse,* p. 14, 1991.
16 Fell, op. cit. *p.* 151.
17 In 'The Great Debate: A breed or a type', *Irish Draught Horse Society Yearbook* 1981, *p.* 17-18.
18 Martin Collins' Chairman's Review, quoted in Elizabeth Deane and Ann Loughnane (eds), *Irish Draught Horse Society 25 Years*, Irish Draught Horse Society, Co. Westmeath, *c.* 2003.

Chapter 1 – Archaeology: The Horse in Early Ireland

1   D. W. Anthony, 'The earliest horseback riders and Indo-European origins: new evidence from the Steppes', in B. Hänsel and S. Zimmer (eds.), *Die indogermanen un das pferd* (Budapest, 1994).
2   Ibid.
3   F. McCormick, 'Faunal remains from prehistoric Irish burials', *Journal of Irish Archaeology*, 3 (1985-86), pp. 37-48.
4   P.J. Hartnett, 'Excavation of a passage grave at Fourknocks, Co. Meath', *Proceedings of the Royal Irish Academy*, 58C (1957), pp. 197-277.
5   L.H. van Wijngaarden-Bakker, 'Horse in the Dutch Neolithic', in A.T. Clason (ed.), *Archaeozoological Studies* (Amsterdam, 1975), pp. 341-4.
6   Anthony, op. cit. p. 191.

7   L.H. van Wijngaarden-Bakker, 'The animal remains from the Beaker settlement at Newgrange, Co. Meath: Final report', *Proceedings of the Royal Irish Academy*, 86C (1986), p. 84.

8   G. Coffey, 'On the excavation of a tumulus, near Loughrea, Co. Galway', *Proceedings of the Royal Irish Academy*, 25C (1905), pp. 14-20.

9   G. Coffey, 'Two finds of late Bronze Age objects', *Proceedings of the Royal Irish Academy*, 26C (1906), pp. 119-24.

10 J. Waddell, *The Prehistoric Archaeology of Ireland* (Galway, 1998), p. 296.

11 B. Raftery, *Pagan Celtic Ireland* (London, 1894), p. 99.

12 F. McCormick, 'The animal bones from Tara', *Discovery Programme 6* (2002), pp. 103-16.

13 R.B. Warner, 'The archaeology of early historic Irish kingship', in S.T. Driscoll and M.R. Nieke (eds.), *Power and Politics in Early Medieval Britain and Ireland* (Edinburgh, 1988), pp. 47-68.

14 J.J. O'Meara (ed.), *Gerald of Wales: the history and topography of Ireland* (Harmondsworth, 1982), p. 110.

15 J. Puhvel, 'Aspects of equine functionality', in J. Puhvel (ed.), *Myth and Law Among the Indo Europeans* (University of California Press, 1970), pp. 157-72.

16 Ibid. p. 161.

17 Ibid. p. 162.

18 F. McCormick, op. cit.

19 Information from Cluny Johnston, personal communication.

20 L. Bieler, *The Irish Penitentials* (Dublin, 1975), p. 161.

21 F. McCormick, 'The animal bones', in C. Manning 'Excavation at Moyne graveyard, Scrule, Co. Mayo', *Proceedings of the Royal Irish Academy*, 87C (1987), pp. 60-7; G. Roche 'Report on the zoological material', in M.J. O'Kelly, 'Church Island near Valentia, Co. Kerry', *Proceedings of the Royal Irish Academy*, 59C (1958), pp. 133-4; F. McCormick 'The animal bones from ditch 1', in J. Barber, 'Excavations at Iona 1979', *Proceedings of the Society of Antiquaries of Scotland*, 111 (1981), pp. 282-380.

22 D.A. Binchy, 'Bretha Crólige', *Eriu* 12 (1938), pp. 1-77.

23 F.J. Simoons, *Eat Not this Flesh* (Wisconsin, 1994), p. 187.

24 E. Emerton, *The Letters of St Boniface* (New York, 1940), p. 58.

25 R.A.S Macalister, *The Latin Lives of St Ciaran* (New York, 1921), p. 20.

26 O. Bergin and R.I. Best, 'Tochmarc Étaíne', *Eriu* 12 (1938), pp. 137-96.

27 F. Kelly, *Early Irish Farming* (Dublin, 1997), p. 478.

28 D. Jenkins, 'The horse in the Welsh law texts', in S. Davis and N.A. Jones, *The Horse in Celtic Culture: medieval Welsh perspectives* (Cardiff, 1977), pp. 64-81.

29 A. Hyland, *The Horse in the Middle Ages* (Stroud, 1999), p. 43.

30 Because of the now universally accepted prohibition of eating horse flesh.

31 A.T. Lucas, 'Irish ploughing practices' (part 2), *Tools and Tillage*, 2 (2), 1973, pp. 67-83.

32 Ibid.

33 Kelly, op. cit. p. 96.

34 Ibid. p. 538.

35 Ibid. p. 99.

36 Ibid. p. 9.

37 Ibid. p. 91.

38 Ibid. p. 498.

39 Ibid. p. 90.

40 Ibid.

41 M. Dillon, *Lebor na Cert: the book of rights*, Irish Texts Society, xlvi (Dublin, 1962), p. 97.

42 A. Hyland, op. cit. p. 4.

43 Ibid. p. 14.

44 H.S. Sweetman (ed.), *Calendar of Documents Relating to Ireland 1171-1251* (London, 1875), p. 5.

45 A. Hyland, *The Warhorse 1250-1600* (Stroud, 1998), p. 54.

46 Kelly, op. cit. p. 98.

47 Ibid.

48 R. Kavanagh, 'The horse in Viking Ireland', in J. Bradley (ed.), *Settlement and Society in Medieval Ireland* (Kilkenny, 1988), pp. 89-123.

49 Ibid. p. 110.

50 J. Clarke, *The Medieval Horse and its Equipment* (London, 1995), p. 79.

51 Ibid. p. 94.

52 O'Meara, op. cit. p. 101.

53 P. Harbinson, *The High Crosses of Ireland*, vol. 2 (Bonn, 1992), fig. 66.

54 M.T. Flanagan, 'Warfare in twelfth-century Ireland', in T. Bartlett and K. Jeffery (eds.), *A Military History of Ireland* (Cambridge, 1996), pp. 52-75.

55 Ibid.

56 Ibid.

57 H. Berry, *Statutes and Ordinances and Acts of the Parliament of Ireland King John to Henry V* (Dublin, 1907), p. 435.

58 J. Webb, 'Translation of the French metrical history of the description of the deposition of King Richard the second ...', *Archaeologia*, 10 (1824).

59 M.T. Flanagan, op. cit. p. 64.

60 R.H.C. Davis, *The Medieval Warhorse* (London, 1989), p. 26.

61 J.F. Lydon, 'The hobelar: An Irish contribution to medieval warfare', *The Irish Sword*, 2 (1954-56), pp. 12-16.

Chapter 2 – Manuscripts: The Horse in Early Irish Society

1 This chapter is an expansion of the section on the horse on pp. 88-101 of Fergus Kelly's *Early Irish Farming: a study based mainly on the law texts of the 7th and 8th centuries AD,* Early Irish Law Series, vol. 4 (Dublin, 1997; repr. 2000).

2 Most of the texts quoted in this chapter are from the Old Irish period (approximately seventh to ninth centuries). For this reason the Old Irish spelling system is employed. It differs in some respects from modern Irish orthography; for example, Old Irish *ech* corresponds to Modern Irish *each*.

3 P. Woulfe, *Sloinnte Gaedheal is Gall: Irish names and surnames* (Dublin, 1923), pp. 356, 358.

4 M.A. O'Brien (ed.), *Corpus Genealogiarum Hiberniae*, vol. 1 (Dublin, 1976), pp. 608-9, 613-17.

5 E. Hogan, *Onomasticon Goedelicum* (Dublin, 1910; reprinted 1993), pp. 393, 482. For a sample of place names formed from words meaning horse, mare, colt, foal, etc. *see* P.W. Joyce, *Irish Names of Places,* vol. 1 (Dublin, 1869), pp. 474-5; vol. 2 (Dublin, 1875), pp. 309-10.

6 D.A. Binchy (ed.), *Críth Gablach,* Medieval and Modern Irish Series, vol. 2 (Dublin, 1941; repr. 1970), p. 158.

7 Ibid. pp. 345-6.

8 O. Bergin, 'What brought the Saxons to Ireland', *Eriu* 7 (1914), p. 244.

9 G. Murphy (ed.), *Early Irish Lyrics* (Oxford, 1956), p. 90.

10 The correct translation of the word *airthenn* (*airthend*) is given in the 2000 reprint of F. Kelly, *Early Irish Farming* (Dublin, 1997), p. 42.

11 R.M. Kavanagh, 'The horse in Viking Ireland', in *Settlement and Society in Medieval Ireland,* J. Bradley (ed.) (Kilkenny, 1988), pp. 89-121.

12 A.T. Lucas, 'Irish ploughing practices' (part 2), *Tools and Tillage,* 2 (2), 1973, p. 68.

13 For detailed discussion on the construction of the early Irish chariot, *see* D. Greene, 'The chariot as described in Irish literature', in *The Iron Age in the Irish Sea Province,* C. Thomas (ed.), Council of British Archaeology Research Report 9, 1972,

pp. 59-73; P. Harbison, 'The Old Irish "chariot"', *Antiquity* 45 (1971), pp. 171-7; W. Sayers, 'Old Irish *fert* "tie-pole", *fertas* "swingletree", and the seeress Fedelm', *Études celtiques,* 21 (1984), pp. 171-83.

14 This text is edited and translated in F. Kelly, op. cit. pp. 537-44.

15 W. Stokes (ed.), 'The voyage of Máel Dúin (1)', *Revue celtique,* 9 (1888), p. 466.

16 S. Mac Airt (ed.), *The Annals of Inisfallen* (Dublin, 1951), p. 304.

17 S. Mac Airt and G. Mac Niocaill (eds.), *The Annals of Ulster* (Dublin, 1983), p. 334.

18 Ibid. p. 158.

19 Mac Airt, *The Annals of Inisfallen,* p. 358.

20 B. Ó Cuív (ed.), 'Fragments of Irish medieval treatises on horses', *Celtica,* 17 (1985), pp. 113-22.

21 This is the interpretation in Plunket's Latin-Irish dictionary of 1662; *see* B. Ó Cuív (ed.), 'Fragments of two mediaeval treatises on horses', *Celtica,* 2 (1952), p. 59.

22 A.M. Freeman (ed.), *Annála Connacht: the Annals of Connacht* (Dublin, 1944), p. 518.

23 On the other hand, N. McLeod's 'Early Irish contract law', *Celtic Studies,* 1 (Sydney, 1992), p. 321, suggests that it refers to bone spavin.

24 J. O'Donovan (ed.), *Annala Rioghachta Éireann: Annals of the Kingdom of Ireland by the Four Masters,* vol. 4 (Dublin, 1856), p. 1,184.

25 S. Mac Airt and G. Mac Niocaill, *The Annals of Ulster,* p. 434.

26 B. Mac Carthy (ed.), *Annála Uladh: Annals of Ulster,* vol. 2 (Dublin, 1893), p. 390.

27 Ibid. p. 236.

28 P. Mac Cana, *Celtic Mythology* (Hamlyn, 1970), pp. 51, 55, 77, 91.

29 R.I. Best and O. Bergin (eds.), *Lebor na hUidre: Book of the Dun Cow* (Dublin, 1929; repr. 1992), 262.8659-263.8670.

30 A.G. Van Hamel (ed.), *Compert Con Culainn and Other Stories,* Mediaeval and Modern Irish Series, vol. 3 (Dublin, 1933; repr. 1978), p. 117.

31 Ibid. p. 116.

32 K. Meyer, *The Triads of Ireland,* Todd Lecture Series xiii, Royal Irish Academy (Dublin, 1906), p. 30.

Chapter 3 – The Horse in Irish Myth and Folklore

1 Michael Herity and George Eogan, 'Archaeological evidence of horses in Irish prehistory', *Ireland in Prehistory* (London, 1977), p. 292; John Waddell, *The Prehistoric Archaeology of Ireland* (Bray, 2000), p. 421.

2 Dáithí Ó hÓgáin, *The Daghdha and Eochaidh: myth, legend and romance* (London, 1990), pp. 145-7, 178-81; this work will hereafter be referred to as *MLR*; *see* also Dáithí Ó hÓgáin, *The Sacred Isle* (Cork, 1999), pp. 59-64, 189; this work will hereafter be referred to as *SI*. Full references to sources are given in both works. The asterisk before a word indicates that the actual word form is not attested, but has been reconstructed through linguistic analysis.

3 Irish gods and goddesses in relation to horses: *MLR*, pp. 195-7, 283-5; *SI*, pp. 173-8.

4 Francis J. Byrne, 'Horses in kingship rituals of early Ireland', *Irish Kings and High-Kings* (London, 1973), pp. 17-18; Brian Smith, *The Horse in Ireland* (Dublin, 1991), pp. 29-32; *SI*, pp. 156-9.

5 The myth of Conaire, *MLR*, pp. 99-101; *SI*, pp. 159-63.

6 Donn: Käte Muller-Lisowski in *Béaloideas,* 18 (1948), pp. 146-53, 189-91; *MLR*, pp. 165-7; *SI*, pp. 54-9, 126-7.

7 Lugh: *MLR*, pp. 272-7; *SI*, pp. 137-46.

8 Lugh and horse-racing: R.A. Stewart Macalister, *Lebor Gabála Érenn,* vol. 4, Irish Texts Society (Dublin, 1941), p. 160; Brian Smith, op. cit. pp. 33-7.

9 Donn Fírinne in folklore: Kate Muller-Lisowski, op. cit. pp. 153-68; *MLR*, pp. 166-7.

10 Water-horses: Bo Almqvist in *Béaloideas,* 59 (1991), pp. 236-9; *MLR*, p. 25; general: p. 197-8; Féichín: pp. 289-90; Maodhóg: pp. 377-8, Ruán: pp. 52-3; Brendan: pp. 135; Cú Chulainn: p. 139.

11   The Mare of the Belt: Máirtín Ó Cadhain in *Béaloideas*, 5 (1935), p. 255.

12   Irish Lass, or the 'Paidrín Mare': Michael F. Cox, *History of the Irish Horse* (Dublin, 1897), pp. 107-11; Tony Sweeney and Annie Sweeney, *The Sweeney Guide to the Irish Turf* (Dublin, 2002), pp. 343-4; Dáithí Ó hÓgáin, 'An Capall i mBéaloideas na hÉireann', in *Béaloideas*, 45-7 (1977-79), pp. 236-7; the latter reference is to an article in *Béaloideas*, 45-7, based mostly on sources in the Irish Folklore Department of University College, Dublin, hereafter referred to as 'An Capall'.

13   Supposed anatomical wonders: 'An Capall', pp. 237-8.

14   Piaras Feiritéar and horses: *MLR*, pp. 200-1; 'An Capall', pp. 204, 230-1.

15   Fairies stealing horses: 'An Capall', pp. 204-5, 208-10.

16   True mares: 'An Capall', pp. 210-14.

17   Horses and ghosts: Kevin Danaher, *Irish Country People* (Cork, 1966), pp. 102-3; 'An Capall', pp. 200-3.

18   Horses taken at night: 'An Capall', pp. 205-7.

19   Horses and the evil eye: Risteard Ó Foghludha, *Éigse na Máighe* (Dublin, 1952), p. 85; George A. Little, *Malachy Horan Remembers* (Cork, 1976), pp. 74-6; 'An Capall', pp. 207-10.

20   Horse-whisperers: Thomas Crofton Croker, *Fairy Legends and Traditions of the South of Ireland* (London, 1828), pp. 199-202; William Youatt, *The Horse* (London, 1885), pp. 503-5; George A. Little, op. cit, pp. 76-7; Kevin Danaher, op. cit. p. 104; George Ewart Evans, *The Horse in the Furrow* (London, 1967), pp. 240-1; 'An Capall', pp. 224-9; Josephine Haworth, *The Horsemasters* (London, 1983), pp. 15-19.

21   Singing and whistling to horses: 'An Capall', pp. 222-3.

22   Traits and colours of horses: Brian Ó Cuív, 'Fragments of two mediaeval treatises on horses', *Celtica*, 2, pp. 30-57; the cited passages are on pp. 42, 44, 56; 'An Capall', pp. 229-36. Versions of the triads concerning traits of bull, hare and woman are in Brian Ó Cuív, ibid. p. 56; 'An Capall', pp. 233-4 (these from Irish Folklore Department, MSS 43:194, 211:106-7, 407:344). The English version dates from the year 1523 and is published in Dorian Williams, *The Horseman's Companion* (London, 1967), pp. 109-10.

23   Horses and portents: 'An Capall', pp. 218-20.

Periodicals cited:
Béaloideas (Dublin, 1927-), the Journal of the Irish Folklore Society.
Celtica (Dublin, 1950-), the journal of the Celtic School at the Dublin Institute for Advanced Studies.

Chapter 4 – Images of the Horse in Irish Art

1   'The Wooing of Emer' from the Ulster Cycle; this description is thought to be a later addition to the original document.

2   Richard Stanihurst, *De rebus in Hibernia gestis*, 1584, translated by Colm Lennon in *Richard Stanihurst, the Dubliner 1547-1618* (Dublin, 1981).

3   Ibid.

4   German picture of an Irish procession in Stuttgart: *Kurtze Beschreibung desszu Stutgarten bey den Fürstlichen Kindtauf und Hochzeit Jungstgehalten Frewden-Fests*, George Weckherlin (1617).

5   Gervase Markham, *A Discource of Horsemanshppe* (1593), and other treatises.

6   George Weckherlin, op. cit.

7   Ann Hyland, *The Warhorse 1250-1600* (Sutton Publishing Limited, 1998), pp. 32-3.

8   Richard Stanihurst, op. cit.

9   Alexander Mackay-Smith, *The Colonial Quarter Race Horse* (Virginia, 1983).

10   www.the jockeyclub.co.uk

11   Currently hanging in the dining room at the K Club, Straffan, County Kildare.

12 Sally Mitchell, *Dictionary of British Equestrian Artists* (Antique Collectors' Club, 1985).

13 Arthur Young, *Tour of Ireland* (London, 1780).

14 David Broderick, *The First Toll Roads* (Cork, 2002), p. 64.

15 Ibid. p. 154.

16 Ibid.

17 www.ilng.co.uk

18 A.J. Munnings, speech at Royal Academy banquet, 1959.

19 Artist's note to *The Táin*, translated by Thomas Kinsella (Dublin, 1986).

Chapter 5 – Horses: Working on the Land

1 Mary A. Hutton's verse translation of *The Táin* (Talbot Press, 1907).

2 Ibid. p. 180.

3 Quoted in A.K. Longfield, *Anglo-Irish Trade in the Sixteenth Century* (London, 1929).

4 R. Gough (ed.), *Chorographical Description of England, Scotland and Ireland* (London, 1806), p. 218.

5 J. Dymmok, *A Treatise of Ireland* (1600).

6 John Feehan, *Farming in Ireland: History, Heritage and Environment* (UCD Faculty of Agriculture, 2003).

Chapter 6 – For Everything there is a Season

1 Timothy O'Neill, *Life and Tradition in Rural Ireland* (London, 1977), p. 83.

2 A.T. Lucas, 'Irish ploughing practices', in *Tools and Tillage*, vol. 1, no. 1 (1972), pp. 52-62; vol. 2, no. 2 (1973), pp. 67-83; vol. 3, no. 3 (1974), pp. 149-60; vol. 3, no. 4 (1972), pp. 195-210.

3 E.E. Evans, *Irish Folkways* (London, 1957), p. 129.

4 Ibid. pp. 127-34.

5 Mervyn Watson, 'The role of the horse on Irish farms', in *From Corrib to Cultra* (Institute of Irish Studies, Queens University, Belfast, 2000), pp. 122-135.

6 W. Shaw Mason, *The Statistical Account or Parochial Survey of Ireland* (Dublin, 1816).

7 L.M. Cullen, *Life in Ireland* (London, 1968).

8 *Irish Draught Horse Book: Register of Mares*; archival document housed at Irish Horse Board.

9 The author still owns the brougham in which her father drove his father to race meetings during the Emergency.

10 Conversation with Norma Cook, May, 2004.

11 Conversation with Tom Berney, Kilcullen, 2001.

12 Seamus Murphy, *Stone Mad* (London, 1966).

13 From collection of 'Broddie' Corcoran, veterinary surgeon, County Westmeath.

14 Traditional, from the Irish.

15 Patrick Kavanagh, *Tarry Flynn* (London, 1948).

16 By kind permission of the Trustees of the Estate of the late Katherine B. Kavanagh, through the Jonathon Williams Literary Agency.

Chapter 7 – Economic Role of the Workhorse in Nineteenth-century Ireland

1 F.M.L. Thompson, 'Nineteenth-century horse sense', in *Economic History Review*, 29 (1976), p. 61.

2 Edward Wakefield, *An Account of Ireland, Statistical and Political*, 2 vols. (London, 1912), p. 308.

3 William Coyne (ed.), *Ireland Industrial and Agricultural* (Dublin, 1902), p. 327.

4 The Suffolk Punch was an ancient, relatively clean-legged East Anglian breed which had been introduced into Ireland as early as 1800 under the Dublin Society's premium scheme. *See* the *Report of the Commission on Horse Breeding, Ireland* (Dublin, 1897), p. 21. At that time the average Suffolk was about 15 hands; John Lawrence, *The Sportsman, Farrier and Shoeing-Smith New Guide* (London, undated); the writer's copy has 1797 on the flyleaf.

5 *Irish Farmers' Gazette*, 13 June 1875.

6 *Report of the Commission on Horse Breeding, Ireland*, op. cit. p. 9.

7 Ibid. p. 20.

8 Colin Lewis, *Horse Breeding in Ireland* (London, 1980), p. 164.

9 In 1871 there were 1,750 licensed cabs operating in the Dublin area; *The Irish Times*, 10 February 1871.

10 Earl of Onslow, 'The Carriage Horse', in Duke of Beaufort (ed.), *Driving* (London, 1889), p. 74.

11 *An Act for the further Amendment of the Act relating to the Dublin Police*, 11 & 12 vict, c. 113.

12 *Economic History Review*, 1976, p. 171.

13 Michael Corcoran, *Through Streets Broad and Narrow* (Leicester, 2000), p. 18.

14 Highway robbery continued to be a problem in Ireland until about the 1820s, when improved policing put an end to it.

15 *A Bill Limiting the Number of Persons to be Carried on Stage Coaches, Etc.*, 17 April 1810.

16 Colonel Rogers HCB, *The Mounted Troops of the British Army* (London 1959), pp. 188, 190.

17 Information from Mary McGrath.

18 M. Bianconi and S.J. Watson, *Bianconi: King of the Irish Roads* (Dublin, 1962), pp. 57-8.

19 *Freeman's Journal*, 1 January 1834.

20 M. Bianconi and S.J. Watson, op. cit. p. 61.

21 This national preference for two-wheeled vehicles has been explained above.

22 Earl of Onslow, op. cit. p. 71.

23 Michael Conry, *Dancing the Culm* (Carlow, 2001), p. 57.

24 Ibid. p. 58.

25 Ibid. pp. 308 ff.

26 Major G. Tylden *Horses and Saddlery* (London, 1965), p. 17.

27 See reports of fairs in the papers.

28 *Irish Farmers' Gazette*, 4 September 1880.

29 Now the seat of the Dáil, the Irish parliament.

30 Now held at the society's premises at Ballsbridge.

31 Denis Bogros, *Les Chevaux de la Cavalerie Français* (Roche-Rigault, 2000), p. 62.

32 Karlheinz Gless, *Das Pferd im Militär Wesen* (DDR Militärverlag, 1980), p. 85.

33 *Proceedings of a Court of Enquiry: Remounts* (HMSO, London, 1902).

34 William P. Coyne (ed), *Ireland Industrial and Agricultural* (Dublin, 1902), p. 258.

35 *Proceedings of Court of Enquiry: Remounts*, op. cit. question 643.

36 Ibid. appendix B., p. 315.

37 Ibid. questions 747, 749.

38 Ibid. question 674.

39 J.P. Mahaffy, 'The introduction of the ass as a beast of burden into Ireland', *Proceedings of the Royal Irish Academy*, vol. 33, C., 1916-17, pp. 535-36.

40 Denis Bogros, op. cit. p. 73.

41 Capitaine L. Picard, *Origines de l'Ecole de Cavalerie, et de ses Traditions Équstres* (Samur, 1890), p. 38.

42 Denis Bogros, op. cit. p. 63.

43 *Irish Farmers' Gazette*, 25 March 1871.

44 Ibid.

45 Ibid. 4 October 1873 (supplement).

46 *Proceedings of Court of Enquiry: Remounts,* op. cit. question 700.

47 Ibid. question 756.

48 *Report of the Commission on Horse Breeding, Ireland,* op. cit. questions 10140-52.

49 Information from the Netherlands' Institute for Military History.

50 John O'Donovan, *Economic History of Livestock in Ireland* (Dublin, 1940), p. 278.

51 *Proceedings of Court of Enquiry: Remounts,* op. cit. questions 700, 705.

52 Ibid. question 756.

53 William Hickey (pseud. Martin Doyle), *The Works of Martin Doyle* (Dublin 1831), p. 29.

54 Permission granted by Margaret Lynch, Navan, Co. Meath.

Chapter 9 – Recognition and Development of the Irish Draught Horse

1 H.C. Casserley, *Outline of Irish Railway History* (Newton Abbot, 1974).

2 T.W. Freeman, *Ireland* (London, 1965).

3 C.A. Lewis, *Horse Breeding in Ireland and the Role of the Royal Dublin Society's Horse Breeding Schemes* (London, 1980); hereafter Lewis, 1980a.

4 Ibid.

5 Ibid.

6 *Annual General Report of the Department of Agriculture and Technical Instruction, Ireland* (Dublin, 1903-04); hereafter *AGR.*

7 *AGR,* 1904-05

8 C.A. Lewis, 'The development and diffusion of the Irish draught', in *Irish Draught Horse Yearbook,* 1979 (Dublin), pp. 24-8.

9 R.G. Carden, in Sir Humphrey de Trafford (ed.), *The Horses of the British Empire* (1907), p. 231.

10 *Hunter Stud Book,* vi, 1983.

11 A. Dent, *Cleveland Bay Horses* (London, 1978).

12 C.A. Lewis, 'Height characteristics of Irish Draught mares', in *Irish Draught Horse Yearbook,* 1980 (Dublin), figure 1.

13 C.A. Lewis, 'Height characteristics of Irish Draught mares', op. cit. pp. 16-22.

14 C.A. Lewis, 'The development and diffusion of the Irish Draught', op. cit. figure 3.

15 A. Fell, *The Irish Draught Horse* (London, 1991).

16 Ibid.

17 N. O'Hare, *The Irish Sport Horse* (Navan, 2002).

18 A. Fell, op. cit.

19 Ibid.

20 Ibid.

21 *AGR,* 1921-22.

22 *AGR,* 1922-23.

23 C.A. Lewis, 'The development and diffusion of the Irish Draught', op. cit. figure 6.

24 C.A. Lewis, *Horse Breeding in Ireland and the Role of the Royal Dublin Society's Horse Breeding Schemes* (London, 1980).

25 *AGR,* 1943-44.

26 *AGR,* 1944-45.

27 A. Fell, op. cit.

28 Ibid.

29 C.A. Lewis, *Horse Breeding in Ireland and the Role of the Royal Dublin Society's Horse Breeding Schemes,* op. cit.

30 *Yearbook of the Irish Horse* (Dublin, 1975).

31 H. O'Toole, *Characterisation of the Irish Draught Horse Population in Ireland,* unpublished M.Agr.Sc. thesis, National University of Ireland, University College, Dublin, 2001.

32　E. Deane, 'Dick Jennings', in A. Loughnane and E. Deane (eds.), *Irish Draught Horse Society – 25 Years*, Irish Draught Horse Society (Dublin, 2003), pp. 21-3.

33　Quoted in E. Deane, 'Dick Jennings', op. cit.

34　C. Moore, *Irish Draught Stallions, 1911-1993* (Dublin, 1993).

35　J. Quinlan, 'Mary Joyce Quinlan, 1912-1994', in A. Loughnane and E. Deane, op. cit. pp. 24-6.

36　*Irish Draught Horse Yearbook*, 1978 (Dublin).

37　M. Kennedy, 'Why the government thinks a million of its horses', in Q. Doran-O'Reilly and M. Kennedy (eds.), *Horses of Ireland* (Dublin, 1982), pp. 201-6.

38　*Irish Draught Horse Yearbook*, 1982 (Dublin).

39　C.A. Lewis, 'Changes in the distribution of registered Irish Draught mares between 1917-19 and 1978', *Irish Draught Horse Yearbook*, 1981 (Dublin), pp. 56-61, figure 7.

40　F.K. O'Neill, U. Shanahan, M. Kennedy and T. McStay, *A Study of the Non-thoroughbred Horse Industry*, An Foras Taluntais (Dublin, 1979), figure 9.

41　B. Cotter, 'History of the Society', in A. Loughnane and E. Deane, op. cit. pp. 28-30.

42　C.A. Lewis, 'Irish horse breeding and the Irish Draught horse, 1917-1978', *Agricultural History Review*, 31, 1983, pp. 37-49.

43　*Irish Draught Horse Yearbook*, 1982, op. cit.

44　N. O'Hare, *The Irish Sport Horse*, op. cit.

45　H. O'Toole, op. cit.

46　G. Willis, *The World of the Irish Horse* (London, 1992), p. 19.

47　H. O'Toole, op. cit.

48　*Irish Horse Register*, 1995 (Dublin).

49　N. O'Hare, *The Irish Sport Horse*, op. cit.

50　N. O'Hare, *King of Diamonds* (Navan, 2002).

51　H. O'Toole, op. cit.

52　L.I. Aldridge, *Genetic Evaluation of Showjumping Horses in Ireland*, Irish Horse Board (Dublin, 2000).

53　N. O'Hare, *The Modern Irish Draught* (Navan, 2002).

54　J. Walsh, 'Foreword', in A. Loughnane and E. Deane, op. cit.

Chapter 11 – Present-day Competition Horse

Thanks to the Irish Horse Board for providing information on pedigree and performance records.

1　The IHB/Irish Draught Horse information leaflet, 2002.

2　Michael Slavin, *Showjumping Legends* (Colorado, 1999).

3　Agricultural statistics from various years from Central Statistics Office (CSO), Dublin.

4　CSO Farm Structures Survey, 1985.

5　*A Study of the Non-thoroughbred Horse Industry*, An Foras Taluntais (Dublin, 1979).

6　Step-Up Project under EU Interreg Programme: The Sport Horse Industry in North-west Ireland, 1994.

7　*Horse and Hound*, 10 July 2003.

8　Alison F. Corbally, *The Contribution of the Sport Horse Industry to the Irish Economy* (Dublin, 1996).

9　*Horse International*, October 2002.

Conclusion

Statistical information provided by the Irish Horse Board, Dublin, 2004.

Index

Italicised numbers refer to picture and illustration captions.
Names of horses are listed under the heading 'Horses'.

Suffolk Punch (horse breed) 107, 220
Suir Bridge (Co. Tipperary) 128-9
Sullivan, James 52-4
Suma Stud 226, 232
Summary of Achievements of Irish Sport Horses in 2003 187
Survey Team on the Horse Breeding Industry 162
Sussex (England) 136, 163
Swail, Conor 193
Sweden 189, 193, 220
Sweely, Robin 189
Swinford (Co. Mayo) 189
Swiss military 140-1
Swiss police force 140
Switzerland 130, 140-1, 191, 199
Swords, Michael 225

Tailtiu (Co. Meath) 46
Táin Bó Cuailnge (story) 39, 79, *79*, 80
Tallaght (Co. Dublin) 51, *209*
Tallow (Co. Waterford) 133, 140, 156
Tallow Road (Tallow, Co. Waterford) 133, 140
Tara (Co. Meath) 20-1, *21*, 22, 37, 45
Tara Street (Dublin) *109*
Tarry Flynn (book) 99
Tartar (horse breed) 228
Teagasc 8, 224
Temple, Sir William 216, 222
Templemore (Co. Tipperary) 133, 192
Thompson, F.M.L. 105
Thompson, G.B. *70*
Thoroughbred Stud Book 65
Thurles (Co.Tipperary) 112, 127-8, 130, 133, 142
Timoleague (Co. Cork) 133
Tipperary, Co. 20, 46, 60, *60*, 130, 133, 136, 150, 156, 158, *159*, 163, *165*, 167, 191-2, 223
Tír Conaill (Ulster) 39
Tiwes (sky-god) 45
Tone, Wolfe 132
Toorkoman (horse breed) 228
Topographica Hiberniae (Topography of Ireland) *34*, *38*, 39
Torres Garcia, Cristino 192
Tralee (Co. Kerry) 158
Trooping of the Colour 141
Tuam (Co. Galway) 114
Tudor-Stuarts 91
Tullamore (Co. Offaly) 114
Tullow (Co. Carlow) 92, 133
Tulsk (Co. Roscommon) 148
Turloughmore (Co. Galway) 133
Turn-pike Road Act 70
Tyrone, Co. *19*, 182, 191

Ua Conchobair, Ruadirí 27
Uí Eachach (ancient sept) 44
Ukraine 17, 80
Ulster 22, 44, 47, 79, 105, 108, 116, 125, 148-9, 152, 158, 230
Ulster Cycle 79

Ulster Lakeland Equestrian Park (Co. Fermanagh) 230
United Nations Food and Agriculture Organisation 171
United States of America (US) 99, 123, 189, 193, 195, 199, 226, 230
University College, Dublin 8, 178, 223

van Wijngaarden-Bakker, L.H. 18
Vaughan, Denis 157
Vejer De La Frontera (Spain) 192
Vikings 24-6
Virginia (Co. Cavan) 191
Voorn, V. 190
'Voyage of the Boat of Máel Dúin' (story) 35

Wales 46, 107
Walker, H. *67*, 69
Walsh, William 191
War Office 149
Waterford, Co. 17, 25, 54, *89*, 97, *118*, 124, 133, 140, 156, 158, 191
Waterford city 137, 140
Waterloo, Battle of 119, 135, 146
Watson, Mervyn 92, 224
Weatherby's (blood-typing laboratory) 178, 198
Weaver, Leslie 137
Weinberg, Wilhelm 176
Wellington (New Zealand) 118, 123, 135, 190
West Riding (Yorkshire, England) 141-2
Westmeath, Co. 46, 119, 192, *201*
Westport (Co. Mayo) 133
Wexford, Co. 46, 125, 130, 150, 152, 193-4
Whitchurch (England) 196
White, Jack 137
Wicklow, Co. 71, *88*, *100*, *102-3*, 133, 136-7, 152, 158, 190
Wicklow Mountains 152
Widger, John 124
William IV, King 119
Willis, Grania 214, 230
Woodlands Equestrian Centre (Co. Sligo) 195
Woods, Peter *209*
'Wooing of Etain' (story) 23
Wootton, John 65, *66*
World Breeding Federation of Sport Horses 183, 186

Yahoo groups (Internet) 232
Year of the Breeder 167
Yearbook (Department of Agriculture) 137, 163
Yearbook (IDHS) 218-9, 221-2, 224-5, 229
Yeats, Jack 77, *78*
Yeats, William Butler 77
Yorkshire (England) 141-3
Youatt, William 217
Youghal (Co. Cork) 156
Young, Arthur 69

Zetterman, Royne 194
Zeus (sky-god) 45